LIFELINE IN HELMAND

RAF Battlefield Mobility in Afghanistan

LIFELINE IN HELMAND

RAF Battlefield Mobility in Afghanistan

by
Roger Annett

Pen & Sword
AVIATION

First published in Great Britain in 2010 by
Pen and Sword Aviation
An imprint of
Pen and Sword Books Ltd
47 Church Street
Barnsley
South Yorkshire
S70 2AS
Copyright © Roger Annett 2010
ISBN 978 1 84884 274 8

The views and opinions expressed in this book are those of the author and
contributors alone, and should not be taken to represent those of HMG, MoD, the
RAF or any government agency.

Typeset by David L Hemingway
Printed in China through Printworks Int. Ltd

Pen and Sword Books Ltd incorporates the imprints of Pen and Sword Aviation,
Pen and Sword Maritime, Pen and Sword Military, Wharncliffe Local History, Pen
and Sword Select, Pen and Sword Military Classics and Leo Cooper.

For a complete list of Pen and Sword titles please contact
PEN AND SWORD BOOKS LIMITED
47 Church Street, Barnsley, South Yorkshire, S70 2AS, England

Contents

Author's Note 7

Foreword 9

Glossary of Acronyms 11

Chapter 1   Dress Rehearsals...15

Chapter 2   Towards the Airbridge 41

Chapter 3   Afghanistan, Theatre of Conflict 58

Chapter 4   Kandahar Base 77

Chapter 5   Hercules into Action 109

Chapter 6   Forward to Camp Bastion..................................121

Chapter 7   Operation Diesel...137

Chapter 8   Air Resupply 150

Chapter 9   Joint Operations 162

Chapter 10   Links with Home Base..188

Chapter 11   Where is All This Getting Us? 205

Chapter 12   Getting On With the Job 217

Chapter 13   Reliefs in Place 237

Chapter 14   On and On ... and On 261

Index 279

Author's Note

This book is about people at war, with the focus on Royal Air Force men and women of all ranks and trades, operating alongside partner Services from many nations in combat air-supply in Afghanistan.

Whatever the rights and wrongs of the conflict, the military in this narrative have taken an oath of allegiance to the Crown – to do their duty, no matter what. That means long periods away from home base and loved ones, in an alien environment and among a populace where the welcome is uncertain, and where the threat of hostile fire is ever-present. And they go back time and time again.

The Americans and the British entered this theatre in 2001 and many of the air and ground crews, medics and support personnel in this story have returned there every year since. That takes a special commitment, and courage. Of course, the same or greater demands are made on the ground troops posted to this vicious and frightening battle, including those from the RAF Regiment, the Army and the Royal Marines who have contributed to this narrative. Many of them are airmen too, serving either in the supply-dropping transports, or flying in vulnerable helicopters on air-support operations.

I am hugely indebted to the serving men and women who have shared their experiences with me for this book. My special thanks go to 'the Boss' of 27 Squadron 'C' Flight, and the Media and Communications Officers of RAF Odiham and Lyneham, Flight Lieutenants Leigh Shaughnessy and Louise Daly – all three exceptionally helpful in getting the project started and completed. Thanks are also due to their chiefs at Air Command and the Ministry of Defence for their assistance in steering the book through the hoops of contractual and other processes. One of those was Group Captain Andy Turner, who has not only kindly contributed a Foreword, but also, along with the Boss and my son and my painstaking wife, kindly took the time to read and edit the manuscript in draft.

Roger Annett

Foreword

Roger Annett's *Lifeline in Helmand* is a vivid account of one of the most challenging operations that has been undertaken by the UK in the contemporary past. Set in one of the most beautiful and beguiling parts of the world, among an ancient and honourable people and pitched against an illusive, fleeting and tenacious enemy who is not particularly disposed to respect either the Geneva Convention or the Law of Armed Conflict, the trade in blood and treasure is tangible, but the purpose is deeply honourable.

Operation Herrick, the UK Government's name for military operations in Afghanistan, blends the very best of the Royal Navy, Royal Marines, the British Army and the Royal Air Force into a tight-knit force under the command of NATO. The endeavours of the UK Armed Forces are more often than not audacious, but always highly courageous, where the enemy is constantly battered, bruised and always kept on the back foot. While the kinetic tit-for-tat has the international media's interest, our focus is not the enemy but the population for whom peace, stability and self-determination, which have so rarely been tasted, are deeply sought.

In this dusty mêlée, the unparalleled bravery and energy of the men of 42 Commando Royal Marines stands out a mile. The marching motto that 'there is nothing that a small band of determined men cannot achieve' rubs off and acts as a talisman and a sort of moral compass for the RAF Chinook and Hercules Forces deployed in Afghanistan. It drives our tenacity to get essential food, water, ammunition and fuel into the remote and sometimes isolated forward bases, it is a critical impetus when on immediate-response standby to extract casualties, it propels the planning of deliberate operations at the vanguard of Task Force Helmand's operational design and it drives the RAF machine at Odiham and Lyneham to maximize Chinook and Hercules effort in the field.

In *Lifeline in Helmand* Roger Annett has captured all of this, in a style that shines a light on a very great deal of detail of daily life. The narrative tracks a small group of Chinook crews, who will ultimately adopt the prestigious mantle of 1310 Flight on arrival in 'the Stan', from the early part of 2009, and follows them through their tour of duty. It starts as they transition through their pre-deployment training in Scotland, follows them along the Airbridge into 'theatre' and reflects on their trials and tribulations throughout their tour. It sets out their feelings and thoughts, the bravery and self-doubt, and is a window on their raw ability to pilot and crew the mighty 'Wokka' around the dusty high-altitude deserts of Southern Afghanistan. It is an honest account of life on the front line, drawing the reader into the cockpit and across the deserts of Helmand, but above all it is an important account of the bravery and courage of the crews of the UK Chinook Force.

Group Captain A.M. Turner
OBE MSc BA MRAeS RAF
Officer Commanding RAF Odiham
UK Chinook Force Commander

Glossary of Acronyms

47AD	–	47 Air Despatch Squadron
A&E	–	Accident and Emergency
AAC	–	British Army Air Corps
AH	–	Attack Helicopter
AMW	–	Air Mobility Wing
ANA	–	Afghan National Army
ANSF	–	Afghan National Security Force
ANP	–	Afghan National Police
AFT	–	Advanced Flying Training
AUW	–	All Up Weight
BFT	–	Basic Flying Training
BSN	–	Camp Bastion
CCAST	–	Critical Care Air Support Team
CCF	–	Combined Cadet Force
CDS	–	Container Delivery System
CINS	–	Chinook Integrated Navigation System
CO	–	Commanding Officer
COM	–	Commander
CR	–	Combat Ready
DARTS	–	Deployable Aeromedical Response Teams
DAS	–	Defensive Aids Suite
DFC	–	Distinguished Flying Cross
DZ	–	Drop Zone
EAW	–	Expeditionary Air Wing
ECL	–	Engine Control Lever
ECM	–	Electronic Counter-Measure
EFT	–	Elementary Flying Training

ER	–	Emergency Room
ExCES	–	Expeditionary Chinook Engineering Squadron
FAM	–	Fighting-Aged Male
FM	–	Frequency Modulated
FOB	–	Forward Operating Base
FP	–	Force Protection
GDA	–	Ground Defence Area
GPMG	–	General Purpose Machine-Gun
GPS	–	Global Positioning System
HALS	–	Hardened Aircraft Landing Strip
HLS	–	Helicopter Landing Site
HRF	–	Helmand Reaction Force
IED	–	Improvised Explosive Device
IOT	–	Initial Officer Training
IP	–	Insertion Point
IR	–	Infra Red
IRT	–	Immediate Response Team
IQA	–	Internal Quality Audit
ISAF	–	International Security Assistance Force
ISO	–	International Standards Organisation
ISTAR	–	Intelligence Surveillance Target Acquisition and Reconnaissance
JADTEU	–	Joint Air-Delivery Test and Evaluation Unit
JAG	–	Joint Aviation Group
JHC	–	Joint Helicopter Command
JHF(A)	–	Joint Helicopter Force (Afghanistan)
JHSU	–	Joint Helicopter Support Unit
JMB	–	Joint Mission Brief
KAF	–	Kandahar Airfield
LEC	–	Locally Employed Civilian
LUP	–	Lying-Up point
MAOTS	–	Mobile Air Operations Teams
MERT	–	Medical Emergency Response Team
MoD	–	UK Ministry of Defence
MDHU	–	Ministry of Defence Hospital Unit
MRX	–	Mission Rehearsal Exercise
NATO	–	North Atlantic Treaty Organization
NCO	–	Non-Commissioned Officer
NHP	–	Non-Handling Pilot
NVD	–	Night Vision Device

NVG	–	Night Vision Goggles
OC	–	Officer Commanding
OCF	–	Operational Conversion Flight
ORs	–	Other Ranks
PADS	–	Precision Airdrop System
PDT	–	Pre-Deployment Training
PJHQ	–	Permanent Joint Headquarters
PNF	–	Pilot Non-Flying
PUP	–	Pick-Up Point
R and R	–	Rest and Recreation
RBG(S)	–	Regional Battle Group (South)
RC(S)	–	Regional Command (South)
REME	–	Royal Electrical and Mechanical Engineers
RiP	–	Relief in Place (the changeover of troop duty on the Herrick Task Forces)
RLC	–	Royal Logistics Corps
RoE	–	Rules of Engagement
RPG	–	Rocket Propelled Grenade
RRCC	–	Rotors Running Crew Change
RV	–	Rendezvous
SAC	–	Senior Aircraftman
SAMO	–	Senior Air Movements Officer
SARBOX	–	Search and Rescue Box
SERE	–	Survival Evasion Resistance and Extraction
SH	–	Support Helicopter
SITREP	–	Situation Report
TACAN	–	Tactical Air Navigation
TCAS	–	Traffic Collision Avoidance System
TRIM	–	Trauma Risk Management
TQ	–	Theatre Qualified
UAS	–	University Air Squadron
UAV	–	Unmanned Aerial Vehicle
UHF	–	Ultra High Frequency
U/S	–	Unserviceable
USL	–	Underslung Load
VHF	–	Very High Frequency
VHR	–	Very High Readiness
WMIK	–	Weapons Mounted Installation Kit

CHAPTER 1

Dress Rehearsals

AUTUMN/WINTER 2008/9

CHINOOKS IN THE SNOW

Soon after a December dawn, a team of mechanics swarms over a trio of RAF Chinook helicopters standing massively in line astern on the Lossiemouth dispersal. The upwind aircraft has its twin rotors roped down against the freshening breeze off the Moray Firth, but the other two are being made ready for flight. Engine-covers are lifted off, electronics checked for gremlins and hydraulics tested for leaks. These heavy-lift machines, painted drab green and designed for the battlefield, will soon be ready for action in the Scottish snow.

In an Operations Room fifty yards across the grass from the tarmac, there's an air of expectancy – a score or more aircrew in olive-green flying-suits are making final preparations for their morning missions. Accompanied by ground-crew, they ferried the three Boeing support helicopters up from their Odiham base at the weekend, two days ago – four bum-numbing hours from Hampshire at 6,000 feet. These are the young men and women of 'C' Flight, 27 Squadron RAF.

In a couple of months, the flight will be thousands of miles away in Central Asia, on yet another ten-week deployment in southern Afghanistan, operating, along with some 8,000 other British servicemen and women, in the NATO-led force tasked with establishing security in Helmand – a province getting on for the size of Scotland, and in its northern parts even more mountainous. For many of those in the Ops Room, this will be their first trip – others will have been deployed up to five times already. 'C' Flight was last there from March to May, sweating on the plains in 35 degrees

Celsius – this time, it will start off icily cold, with temperatures in the mountains dropping to as much as 25 degrees below. That's why, as part of their Pre-Deployment Training (PDT), they're up here for five freezing days in the Scottish Highlands.

'C' Flight has the use of a large, square, briefing table, a line of cupboards, aircrew lockers, a sofa and chairs, and a laptop computer installation. Shelving runs along one wall, laden with the accumulated clutter of a flight office: aircraft operating manuals, lunch-bags and domed olive-green helmets next to a hot-water urn for tea, coffee and packet soup. The chat is about yesterday's airborne exploits, football results, and the after-effects of an epic curry dinner in Elgin.

Pinned to a cupboard door alongside an array of maps is a poster depicting a Chinook barrelling along a mountain valley at low level. The caption commends the joys of helicopter 'BLADE SLAP – because jet noise is boring'. There's always some rivalry between rotary crews and 'fighter boys', and 'Lossie', home to four squadrons of ground-attack Tornadoes, is the largest and busiest fast-jet base in the RAF.

Two crews – each with two pilots up front and two crewmen in the rear cabin – finish their pre-flight briefing before gathering up maps and helmets and clattering through the door to the airfield. They're off on the early mission, a two-ship formation patrol up to Cape Wrath, 100 miles to the north-west on the farthest tip of Scotland. Alongside their operational tasks they've been asked to look out for the National Park Warden's collie that's gone walkabout. As part of their route lies over the sea, they've struggled

BLADE SLAP

Because jet noise is boring.

Crew-room poster - RAF Lossiemouth (Crown Copyright 20..

into green rubber survival suits – trudging in heavy-duty flying-boots out to their machines, they look not unlike deep-sea divers.

'C' Flight Commander, 'the Boss', a squadron leader with four Afghan detachments already under his belt, gathers another pair of crews around the table and starts the briefing for the second mission of the morning:

> In line with what we'll be doing in Helmand, it's to be a simulated
> Deliberate Ops sortie, in support of an overt show of force by our

ground troops. It's designed to let the hostiles know what the British Task Force can rustle up when it wants to.

('Simulated' conditions and procedures are real, but without actual participants and equipment other than the crews and their Chinooks.) He reads from a sheet of A4 lifted from the printer:

We've been allocated Air Mission Request 10/01. It calls for a high-readiness pair of Chinooks to carry out practice supply deliveries, reconnaissance, and casevacs in the front line. We'll be operating in the Cairngorms Search and Rescue Box – the SARBOX.

He indicates the map on the wall:

The box is twenty miles square and gives us plenty of scope to fly the Cabs at low level above the snowline. Just right for the Helmand mountains.

This sortie's designed to be an exercise in comms between the two crews in the pair as well as between the pilots in front and crewmen in the back – and also with Ops Control. They'll throw emergency tasks at us mid-mission. Of course it'll be me making the calls, using the FM to simulate the secure radio. But remember, these calls and tasks may well be mocked-up today, but in a couple of months they'll be for real.

['Cabs' – Chinook crews spend a lot of their time driving the Army around.]

The Boss is to fly as Number Two in the formation – it will be led by a flight lieutenant who, because of his chiselled features and powerful build, is known to all as 'German'. Many of the Chinook aircrew sport nicknames on their flying-suits – it's to relax the formality and, with it, the tension.

German takes over the briefing, reading from the Tasking Sheet, which out in Helmand would be issued jointly with the Army:

For the purposes of the exercise, simulated factors will be as follows. Friendly forces are positioned in the north-west of the SARBOX. We'll get support from the Army Apaches today – they'll give us a shout of 'Madras' if a landing-site is hot, and 'Korma' if it's safe to go in. Any incoming groundfire is to be reported to Playmate on UHF – and a full contact report on secure radio to the simulated operational base in Helmand. For real, when breaking away, make every effort to keep Playmate in sight, and avoid going blind. And if either of us gets lost, the RV point is Glenmore Lodge estate.

[Apache – Army Air Corps (AAC) AH64 attack helicopter.]

Chinook crew – kitted out and ready to go (Photograph by POA (Phot) Tony Leather, RN © Crown Copyright/MoD, image from www.photos.mod.uk)

['Playmate' – Other aircraft in the formation.]

He then reads from a sheet of local met reports, issued by the Tain weather centre:

> Surface wind 280 degrees at 10 knots gusting 15 to 25, and 30 at higher levels. Within 10 kilometres of the airfield, broken cloud from 2,000 to 18,000 feet – later in the day, showers with the chance of thunderstorms and cumulonimbus. Outside those, visibility should be good – but icing will be a distinct possibility within cloud.

That gets everyone's attention – icing in cloud is a real hazard for helicopters. The trick is basically to get out of it as soon as possible. Hot engine oil pumped around the air intake, together with windscreen heating, gives the Chinook some protection, but ice on the rotor blades dramatically reduces lift, and the only sure way out of it is to descend – not usually an option in mountains:

> Remember, safety height in the SARBOX is 6,500 feet. The best direction for lower ground is to the east and the north.

The mission route is outlined on a 'Kill Box' map. This system was set up by the United States Department of Defense in the late 1980s, for co-ordinating fire support. Now, based on a Common Grid Reference System, it provides virtual air-traffic control for American and allied forces in operational theatres across the globe. Each box is subdivided into 'Keypads' numbered 1–9:

> Lossiemouth will have cleared its Tornado fighter-bombers and Sea King search-and-rescue helicopters from the SARBOX for the period of the sortie, scheduled to be two hours and thirty minutes. Mission callsigns are 'Gambit One' and 'Gambit Two'. Take-off at noon.

The formation briefing complete, the two crews set to, working from maps and radio logs, to put together the combat mission plan. Every last detail has been checked and rechecked by the time the distinctive beat of returning Chinooks is heard in the distance. In response, the Boss's men grab helmets, bundle up flight documents, and troop across the tufted airfield grass to meet the incoming aircraft.

Lossiemouth is the perfect place for an air base – sea beyond the north perimeter and coastal plain to the south. The returning Cape Wrath formation pair approach the dispersal on a slow forward hover into the strengthening northerly wind. The Odiham mechanics, up here for the week, have their office in a line-hut alongside the tarmac. They're from the centralized Expeditionary Chinook Engineering Squadron (ExCES), and they, too, are getting ready for the Afghan winter. The captains examine the Forms 700 that confirm both aircraft are fit to fly, before signing to take responsibility for the multi-million-pound airframes. They're standing ready for a rotors-running crew change (RRCC), and the crews split off to man their machines, pulling on helmets for protection against the noise and downdraft.

The Chinook's 30 ft carbon-fibre blades, three on each pylon, contra-rotate at a constant 225 revolutions per minute, and even though the two Avco Lycoming Turboshaft jet turbines below the aft rotor are idling at just twenty per cent of their power, the downwash is boisterous, to say the least. The crews avoid the forward door into the cabin, as the forward rotor tilts down 9 degrees, and a strong gust of wind could bring a blade down to head-lopping height. Preferred access is over the rear ramp.

In the box-like cabin – at over nine metres long and two metres square, big enough to transport forty-four fully armed troops or two Land Rovers – the incoming crew report that happily the Warden's collie has been found, and the new team takes up stations. Number One crewman stays by the ramp controls. He's a Master Aircrewman with a proud record of 5,000 hours' flying time on the Chinook fleet. His rank is a warrant officer equivalent, and he's known respectfully to his colleagues as 'Mister B'. Number Two, 'Ginger', a flight sergeant who's also an experienced aircrewman, moves up to behind the forward bulkhead, by the side doors.

The pilots clamber forward into the cockpit, and strap themselves into their armoured seats, the Boss on the right-hand side, in the captain's position. Instruments surround them on the panel in front, above their heads and along a central pedestal. Feet rest comfortably on the foot pedals, for controlling yaw in flight. A cyclic control stick, which changes the angle of attack of the rotor blades for turn and pitch, stands between each pilot's knees, and a collective lever, which changes the level of upward thrust, is at each left hand.

All four plug into the intercom, the crewmen's long spiral cables trailing behind them as they move around the cabin. Black leather flying-gloves dart around switches, levers and dials, checking fuel levels, engines and instruments. The engine control levers (ECL) overhead are at 'Flight', with the twin 5,000-horsepower Turboshafts ready to deliver maximum torque.

From Ginger: 'Ramp up, chocks removed – fifteen six-hundred all-up weight – clear above and behind.'

From the Boss: 'Temperatures and pressures within limits, harnesses locked and tight. Let's go.'

He releases the brake on the collective and eases the lever upwards. The magnificent rotors tilt to chop the air, and there's the blade-slap, a distinctive 'wokka-wokka' rhythm as the 16 tonnes of Chinook are hauled smoothly towards the sky. The Boss checks the ascent at 20 feet and hovers, nose slightly higher than tail, over the tarmac and behind the formation leader's aircraft below.

German signals that he's about to lift off, too, and up goes Gambit One, clearly seen through the all-round window panels below the Boss's feet, as he brings Gambit Two into position two rotor spans astern. The Chinooks dip forward and they're off. At about 40 knots, the giant rotors transition effectively to a single high-lift aerofoil, performing like a fixed wing. Speed increases, and the formation turns low over the grass – flushing a pair of startled hares from cover – before setting course to the south, over the fields and woods of northern Morayshire.

Clearing the airfield, the cruising speed builds to 140 knots and the airframe begins to judder – the leader holds it there, at the limit for comfortable flight. Within minutes the pair are in sight of the SARBOX, and flying over the 1,000 ft foothills of the Cairngorm range.

In the left-hand seat, the non-handling pilot (NHP) is busy with his maps. 'Morts' is a young flight lieutenant in training for his first detachment to Helmand, where his prime responsibilities will be radio and navigation. He has all he needs to calculate the aircraft's position – Global Positioning System (GPS), together with a Doppler radar transceiver giving a constant check on track and groundspeed. But for this sortie he's carrying three charts: a large-scale map of the Braemar area for plotting the route, a Kill Box plan of the exercise region, and the one he's using now – a hill-walking-scale map for low-level work.

'Aviemore Ski Centre at nine o'clock,' he reports, 'two thousand feet above sea level – SARBOX in two miles.'

In the Box, Gambit One lets down to 50 feet, and starts to fly evasion tactics, weaving among the tree-tops, the airspeed indicator swinging between 120 and 150 knots. Houses, cattle, rivers and woods flash by below, and a herd of buffalo grazes through the snow by a frozen loch. Birds appear momentarily above. There are few worries about bird-strikes on the cockpit,

The Boss searches for a ridge to climb – Cairngorms. (The Boss & Friends)

as the windscreens in front of the pilots are reinforced against much worse – gunfire. The Boss has to work to hold position, and from time to time he hauls the Chinook round in a shuddering S-bend to avoid closing up in the turn. To maintain height, he manoeuvres the aircraft effortlessly up or down with the collective, and 'wokka-wokka' echoes through the Cairngorm glens.

In the cabin, Ginger keeps lookout to the right from the open upper half of the starboard door. Mister B does the same on the left and right from the bulbous all-round observation windows at the rear. He braces to keep upright – formation-keeping pulls heavy G-forces down the back.

After ten minutes of skimming the ridges and cairns of the National Park, Mister B speaks up: 'Boss, we haven't had much recirculation practice lately.'

'Correct.' The Boss presses the UHF radio transmit button on the cyclic stick. 'Gambit One from Gambit Two – clearance to break off for ridge practice.'

German acknowledges, and the formation splits for individual hill flying. The Boss pulls the nose up to flare the rotors and trade speed for height, and the Chinook powers up through a rocky gulley to the snowline, with towering crags and peaks filling the horizon ahead.

The pilots search for a suitable ridge, and find one a mile long at 3,000 feet above sea level. Morts is shown the best way to climb up to the top, with the slope to the left, and the valley to the right in the captain's full view – an escape route should it be needed. Up here, at about the same altitude as the Helmand Plateau, the air is rarified and the rotors less efficient, but the lightly loaded Chinook has plenty of power to spare.

On the crest of the ridge the Boss brings the aircraft down with the collective, before going into the hover a few feet above the snow. The downwash throws up a veritable blizzard – this is 'recirculation'. Ice clouds shower through the side-door openings and drift into the cockpit. Morts switches on the wiper blades as, in the face of a strongly gusting wind, the machine touches down. The challenge now is to lift off again, in the self-generated white-out.

As he coaches Morts in bad-weather flying, the Boss refers to the Sea King recently forced to land in these mountains when the weather took a turn for the worse:

The crew walked out – had to come back for the aircraft three days later. We wouldn't want to do that, so we make sure we take a firm bead on the escape route coming in, and land into wind to maximize rotor performance. Then we set our incoming track on the compass bar, for

'If there's not room for all the wheels, use the ones at the back...'
(Photograph by POA (Phot) Tony Leather, RN © crown copyright 2010/MoD, image from www.photos.mod.uk)

orientation. We know we can fly the reciprocal to find an escape route on the way out. OK?

The Boss lifts the Chinook off the ridge, carefully turning through 180 degrees, and the compass guides him back to the valley.

'Works every time!' from Mister B.

'The technique's the same for a ridge, saddle or summit', explains the Boss. 'If there's not room for all the wheels, use the ones at the back and float the ramp to let the pax on or off.'

['Pax' – Passengers.]

He flies across to a ridge below the snowline, and sits the rear wheels on a rocky cairn to demonstrate. It's a technique used in the Helmand mountains to insert troops directly into their combat positions.

'There are four ways for unloading troops', he reminds Morts. 'The hover-jump from not more than four to six feet, swarming down ropes from up to twenty, and for the bravest, abseiling from a hundred and twenty. Then there's this – landing on and getting them out over the ramp. It's the one we use all the time in Helmand.'

Back in the valley again, the Boss settles the Chinook in the hover – it's time to put out a call on the simulated secure FM radio. 'Gambit Formation – scramble to Kill Box location Golf Charlie India, Kilo Sierra Echo – uplift two medical teams, Charlie One and Charlie Two – further instruction to follow. Over.'

'Roger, Ops', acknowledges German, and reads the message back in confirmation, before calling Gambit Two to rejoin formation. The Boss slots his Chinook back in behind the leader's engine tailpipes, and the pair swoop down across the mountainside.

The pick-up location has been given in code. Morts uses the day's keyword to decipher it, and plots the spot on his Kill Box map. It turns out it's the helicopter landing site (HLS) by the paper mill at Fort William, seventy miles away at the southern end of the Great Glen. So at high speed the formation sets course through the Cairngorms National Park, and snakes down to the sunny Spey valley at Kingussie – where the leader flies low, climbing only for power lines.

'This low-level stuff is mainly for navigation practice, Morts', explains the Boss. 'In theatre, we'd mostly be flying high, out of range of small-arms fire.'

Morts and the crewmen co-operate on map-reading, while the Boss concentrates on the demands of flying the machine. 'You know, I'm very happy in my work', he grins, as he deftly swings the Chinook through the curves. 'Couple of horses ahead – no riders', he adds. Horses grazing on their own can be ignored, but horses with riders are to be avoided.

From time to time, leaning into the cockpit, Ginger calls out the instrument scan checks for Morts to respond. 'Forty-five minutes loiter time', he reports – a reassuring safety margin of fuel over and above scheduled mission duration.

As the Chinooks hurtle alongside the railway line from Kingussie, Ginger transmits further confirmation of task over the secure radio. Gambit Formation is to land at the Paper Mill and simulate uplifting five Immediate Response Team (IRT) medical staff plus their kit – 200 kg of freight per load

– and then return to the SARBOX, back above the snowline, to winch casualties on board.

Crags rise on either side up to 3,500 feet as the rotor downwash carves patterns on the waters of Loch Laggan. 'Touch of the Dambusters here', murmurs the Boss.

Over Tulloch Station and then veering left 20 degrees at Spean Bridge it's, 'Ten miles to run', from Morts.

Mister B comes on the intercom with an item of simulated Intelligence. 'Boss, Cabs came under fire here the other day – mortar shells for five to six minutes.'

'Roger, understood', responds the Boss. After a moment, he enquires, 'Any more to be learned from secure traffic lately?'

Ginger takes the cue. 'Ah yes – friendly patrol despatched from the paper mill – look out for insurgents to the north.'

At around 1300, an hour into the mission, Fort William shows up ahead, hugging the northern reach of Loch Linnhe, wreathed in Scotch mist. Keeping east of the town to avoid possible hostiles, the helicopters swoop along the slopes of Glen Nevis, the mighty Ben towering into the clouds above.

'A bit like Kajaki Lake in Helmand, but not quite as blue', the Boss tells Morts as the Chinook goes into a holding pattern behind the leader.

Then a further call – this time on UHF from an Apache simulated up above – reports the HLS all clear for landing. German breaks away to the west bank of the loch, to put his machine down in a compound no more than 200 feet square, with tall floodlight masts guarding opposing corners.

Ginger reports: 'Increased chatter on secure radio – TiC in Keypad 9.' (In one of the grid locations in the Kill Box to the north of Fort William, the friendly patrol has gone into action against the hostiles.)

[TiC – Troops in Contact.]

Gambit One lifts off from below, and with a downward thrust on the collective, and a push to the left on the cyclic, the Boss launches Gambit Two down to the loch. Bringing the machine in on a steep left-hand curve, he threads through the floodlights, flares the rotors and touches down.

From the rear, Mister B calmly reports: 'Ramp down – I've got five medics and a stretcher heading our way – they're on the ramp.' And then, urgently: 'Incoming mortars!'

Up front, the pilots can only wait. Nothing to be done until: 'Clear of the ramp – ramp up!' from the back.

Then it's maximum torque, collective fully up, and maximum-rate lift-off. With Morts watching out for those floodlights, the Boss throws the Chinook into the steepest of left-hand turns and skims over the water, away from the mill and the imagined mortar shells.

The crewmen grip any handhold they can as, low over the loch, the Boss carries out a series of 'Wells' manoeuvres, named after the boffin who invented them. It's a string of co-ordinated height, speed and attitude changes in short succession so as to throw hostiles with anti-aircraft projectiles off their aim. It's spectacular flying – and, as the Boss knows from experience, highly effective.

'God knows what they thought of that down in Fort William', he grunts as, skirting the town and repositioning in formation, the pair speed away, keeping well clear of the area they now know is active.

'Pax and kit all secure', from Mister B, as the Gambit pair soar up Neptune's Staircase – nine locks climbing up to the Caledonian Canal – and flies low, very low, along the Lochy river valley, out of harm's way.

'Well, that was as realistic a taste of combat you're likely to get, Morts,' comments the Boss, adding, 'before the real thing.'

Morts gets back to his maps. He reports, 'Fifteen minutes to SARBOX.' Then, urgently, 'Wires two-fifty feet high round this bend, Boss!'

'Got them visual', is the response, but German appears not to have spotted the power lines.

'Wires ahead, Gambit One!'

It's a heart-stopping moment, but the power of the collective torque pulls the lead machine over the pylons, and the formation surges onwards, along the Great Glen.

Mister B comes on the intercom: 'One and a half tonnes of fuel remaining.'

Ginger sends a contact report to the operational base on the simulated secure radio: 'From Gambit Two as at thirteen-thirty – contact at grid reference Golf Charlie India, Kilo Sierra Echo – mortar fire incoming from north – support required nil – damage nil. Over.'

Ops acknowledges receipt as the two-ship barrels down the River Oich section of the Caledonian Canal, its locks and motorboats not far beneath the pilots' feet. As the stately stone facade of the Inchnacardoch Hotel flashes by to port, the leader breaks to starboard, and they're again climbing up to the Cairngorms.

Back in the SARBOX, they rise up to the snowline, preparing for more recirculation – this time with winching practice. The grid location for the pick-up is on the crest of a long and rocky saddle, not far below the now extensive cloudbase. It's the Boss's turn to go in first, and as German hovers off to the side to observe, he brings Gambit Two in with crags to the left and valley to the right as before, while the crew keeps a keen look-out all round.

'Prepare for winching', directs the Boss. 'Morts, switch hoist to cabin.'

The Chinook is taxi-hovered forward to a level stretch. It's now recirculating good and strong, and the outside air temperature is a fraction above zero – just right for icing. Sure enough, there's the white stuff on the windscreens, and it's Morts to the wipers again.

Ginger takes over direction-giving from the starboard door hoist position. He guides the machine to downwind of the simulated casualty, and then edges it sideways towards the target. At the same time he winds down the winch, simulating Mister B's presence on the end of the cable:

> Winching out – right – five, four, three, two, one – steady! Height is good – crewman on ground – working with casualty – crewman and casualty on hoist, winching in – hook at the door – survivor on board – crewman in cabin – all safe and sound.

Satisfied, the Boss flies off to hover over the valley and keep an eye on Gambit One's winching. That goes without a hitch, and the formation breaks for individual snowline practice.

'Let's go further up the saddle and do some more above the tree line.'

He climbs towards the summit, where only the most prominent rocks give any reference points. Up here, the blizzard flies up in the downwash and the clouds close in above. Just as all perspective is lost in a complete white-out, the Boss settles the wheels into the snow. He knows what he's doing. 'Now we turn the aircraft 180 degrees like before, and go out the way we came in, along a known safe route.'

By correct use of foot pedals, cyclic and collective all together, the versatile Chinook can be rotated around its centre point, its nose or its tail. So, relying partly on instruments and partly on glimpses of the slopes below his feet, the Boss gently lifts off, and in the hover turns the machine about the nose, the tail swinging round into a known clear area. But, just at the moment when his captain's attention is focused on the snow below, Morts resets the compass bar – for the course back to Lossie. In clear weather that would be helpful, but in this white-out it has lost the Boss his escape datum. On top of that, they are icing up again. The Boss holds in the hover, his mind racing – he really doesn't fancy the embarrassment and discomfort of foot-slogging it down off these hills.

'This is getting interesting', from Mister B at the back, peering through the blizzard for references. 'Are we going to make it back for tea?'

The Boss then shows his mettle. He crabs sideways, still in a low hover, looking for the imprint the tyres made on landing, a minute ago. There they are – two each side at the front and one each side at the rear. He's got his bearings again. He lines up on the pattern and thumbs the compass bar back to the datum. Now all they have to do is get off the mountain.

'Good references to the right, Boss!' reports Ginger as the aircraft inches forward, and the rocky landmarks loom out of the ice cloud. Then it's, 'Playmate at nine o'clock', from Mister B at the rear, as they escape to the open valley.

It's been a close-run thing and the crew's banter is lower-key as Gambit Formation joins up again for the flight back to Lossie. 'We'll talk about this on the ground', says the Boss. The crew knows that it's down to his experience, and the trusty Chinook, that they've got safely off that saddle.

The weather presents a further challenge in the valleys, but the leader flies as straight and level as he can to assist the crewmen in their next task, preparing for cargo-handling practice back on the tarmac. Nevertheless, it's far from comfortable in the cabin. Simulating combat mode, the upper halves of the two forward doors are fully open, providing space for six-barrel Miniguns. Added to that, the upper section of the ramp is also wide open, the 'tongue' retracted into the lower section to give a field of fire for the M60 machine-gun, mounted there in theatre. The result is that in the cruise, a continuous gale howls straight through. The whine of the transmission shafts overhead – a penetrating 91 dB below the forward rotor, and 110 aft – adds to the racket.

The crewmen move with practised skill around the fixings and the heaped up survival kit, looking for handholds, like rock climbers. They check out the two palleted packs secured to the floor, ready to be rolled off the ramp at Lossie dispersal. In theatre, they could be carrying up to five pallets of 1 tonne (1,000 kg) each, but today it's a practice low-level 'get in, get out quick' resupply. Then, on the retractable central hook of the three fitted below the machine, they'll carry out a heavy lift.

On a signal from the cockpit, Mister B moves a switch-lever, and the ramp drops to the open position, flat in line with the cabin floor. The woods and fields of Morayshire unroll below.

Over the VHF radio comes an instruction from Approach Control to switch to Lossiemouth Local, where a friendly female voice clears Gambit Formation to join the circuit. With Gambit Two approaching the dispersal, the crewmen crouch by the load to release the ratchet strops on the lateral restraints. They unsheathe their aircrew knives and, as the tarmac slides beneath the ramp, confidently slice through the remaining fore and aft webbing. Off trundle the pallets, to bump down the few inches to the surface as the Chinook taxis slowly forward.

In action, the Boss would now soar away – doubtless doing a bit of evasive Wellsing as he went – but today, air-traffic control instructs Gambit Formation to land on without delay. A Learjet carrying a visiting prince of the realm is in the circuit and having a bit of trouble with its nosewheel. All other flying is temporarily suspended, so the underslung load (USL) will have to wait. The Boss reluctantly brings the machine to a halt, moves the ECLs to 'Ground' and pulls on the parking brake. He and his colleagues greet the next crew, clatter down the ramp and tussle with the downwash – back to a quieter, earth-bound world.

In the debriefing, Mister B has a word or two for Morts:

> On Ops, emergencies come at us all the time – they need quick, snap decisions, like at the Paper Mill. And down the back, we get unexpected loads thrown at us with precious little time to work out how best to stow it. We have to trust each other to handle all that sort of stuff. Intercom banter helps. It's a helicopter thing – makes us a team – and helps us relax. Remember, on detachment we'll be on the same crew for weeks.

The Boss calls it one of the best training sorties so far. He tells the Gambit crews:

> We've seen the need for communication within each Cab, as well as between Playmates. We've had hill and valley flying, a run-in with a full white-out, and icing. There's been valuable simulation of combat events – a call-out on a casevac mission, dodging groundfire and mortars, and a winching. The calls with the secure radio seemed realistic enough – we picked up situational awareness from those and from background chatter between other units. All that will come in more than handy for later use.

Everyone is well aware that that will be in the far from simulated battle areas of Afghanistan.

MEDICS IN THE FROST

A few weeks later, very early on a bright Wiltshire morning in January, the thermometer's plummeting to minus 7 degrees. Behind a hangar at RAF

Lyneham where the sun doesn't reach, a group of media folk, sixteen strong, are stamping their feet and waiting for the action to start. The focus of their attention is a black, shed-like construction, squat on the ground and open at the rear end, with a wooden ramp sloping down to the frozen grass. It's an exact-scale mock-up of the fuselage and cabin of a Chinook, and the journalists, TV and radio crews are here to watch Helmand casevac training for real.

It's a pretty good turn-out for so early in the New Year. They're here mainly through the persuasive efforts of the Media and Communications Officer at Lyneham, Flight Lieutenant Louise Daly, but part of the attraction is that the Under-Secretary of State for Defence, Kevan Jones, is to arrive shortly, and he's a cert for a sound-bite. This morning, his tight politician's schedule and the heavy traffic have held him up, and as a result, Flight Lieutenant Matt Haslam steps forward into the breach.

He's a fully qualified Accident and Emergency (A&E) Nurse, and the Training Officer of the Medical Emergency Response Teams (MERT). Today he's in charge of the Rotary Wing Training Facilitator and of this demo. He's to be the ringmaster, the main link for the media invitees, and commentator for the Minister. To get the show rolling, he briefs the waiting jouralists:

> MERTs are manned by experienced tri-Service personnel trained in trauma management, who take Emergency Room intensive care out to the front line in the back of a Chinook. There, their job is to stabilize the condition of the wounded, and get them back to the NATO base hospital at Camp Bastion. The whole aim is to enhance the treatment the patient receives within the 'golden hour' – that's the critical time from point of injury to arrival at ER.
>
> Sessions on this facilitator are a key part of training our men and women for deployment to theatre. The teams of four are made up of one tri-Service anaesthetist or an Emergency Medicine Consultant, together with a combination of RAF Emergency Nurses and paramedics.

He leads the guests into the dummy cabin:

> We all have to be fit and alert – it's a challenge hauling stretchers in and out of the Chinook. Going out, you have to sashay round the machine-gun on the ramp, and then there's the rotor downwash – not to mention the Taliban – trying to knock you over. You have to run the gauntlet all the way back with the full weight of the casualty, then struggle back up the ramp – often manoeuvring alongside a second stretcher-party – and

go into medical action where, as you can see, there's not much room to spare.

The minister's still not in sight, so Matt invites questions. He can answer from experience. Last summer he did six weeks on MERT in the roasting heat of Iraq, and the year before he was in Afghanistan, working in the exceptional cold of November. The resident British Task Force was 45 Commando Royal Marines, and the medics were fully occupied with thirty casevac missions in three months:

There's a maximum of two MERTs in Helmand at any one time. We work with one team per aircraft. For multiple casualties another aircraft would be launched with a second team.

Yes, all of us – and a third of our people are women – are taught how to carry and use weapons. We are issued with rifle and pistol, so as to be ready to defend ourselves in the front line. The aircraft can come under fire, and so can the team when they're on the ground. Our pre-deployment training is comprehensive, lasting six to eight weeks, sometimes longer than the deployment itself. As well as time on the firing range and fieldcraft, we practise immersion, survival and interrogation drills – as well as all the essential advanced trauma techniques.

Yes, we're also trained to operate in minefields – not to defuse mines, but to avoid them wherever possible or to clear a path out if we were to find ourselves in that situation. To ensure the safety of the team, Explosive Ordnance Disposal personnel would be brought in to get us to the site of an incident involving explosives.

You're right. The back of a Chinook isn't the best environment for medical treatment. It's cramped and noisy, and often all over the place in turbulence. It's sometimes dusty and hot, sometimes freezing cold. At night, the only illumination is from chemical flares or blue-light head and finger torches. But, despite all that we're bringing the emergency ward to the front-line, giving proven and highly effective critical care to wounded – often horrendously wounded – soldiers.

Yes, the casualties are not only NATO troops but also from all sections of Afghan society. We carry Afghan soldiers and police, civilian victims of mines and suicide bombs – and the occasional wounded Taliban, too.

We concentrate our care on the living – sadly, there's nothing we can do for the dead.

The minister arrives, and the demo starts. It's set up to provide the trainees – all by now chilled to the marrow, huddled on the side benches in the belly of the dummy Chinook – with maximum realism. A section of four RAF Regiment gunners, the Force Protection Team, sits just forward of the ramp, armed to the teeth and ready to go. Everyone is helmeted and in full, heavy-duty body-armour.

BBC, ITV and Sky cameras roll, and a whistle-blast from Matt kicks it off. Thunder-flashes rend the air, smoke bombs choke the lungs. On another whistle, riflemen scoot down the ramp and fan out over the grass, giving covering fire with ear-shattering blank rounds from their carbines. The MERT teams – two to each of two stretchers – follow, running in the crouch, their rifles swinging clumsily from the shoulder. They make it a full thirty yards to two dummy casualties, crouch beside them, and, as carefully as they can, manhandle them onto the stretchers. Thunder-flashes and the shouts of the riflemen batter their ears and nerves.

Their charges secure, they turn about and haul them back through the smoke to the Chinook ramp. One stretcher party, manned by the youngest trainees, is seen to be struggling, and getting in a tangle with the M60. They stumble and the casualty is close to being dumped on the ground – but they recover and make it safely to the shelter of the cabin.

In reality, the Chinook would now clatter its way back to Bastion, but now it's the press party that moves, crowding around the ramp (the bangs have stopped and the smoke has cleared) to get close-up shots of the medics at work. With the two stretchers on the floor, and the protection force recovered to the cabin, the restriction on operating space becomes immediately apparent. These young guys and girls have a tough job to do. Viewers will later get to see ER care in a dark, cramped box: trainees setting up saline drips from the cabin roof, applying tourniquets and dressings, and carrying out pulmonary resuscitation and heart massage.

After ten minutes, and a simulated landing back at base, Matt moves the onlookers to one side. His whistle brings the MERT personnel humping the stretchers back past the machine-gun, and then at the trot to an ambulance, for the casualties to be handed over to the care of the base medical team, and the facilities of the hospital.

The media people gather round the minister for a series of interviews, and to camera he acknowledges the vital nature of the MERT task and how essential it is to invest in the resources required for doing it. The whole party then climbs into a bus for a visit to one of Lyneham's four-engined Hercules transports (fitted out in medevac rig), their faces and remarks clearly indicating that Louise and Matt's demo has impressed. The realism has been heightened by the below-freezing temperatures, a foretaste of the much greater cold awaiting the trainees in Afghanistan this winter.

HERCULES OVER THE PLAIN

Since 2001, the Hercules turbo-prop tactical transports of RAF Lyneham have been flying the trooping, freight and air-drop missions in Helmand that are a key logistical link in the combat chain. Air-drop services are provided to the Army and the Marines, in fact to any Ministry of Defence (MoD) force that requires it in the field. The business has grown. Air-delivery of supplies reduces pressure on road convoys and helicopters, both of which operate at high risk in the current combat areas.

The Lockheed C-130 Hercules has been in service now for fifty years, and with the RAF since the late 1960s. It is planned to reduce the fourteen-strong fleet of the earlier 'K' Models based at Lyneham to nine by December 2010. Meantime, the force has been strengthened with the more advanced 'J' Model, the 'Super-Hercules', with one-third longer freight cabin, forty per cent targeted increase in range (albeit the 'K' has underwing external tanks, giving it greater range than the RAF's 'J's at present), twenty-one per cent higher maximum speed, and forty-one per cent shorter take-off distance.

Nevertheless, alongside the 'J', the 'K' is still doing sterling work in Helmand. Its four turboprops can haul a maximum load of close to 18,000 kg for a couple of thousand nautical miles at 325 knots. It can cruise out of danger from the current crop of surface-to-air missiles in use by hostile forces in Afghanistan. And it can deliver a wider variety of loads than the 'J' can currently manage. The 'K' will in due course be superseded by the Airbus A400M 'Super-Freighter', but delivery of that is already forecast to be between two and four years late.

The 'K' Model carries an aircrew of five, four of them on the flight-deck at the top of six feet of steep steps – captain and co-pilot, navigator and flight engineer. Up there in the heat of an Afghan summer the temperature can reach 73 degrees Celsius, 'nearly hot enough to casserole a chicken', but on the Lyneham dispersal one November morning in 2008, a training crew is sitting comfortably and cool, their flying-gear set off by white shammy leather gloves. Down in the cavernous cabin – three metres high and the same wide – sits the fifth crew member, the flight sergeant loadmaster. He's overseeing three NCO air despatchers from 47 Air Despatch Squadron, flying to restore their air-drop currency. No. 47AD is an Army unit of the Royal Logistics Corps commanded by a major, but based at Lyneham and manned by all three Services. Its task is to maintain the MoD's air-delivery skills and capabilities, and the inventory of air-drop equipment. They prepare the loads and stow them in the aircraft, and their men, two to four depending on the weight of the delivery, fly on every Hercules air-drop mission, worldwide. At any one time there are a dozen 47AD men and women on deployment in Afghanistan. The soldiers on today's trip, a despatch crew commander and his team of two, are wearing the same kit as their RAF counterparts, distinguishable only by their rank badges and shoulder flashes. The task is simple – a single 70 kg harness pack with its parachute sits shackled to the cargo floor, ready to be dropped onto Keevil Airfield on the edge of the Plain – but the aim is clear. After this drop the despatchers will be requalified for the Afghanistan crewing roster.

The interior of their place of work is a maze of exposed piping and wiring, and packed with stowed equipment, including a large bristled broom hanging halfway up on the forward starboard wall, essential for sweeping foreign objects off the rear ramp after each mission. The porthole-type windows are each no more than a foot square, and lighting is restricted to soft white spots above and red strip illumination below the seats. Today, the rig is a couple of dozen paratroop-type fold-back canvas seats alongside the cabin walls, with red webbing latticework for back and head support, and a central back-to-back bank of two rows of four up front, immediately forward of a powerful electrical cargo winch, and a stack of pallet chocks strapped to the floor. Above the seats hang life-jackets in yellow packs, together with supplies of ear plugs, and much-needed sickbags – Hercules crews can tell you that the atmosphere in here with a full load of vomiting Paras is a challenge for the strongest stomach. There are four urinals with little or no privacy (two at the front on the bulkhead, two at the rear on either side) and a chemical toilet at port rear with just a flimsy curtain – there's no 'Ladies'. This is the standard rig for passengers in this typically American design of military transport – functional, with no room for non-essentials. In this cabin, the C130K can carry 128 troops, or ninety paratroops in full kit – with two tonnes of their equipment on a 'wedge platform' on the upper section of the two-part ramp.

The loadmaster points out the numerous emergency exits in the Hercules, starting with two roof hatches – one forward of the main spar and reached from the flight-deck ('Watch the props as you go out!') and one aft, accessed by a ladder ('Go up the starboard side or you'll get stuck'). Others are the crew door and steps forward and to port ('Again, mind the props – and the exhaust from the APU!'). Two more to starboard, and one to port, complete the escape routes.

[APU – Auxiliary Power Unit.]

For the pre-start checks, the helmeted loadmaster first stalks the cargo floor, trailing a long intercom cable. He has to watch his footing among the matrix of cargo anchorage points. Armed with a powerful torch, as the aircrew read through the list up on the flight-deck he confirms that all is well with the two dozen key pieces of plumbing and electrics in the roof and on the walls. The interior checks complete, still trailing his intercom cable he moves to stand on the tarmac outside the crew door for engine start-up. Upstairs, the captain, from the left-hand seat, pushes the buttons and moves the levers that bring the four turboprops to life. The noise level builds.

The co-pilot calls for clearance from the tower, and the captain takes all four throttle levers into his right hand. The three marshallers are now in position – one in front and one on each wingtip – ready to guide the 100 ft length and 133 ft wingspan of this bulky aircraft, dubbed by Americans the 'Fat Albert', safely off its stand. The captain eases the throttles forward from 'Flight Idle', and over 100,000 lb of airframe and fuel is on the move. A check of the brakes, and then the skipper grasps the nose-steering wheel with his left hand, following the signals of the marshaller until clear and out onto the taxiway.

There are no control locks on this machine, allowing the ailerons and tail surfaces to fly free in any air-turbulence on the ground, avoiding damage. But there's a brisk wind today and it's the co-pilot's job to 'fly' the controls during the taxi, to minimize their movement. The flight engineer, seated behind the two pilots, monitors the temperatures and pressures of the engines and mechanics, and the navigator, sat at the back, checks out the critical Traffic Collision and Avoidance System (TCAS) and its repeater screen in front of the pilots – there's to be a deal of low flying on this mission, and this piece of kit, obligatory these days on civilian as well as military aircraft, will come in more than handy should the weather turn foul.

With brakes on at the end of the runway, the co-pilot calls for take-off clearance and then, on a command from the captain, grasps the propeller pitch levers at his left hand and moves them forward to take-off setting. The skipper opens the throttles to full power, and downstairs, loadmaster and despatchers are buffeted by the roar and vibration. The Hercules then shows its paces as the props haul the machine into the air after just a twenty-second take-off roll.

Undercarriage up, and within another half-minute the captain levels off at 500 feet to clear the local area, before banking steeply to the left over the Wiltshire fields for the short southerly transit to Salisbury Plain. Throttling back for the cruise, engine roar is less, but at the same frequency on the ears, as the constant-speed props maintain control of the revs. With an all-round view through the twenty-three window panels, extending to below foot level either side of the flight-deck, the pilots map-read their way towards Keevil across the familiar landmarks of the countryside – a church steeple or two, here and there a river, and a string of picture-postcard villages.

The airfield, which comes up five miles east of Trowbridge, has three concrete runways, and extensive areas of grass. It was used by both RAF and USAF during the Second World War – nowadays there are no aircraft based there, but the MoD maintains it as a day-and-night exercise field for all helicopters in service, and for short-strip and air-drop practice for the transports. The co-pilot makes contact with the control centre for low-level air traffic over the Plain, and gets clearance for an approach, flying at 250 feet above the long-suffering heads of the good people of Wiltshire.

Downstairs, the despatch team is on the move, preparing for the drop. The loadmaster has been given the signal that it's ten minutes to run to the dropping zone (DZ). The crew commander beckons to the two despatchers, and all three make their way back to the starboard rear paratroop door, knees bent to ride the jolts and shudders in the swaying fuselage. There, they attach one end of their safety lines to anchoring brackets on the floor, and hook the other to their waist harness. They unshackle the lumpy bundle, and at the five-minute signal, attach the parachute static line to the floor. The commander leans into the curve of the door, spying out the land through the porthole window.

On the two-minute warning from the flight-deck, he signals the two men to manhandle the pack to the door and kneel either side of it – leading knee down. With them settled, he heaves the door open, up and over, and the slipstream roars past – fields, villages and farms flying by below at 140 knots. He then shimmies round to crouch to the rear of the load. At one minute to drop, the despatchers manoeuvre the bundle to the edge and swap knees, the outer foot braced against the doorframe. All three men then stand erect, waiting for the lights. At 'Red on', they brace – at 'Green on' they heave the bundle out. The static line cracks, and away goes the load. A quick look to make sure the pack is clear and the 'chute opening, and then in short order it's static line in, door closed and locked, and the Hercules climbs away – job done.

Back in the circuit at Lyneham, the captain takes the chance to practise a tactical landing. He brings the machine in at a noticeably steep angle of approach, with full flap and power on to keep safely above stalling speed. Over the threshold, he pulls the power off and the control-column back, levelling out and touching down almost simultaneously. Immediately, he pulls the throttles back through the gate into reverse pitch, and the propellers become the most effective of brakes. It's a remarkably short landing run. In normal operation the minimum length of runway for the Hercules is a couple of thousand yards, but in the tactical role, as for instance on up-country Afghanistan strips, it can manage with much less than that. In early trials, a Mk 1 C130, stripped down and with minimum fuel, took off from a United States aircraft carrier at sea – and landed back again in one piece.

This has been a short trip, and a basic exercise. But these despatchers and this crew are proficient in all the varieties of air-drop that the Hercules can offer the NATO Coalition in Helmand. Harness packs like the one dropped this morning can be heaved out three at a time from each side door, on a tip-up slide arrangement. Canadian Ski Tubes, 'torpedoes' of up to 317 kg each, can be slipped along the rails and over the rear sill, eight at a go. A system for delivering robust stores over the sill is the 'Para Wedge' one-tonne container, weighing in at up to 1,200 kg with its parachute. With this, water, ammo (including anti-tank shells) and operational ration packs can be followed six seconds later by up to ninety-six paratroops from both side doors. Over water, those paratroops can also gallop in a string off the back, close behind their inflatable boat, rigid raiding craft, or canoes. The men who shove the boat platforms off by muscle-power know to get out of the way sharpish to avoid being caught in the rush.

They are trained to deliver heavier extracted loads, pulled out of the Hercules cabin by a drogue 'chute, allowing the despatch of single loads of up to 7,416 kg, or a double Medium Stressed Platform (MSP) with an all-up weight of approximately 15,000 kg. Up to two of these can be carried, and dropped on up to four 66 ft 'chutes, each taking two Land Rovers, the front wheels of one sitting in the back of the other. One MSP can also deliver one fork-lift truck, one Air-Delivered Forward-Arming and Refuelling Point (AD FARP), or two 105 mm light guns plus ammo, which can be brought to firing readiness within fifteen minutes of landing. With this load, the platform base opens in the descent, and airbags designed to burst cushion the landing. They are extracted with ten tonnes of force, and in the dry words of the manual 'require significant control column movements from the pilot'.

But the workhorse air-drop in Helmand is from the 'J' Model Hercules, using the Container Delivery System (CDS) employed by both British and American forces. Up to eighteen one-tonne containers can be loaded on two rows of rails – the Mark 4 can carry twenty-four, the Mark 5 sixteen – and they can be dropped either in groups or all at one go. These heavy loads almost completely fill the cargo compartment (when double-width base-boards are used they can take a tank engine), and they build up a considerable head of steam on the move. But the system is known for its reliability, and using it the Americans recently set a record for air-drop, two of their C17 transports simultaneously despatching 84,000 lb (49,895 kg) of winter clothing and stores in forty containers onto the one Afghanistan DZ.

It's that kind of capability that has made Hercules air-drop the delivery method of choice for bulk stores for Coalition ground commanders in Afghanistan. This morning's short sortie with a harness-pack, in renewing the currency of another despatch team, has made its contribution to that vital task.

MARINES UNDER THE AIR-DROP

In Helmand, among clients for Chinook and Hercules resupply will be the Royal Marines of 42 Commando, one of the three brigades within 3 Commando Group, the Royal Navy's amphibious infantry. A few weeks before flying out to Kandahar at the end of September 2008 for a seven-month stint as Regional Battle Group (South) (RBG(S)), a troop of newcomers to the unit is dispersed on the grassy expanse between the runways of Keevil Airfield. Two Lyneham Hercules are scheduled to give them first-hand experience of being under a stores delivery by CDS.

At their barracks at Bickleigh in the wooded hills around Plymouth, and in their exercise area on the edge of Dartmoor, routine year-round training keeps the 400 men and women of 42 Commando up to speed and ready for battle. But for Southern Afghanistan, there's a six-month process for sharpening skills particular to the campaign – such as special arms and ordnance handling, briefing on the latest Intelligence, Surveillance, Target Acquisition and Reconnaissance (ISTAR) procedures, and practice in receiving supplies by parachute.

Major Justin Morton is the battalion's Quartermaster, and he'll be the Logistic Officer for the battle group when on deployment. As an old Iraq and Afghanistan hand – he's been to Kandahar before, as a logistic planner in Brigade HQ – he's well aware that supply is the key to successful assault operations, and knows the particular challenges of the Afghan theatre. Along with fuel and ammunition, and batteries for the all-pervasive electronic counter-measure (ECM) equipment, about top of the list of resupply priorities is clean drinking-water. In the summer, the daily requirement for each deployed man is ten litres. In mid-winter this reduces to three to four litres, but in the final months of the Marines' next spell in the Task Force, in the spring, the ambient temperature will increase in the lowlands by 10 degrees Celsius each week, and the minimum requirement per man will increase to six litres. Supplies must be ensured through frequent air-drop, supplemented in part by shipment in, or under the Chinooks.

WO2 David Mallinson runs the Equipment Support Section in barracks, but in Kandahar he'll have the job of Echelon Sergeant Major. The echelon is the support unit that drives out in convoy in the spearhead of the assault, to set up a communications and resupply hub for the troops. He has also operated in Afghanistan before, in the HQ of 42 Commando when it was Battle Group (North), and spent the time resupplying the static Forward Operating Bases (FOBs) by Chinook and Hercules along the Helmand valley. This time, the Commando is slated to carry out mobile air assault operations, for which the mobility of air-supply is an essential. He'll liaise with the Logistic Officer by radio from the field, providing a daily inventory of requirements.

Sergeant Philip Eames is the unit's Armourer, but in theatre he'll be the NCO out on the Drop and Helicopter Landing Zones. Away from the hub, he and his men will draw up an 800–1,200-metre base-line, taking account of the prevailing winds, terrain, enemy action and position of friendly troops. They will then lay out the insertion point (IP) markers as an aid for the aircrews on night approaches. Because of the risks to men and aircraft alike, this task is critical to the success of the mission, and is being practised as part of a Mission Rehearsal Exercise (MRX) at Keevil today. Sergeant Eames briefs the men:

> We've set out the airfield to receive two Hercules transports, each with a full CDS load, to be despatched from 3,000 feet. There are risks in being under an air-drop, both from 1,000 kilos of container straying off-line into your positions close by and from 'chute failures – they're called candles – which happen too often for complete comfort. Around one and a half per cent of parachutes fail, and in free-fall from over half a mile high at a terminal velocity of 120 mph, a plummeting container of water is a frightening thing. The impact is enormous and the whole thing goes up like a bomb, hurling the bottles anything up to 300 metres.

Mister Mallinson adds his own experience. 'At night, it's something else again. You lie there listening, hugging the ground, counting the thuds as the loads come down, and hearing the booms as the candles hit the deck.'

One of the riflemen, Lance Corporal Danny Cole – in Plymouth, he's the Commanding Officer's driver – knows all about that: 'It's surreal. You don't twig the aircraft at first – you just all-of-a-sudden hear this whole lot of wallops out in the desert. Then you grope your way in the dark to find the containers, and lug them and the parachutes in.'

The first Hercules appears. It's a 'J' Model, which the lads recognize primarily from its extra fuselage length and the absence of underwing tanks, droning over from the north-east into the prevailing wind. The pilot has set the aircraft up in a shallow climb, and at 'Green light on!' the loadmaster starts the two lines of containers – bulked up with their webbing and 'chute packs, and each filled with gravel to simulate supplies – rolling down to the open ramp, drawn by gravity along the tracks to the sill. Over the edge, static lines thwack, 'chutes billow out, and the loads float free, silently down to the troops below. The aircrew have judged the winds at height just right, and the whole delivery lands within the triangle of Keevil's runways. There are no candles in this despatch. Eighteen thumps mean a full load's arrived.

'All right, lads,' from Mister Mallinson, 'time to let the dogs loose. Go get 'em! There'll be another one coming in an hour or so.'

All the experienced hands know that this exercise, in good weather and in the secure surroundings of the Salisbury Plain, is far removed from the real thing the Marines will get in Afghanistan, with dust, storms, and enemy action – and usually in darkness.

'But it practises the drills,' says Sergeant Eames, 'and gives the newcomers the basics. They'll learn much more on the job in Helmand, and before very long it'll all become second nature.'

'Of course,' adds Mister Mallinson, 'once we're established out in the field, and the area and our road links have been secured, ground convoys can bring in many tons of supplies and take the pressure off the aircrews somewhat. But without the air-supply assets there'd be precious few assault operations.'

Major Morton is quick to endorse that. 'As we see it, the air-resupply guys in Afghanistan, including the RAF in their Hercs and Chinooks, are doing a fantastic job for us. They're our lifeline.'

CHAPTER 2

Towards the Airbridge

OCTOBER 2008

INTERNATIONAL SECURITY ASSISTANCE FORCE

Some 50,000 servicemen and women from thirty-one countries currently make up the International Security Assistance Force (ISAF) in the landlocked and mountainous country of Afghanistan. At 21,000, American troops form the largest contingent, followed by the British with 6,500. According to its official website, ISAF is 'a key component of the international community's engagement in the Islamic Republic, assisting the Afghan authorities in providing security and stability and creating the conditions for reconstruction and development'. Mandated by the UN, it began operations in January 2002, following the Al Qaeda suicide attacks on New York the previous September and the subsequent United States–Great Britain Coalition assault on the country from October to December. This operation, carried out with air support, was aimed at ferreting out Osama bin Laden, the Al Qaeda warlord, and ejecting the hard-line Taliban. In that action – which failed in the former task but had success, for the time being, in the latter – key Coalition assets were the Chinooks and Hercules of the RAF.

CHINOOK AND HERCULES ARRIVAL

Chinooks have been at RAF Odiham since August 1981. In addition to Afghanistan, they've seen service in the Falklands, Northern Ireland, the Gulf and Iraq. They've been with the peacekeepers in the Balkans, on evacuation sorties in Sierra Leone and the Lebanon, and on famine-relief operations around the globe. The original HC1 fleet, with airframes dating from the early 1970s, was upgraded during 1993 and '94 to the HC2 with enhanced avionics and more powerful engines. These were the aircraft in action in the 2001 Afghan campaign. From the start, their designated battlefield tasks have been the tactical transport of troops, weapons, ammunition and stores – frequently into difficult forward positions and often in emergency response – together with search and rescue, and evacuation of casualties from the front line.

The Hercules have been at RAF Lyneham since August 1967, and they, too, have subsequently seen service in all British forces' campaigns. In the Falklands in the early 1980s, their 3,900-mile route from Wiltshire to Ascension Island in the mid-Atlantic staged through Gibraltar and Dakar. In the first three weeks of the operation the Hercules carried more than 1,600 tonnes of freight to Ascension, and flew on to air-drop supplies to the Task Force at sea. Later, the aircraft were fitted with refuelling probes, and some with extra fuel tanks in the freight bays, so that, supported by airborne Victor tankers, they could make the extra 3,900 miles down to the Falklands – and back, non-stop. On the first of these flights, 16 May 1982, the crew dropped paratroops and their stores and then returned to Ascension, clocking up twenty-four hours and five minutes in the air. Just before the campaign, the first CMK3 conversions had come into squadron service, with an extra fifteen feet of length spliced into the fuselage and freight bay. By 1985 all (save for a number of Mk 1 'shorties') had been converted, and were available to fly in support of the 2001 Afghanistan action, where their tactical take-off and landing capabilities came to the fore on the short, rough desert airstrips, as they flew air-drop, troop insertion and resupply missions.

Both types of aircraft are fulfilling the same roles in Afghanistan today, within ISAF, and now with NATO.

NATO IN CONTROL

On taking up his post in January 2004, General Jaap de Hoop Scheffer, the eleventh Secretary-General, gave the rationale for the involvement of the North Atlantic Treaty Organization: 'The immediate priority is to get Afghanistan right – we cannot afford to fail. If we do not go to Afghanistan, Afghanistan will come to us.'

Following the 2001 Coalition invasion, the Taliban and their supporters melted away, mostly over the southern border with Pakistan. In August 2003, NATO assumed authority over the UN-mandated ISAF mission, in its first operational commitment outside Europe. In October it extended its activities outside Kabul, initially in the Northern Region. In February 2005, it entered

HELMAND PROVINCE
(AFGHANISTAN)

WORLD BRIEFING MAPS

Series	GSGS 5865
Sheet	Helmand Province
Edition	6-GSGS

1459/1151

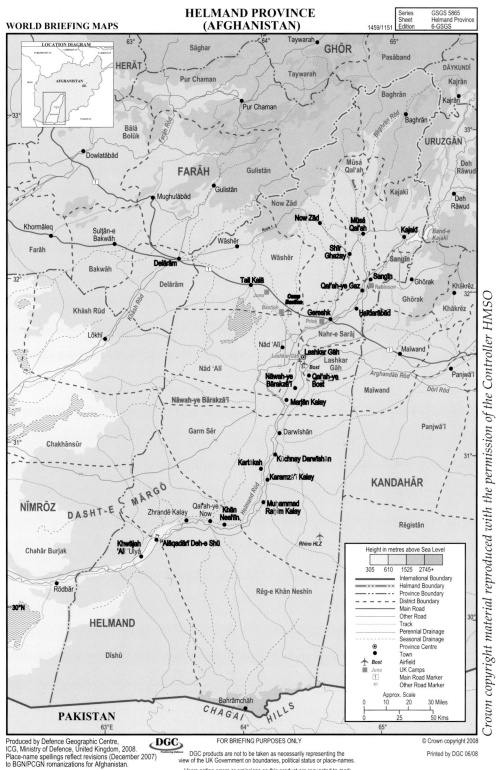

LOCATION DIAGRAM

HERĀT
GHŌR
Săghar
Taywarah
Pasăband
DĀYKUNDĪ
Pur Chaman
Taywarah
Baghrăn
Kajrăn
Pur Chaman
Baghrăn
Kajrăn
Băghrăn Rōd
URUZGĂN
Bălă Bolŭk
Dowlatăbăd
FARĂH
Gulistăn
Mŭsá Qal'ah
Deh Răwud
Kajakĭ
Deh Răwud
Mughulăbăd
Gulistăn
Now Zăd
Khormăleq
Sultăn-e Bakwăh
Wăshēr
Now Zăd
Mŭsá Qal'ah
Kajakĭ
Band-e Kajakĭ
Farăh
Bakwăh
Delărăm
Wăshēr
Shĭr Ghazay
Sangĭn
Khāsh Rōd
Delărăm
Tall Kală
Qal'ah-ye Gaz
Sangĭn
Ghōrak
Khākrēz
Khāsh Rŭd
Juno
Camp Bastion
Gereshk
Robinson
Ghōrak
Khākrēz
Lōkhĭ
Price
Nahr-e Sarăj
Haidarăbăd
Chakhānsŭr
Năd 'Alĭ
Lashkar Găh
Maīwand
Lashkar Găh
Lashkar Găh
Năd 'Alĭ
Bost
Arghandăb Rōd
Panjwă'ĭ
Năwah-ye Bărakză'ĭ
Qal'ah-ye Bost
Dōrĭ Rōd
Năwah-ye Bărakză'ĭ
Marjăn Kalay
Maīwand
Panjwă'ĭ
Garm Sēr
Darwīshăn
Kūchnay Darwīshăn
Kartăkah
Karamză'ĭ Kalay
KANDAHĀR
NĪMRŌZ
DASHT-E MĀRGŌ
Qal'ah-ye Now
Khān Neshĭn
Muhammad Rahĭm Kalay
Zhrandē Kalay
Rēgistăn
Chahăr Burjak
Khwăjah 'Alĭ 'Ulyă
'Alăqadărĭ Deh-e Shŭ
Rhino HLZ
Rēg-e Khăn Neshĭn
Rōdbăr
30°N
HELMAND
Dĭshŭ
Bahrămchăh
PAKISTAN
CHAGAI HILLS

Height in metres above Sea Level

305	610	1525	2745+

International Boundary
Helmand Boundary
Province Boundary
District Boundary
Main Road
Other Road
Track
Perennial Drainage
Seasonal Drainage
⊙ Province Centre
● Town
Bost Airfield
■ Juno UK Camps
① Main Road Marker
⑪ Other Road Marker

Approx. Scale

| 0 | 10 | 20 | 30 Miles |
| 0 | 25 | | 50 Kms |

63°E
64°
65°

Produced by Defence Geographic Centre,
ICG, Ministry of Defence, United Kingdom, 2008.
Place-name spellings reflect revisions (December 2007)
to BGN/PCGN romanizations for Afghanistan.

WARNING
Administrative Divisions may not reflect
those in operation on the ground.

DGC
Publishing Defence

FOR BRIEFING PURPOSES ONLY

the Western Region, and in September of that year the country was able to hold its first parliamentary and provincial elections in more than thirty years, undisrupted by civil disturbance. But in May 2006, a United States military driver lost control of his vehicle in the capital, Kabul, tragically killing several Afghans. In the violent anti-US protests that followed, the Taliban saw their moment to strike back, retaking former strongholds in the south. At the end of July, in response to that threat, NATO took command in the Southern sector. By October 2006, it had taken responsibility for security across the whole of the country.

The 1,500-mile border with Pakistan is mountainous, virtually impossible to secure and a hotbed of insurgent action. As part of a wholesale reorganization of ISAF forces, the Americans took up the lead role in the frontier provinces east of Kabul, while the British forces relocated to Kandahar Province in the south-west, setting up Regional Command (South), RC(S), in an operation codenamed Herrick – now, in 2010, in its fifth year.

RC(S) comprises Kandahar and five more of the thirty Afghan provinces, including Helmand, the most populous and a stronghold of the Taliban. To cover Helmand, an FOB was built by the British Army at Bastion, seventy-five miles north-west of the main base at Kandahar Airfield (known to all who use it by its three-letter identifier, KAF) and a dozen or so miles north of the Helmand provincial capital of Lashkar Gah. The site was chosen not only for its remoteness, which brought an increased measure of security, but also because the Royal Engineers identified a location there for sinking a borehole, which has since given the camp self-sufficiency in water.

In May 2006, the first British Battle Group deployed at Camp Bastion, manned by 3 Parachute Regiment. '3 Para' was handed the challenging task of securing the 'Triangle', the area between Bastion, Lashkar Gah and Gereshk, a fortified town seventy-five miles north-east up the Helmand river from the provincial capital, in order to enable the redevelopment of towns and villages ravaged by twenty-five years of conflict. Instead, the soldiers found themselves marooned in those devastated towns and villages, walled up in further, hastily constructed FOBs and fighting a continuous and bloody battle against scores of determined and well-armed hostiles. The conflict expanded to Sangin, a further eighty miles up the river, and to Musa Qal'eh and Now Zad, remote in the northern Helmand mountains. In the Paras' struggle to hold their extended positions, Hercules air-drops and Chinook resupply became a lifeline.

EXPEDITIONARY AIR WINGS AND 1310 FLIGHT

Since 1 April 2006, the Hercules on Herrick have been operated under the control of the RAF's 904 Expeditionary Air Wing (EAW). These wings were first established in the Second World War to give units a command structure while ensuring the flexibility to mobilize overseas at short notice. The first action for 904 was in 1944, with four squadrons of P47 Thunderbolt ground-attack fighters supporting General Slim's Fourteenth Army in the Burma campaign. It was disbanded in 1946, but has now been reactivated, based at Kandahar with a flight of four Hercules, crewed on a rota basis by the Lyneham squadrons. Each crew member goes for a month or six weeks, on average three times each year, but that could stretch to four or five.

On Herrick operations, the Odiham Chinooks are operated by RAF 1310 Flight. Also first formed in 1944, this was a short-lived command flying Avro Ansons in support of aircraft ferrying operations. Since then, it has been reactivated a number of times, most recently for support helicopter (SH) action overseas: in South America, the Falklands and the Balkans, and in Iraq on Operation Telic, the mobilization in support of the American invasion of 2003, and in the occupation thereafter. Since the spring of 2006, 1310 Flight's role has been to provide the heavy-lift element within the British Forces' Joint Helicopter Force Afghanistan, JHF(A), based at Kandahar and working for RC(S).

In the UK, all MoD helicopters report to Joint Helicopter Command (JHC), which is itself part of Land Command, meaning that operational control and funding lie with the Army. It's an example of the modern commitment to 'jointery', with all three arms of the Services seeking to co-ordinate their efforts for maximum efficiency. Another example is the RAF's Nimrod Maritime Patrol Squadron, which now reports to the Royal Navy.

RAF Odiham offers JHF(A) the largest fleet of Chinooks outside the US Army. Forty HC2/2A Models are in service, at any one time scheduled either for deep servicing, allocated to UK-based training, or on operations. In addition, there are eight Mk 3s in a hangar at RAF Boscombe Down, waiting for modifications to bring them into operational use. Currently, 1310 is manned by the Odiham squadrons, with each of five flights being detached to theatre for ten weeks at a time, every ten months.

The EAW and 1310 Flight structure succeeds in giving these in-and-out warriors an invaluable *esprit de corps*. A formal request has been submitted to Her Majesty the Queen to approve the award of a formal crest to 1310 Flight, and in the citation is the following:

The Flight's conspicuous and meritorious service in the best traditions of the Royal Air Force has been typified by the award of four Distinguished Flying Crosses and numerous other gallantry awards to its personnel serving in Afghanistan in the past two years.

If granted, the badge will bear the Flight's motto: *Quicquid Ubivis Utcumque*, which roughly translates as, 'Whatever, Wherever, Whenever', encapsulating its universal capabilities and flexibility.

1301 Flight Badge – with Royal Approval (crown copyright 2010)

Adaptability and patience are needed in managing the complex chain of command. All deployed UK forces ultimately come under Permanent Joint Headquarters (PJHQ) based at Northwood in Middlesex, but for admin and discipline, the Hercules crews report back to the Lyneham Station Commander and the RAF's Air Command. For operational control the line is to the EAW Commander at Kandahar. It's a similar chain for the Chinook crews, but to Odiham and the JHF(A). They manage the complications, for according to Wing Commander Dom Toriati, OC 27 Squadron and a previous JHF(A) CO: 'There's a light blue streak through the whole chain of command. And these men and women are professional RAF. They know how to keep focused on the job – they've all been through the RAF training mill.'

That training mill has for ninety years been turning out aircrews renowned around the world for their airmanship and commitment to the task. The air-supply crews on Herrick are the latest in a line with a proud tradition.

Chinook people – aircrew

The Boss – 'C' Flight Commander on 27 Squadron, and captain of Gambit Two on PDT in the Cairngorms – is well over six feet tall, lean and dark. Born the son of an RAF pilot, he joined the Combined Cadet Force (CCF) at school and passed flying aptitude tests at RAF Biggin Hill before being sponsored by the RAF to study civil engineering at Birmingham University. He played all the sports and flew with the University Air Squadron (UAS), yet managed to get his degree, before enlisting at the RAF College, Cranwell.

He graduated in February 1995 after six months of Initial Officer Training (IOT), and spent an enjoyable holding detachment at Goose Bay in Canada, where the skiing was good, before reporting to RAF Barkston Heath for Elementary Flying Training (EFT) on the Bulldog, 'pretty much a rerun of UAS flying'. The lottery of RAF postings then sent him for further holding, at Odiham, and his first experience of the Chinook. Rotary-wing flying has been his operational world ever since, for after Basic Flying Training (BFT) on the Tucano, a change of direction took him to the AAC base at Middle Wallop, joining what was to be the final 'all-army' helicopter Advanced Flying Training (AFT) course. For the next four-and-three-quarter years he was seconded, unusually, as 'a flight lieutenant in the Army'.

His first tour with the AAC was in 1998 as a Lynx pilot, with 657 Squadron at Dishforth. On active service in Belize, he flew his first casevac missions. Next came Sierra Leone, where he won the Distinguished Flying Cross (DFC) on a hostage-release mission. In October 2001, following a spell in Macedonia, he organized a path back into the RAF and a place on the next course at the Operational Conversion Flight (OCF) for Chinooks, hosted by 18(B) Squadron at Odiham ('B' for Bomber, reflecting its history). He has now completed four detachments to Helmand – the next, in February 2009, will be his fifth.

German, the leader of Gambit Formation in Scotland, has at the age of just 29 already been on Afghanistan detachment five times. From the Air Training Corps in Essex, he won a coveted Flying Scholarship at Southend. The RAF provided a bursary for a four-year course at Durham, starting in 1998, in Economics and French, the latter giving him a year's study in Aix-en-Provence.

Durham also offered rugby and soccer, and the UAS at Leeming – EFT on Bulldogs and the Grob Tutor. He graduated in 2002 and went up to Cranwell in August, where 'there were a lot of hoops to jump through – and I made a lot of good mates'. He was recommended for multi-engine, but the demands of the Service streamed him instead for rotary. 'I wasn't disappointed, it was something different.' In February 2003, he reported to the Tri-Service Defence Helicopter Flying School (DHFS) at RAF Shawbury. Following six months' common syllabus training, with the air hours on the *Aérospatiale* AS350 Squirrel, the Navy students went off to Yeovilton and the Army to Middle Wallop for their AFT. The RAF pilots remained at Shawbury for theirs, on the Bell 412 twin-engine single-rotor Griffin. Successfully negotiating the course, right through to search and rescue techniques and mountain flying, and now a flight lieutenant, German gained his wings in July 2004.

He arrived at the Odiham OCF in September. After the five-month course – forty per cent of the 'flying' actually took place on the simulator at RAF Benson – he joined 27 Squadron's 'A' Flight. With them he deployed to Helmand for the first time in April 2006, just before the riots in Kabul. It's been non-stop action for him ever since.

The NHP on Gambit Two conforms to the popular image of an RAF pilot – compact and good-looking. Morts is another son of a flying father, and his elder brother is an RAF aviator too. But, set on taking a different direction, he went to Exeter University to study Economics, aiming at City banking – until work-experience in his first long vacation revealed that finance wasn't for him. One lunchtime he walked into an RAF Recruiting Office 'really just to see what the options were'. He found himself channelled straight away into the aircrew selection process. The RAF offered a bursary, and his flying career started at Bristol UAS on the Tutor, 'lovely machine – handles like a glider'. With his EFT completed and degree achieved, Morts entered Cranwell in April 2005: 'I just managed some skiing before hitting the first six weeks' intensive. All the instructors at the UAS had been fast-jet friendly, and keen for us to try for single-seat aircraft – so when the flying started, so was I.'

But priorities and quotas were changing, and of his entry, only one trainee was streamed to fast jets. Eighty per cent went to rotary, and Morts was among them – the sight and sound of a Chinook quickly convincing him that helicopters were the thing. He was successful at Shawbury, and again at the Odiham OCF, where he was chosen by 27 Squadron's 'C' Flight. He joined it in September 2008. 'I'd been at UAS with some of their blokes. We all knew we'd be going to Helmand within a year, but I wasn't too worried about that just then – I went skiing over Christmas without a care in the world.'

Twelve short months later, his first detachment is just around the corner.

Crewman Number One off Gambit Two, Mister B – a fit-as-a-fiddle six-footer with close-cropped grizzled hair and a ready smile – was another 'Services brat', and followed his father into the RAF in 1985, straight from the Sixth Form. Following basic, he qualified for eighteen months' comprehensive air loadmaster training at Finningley and Shawbury. The course covered everything from engineering and service for rotary-wing machines, through defensive weapons suites, USL, and navigation. It even extended to offensive weapons – this on the Westland Wessex, the first RAF helicopter to carry the General-Purpose Machine-Gun (GPMG, or 'Jimpy') – and basic helicopter handling, both 'just in case'.

In 1987, with his loadmaster brevet, and accompanied by his new wife, he was posted for an eighteen-month tour on 18(B) Squadron at Gütersloh, Germany, as crewman on Chinooks.

Mister B has been on Chinooks ever since. Now Crewman Master on 27 Squadron, he has great respect for the aircraft: 'As they say – if the world's going to end, you send for a Chinook.' He has crewed on them in Northern Ireland, in the First Gulf War, in the humanitarian missions to the Kurds in Northern Iraq and Southern Turkey, Kosovo, Sierra Leone – and Afghanistan. He was first there in support of the American–British operations of 2001, and then on Operation Herrick from the start. His next tour, like German's, will be his sixth in the theatre.

Mister B's deputy as Crewman Master is Ginger, blessed with jet-black hair, muscular frame and forthright manner. He was born a few miles up the road from Odiham, where Chinooks were often clattering overhead. From an early age he determined to fly in 'the mighty machine'.

At school, he won a Flying Scholarship, and after A-levels the RAF offered to take him either in ground trades (RAF Regiment, Air Traffic and Provost Branch), where he would get a commission, or aircrew, as an NCO loadmaster. He opted for aircrew, hoping for helicopters, finding the notion of going into the firing-line 'highly motivating'. At the end of three months' basic at Cranwell, he was promoted to aircrew sergeant. Four months of loadmaster generic (fixed-wing and rotary) training followed, which included airmanship studies such as Meteorology and Principles of Flight. He got his hoped-for helicopters, and fourteen months later had his brevet. He reported to the Odiham OCF in the summer of 2000 before joining 27 Squadron in March 2001.

He was immediately on a helicopter carrier in the Indian Ocean, lifting light guns to on-shore Army Commandos, and by August, was detached to the Falklands. Back from the South Atlantic it was up to Fagerness in Norway for February and March 2002, on Arctic Ops and winter survival training. Then he was off again to the Falklands, ferrying heavy radar equipment from MV Brandon, the loads slung under the single deployed Chinook. 'It was South to North Pole and back again in three months.'

The pace didn't slacken. March 2002 saw him operating for the first time in Afghanistan, and he then spent seven months in Iraq, which included the 2003 American-led invasion. In October 2005 he was in Pakistan on earthquake relief in Kashmir, and the next summer evacuating British noncombatants from the Lebanon. Home from that, he transferred to 'C' Flight when it was formed in July 2006. This next detachment will be the fourth time his name has come up on the flight's Herrick rotation.

NOVEMBER 2008
CHINOOK PRE-DEPLOYMENT TRAINING

The Chinooks of 1310 Flight are manned in turn by the three aircrew flights of Odiham's 27 Squadron and the two of 18(B). Each deployment comprises some nine weeks of operations, with handover and travel tacked on at either end. Thirty-four weeks are then spent either away on training and exercise, on standby Ops and routine flying at Odiham, or on annual and 'decompression' leave. In this way, the start of each spell at Kandahar rolls back by a couple of months each year, ensuring a change of season and most likely a change in the intensity of action.

'C' Flight of 27 Squadron will relieve 'B' Flight of 18(B) at the beginning of February 2009. On 3 November, it's due to start its Pre-Deployment Training (PDT), and the Boss calls a meeting to discuss the basics, with Crewmen Leader Mister B, and the Deputy Flight Commander, Frankie.

Trim and straight-talking, Frankie was another born into the RAF, and followed her aircrew father wherever he was based. But the irregularities of schooling didn't prevent her winning an RAF bursary at Nottingham, where she gained a first in Biology and flew on the UAS.

She went up to Cranwell in January 2002, and graduated as a flying officer, her UAS time crediting her with one year's seniority. Streamed already for rotary-wing, she moved on to DHFS, where it was the Army's turn to be in charge. 'There was loads of bull. The RSM demanded proper creases in everything – even in your flying-suit.' She gained her wings in July 2003, and was posted to the OCF at Odiham, becoming the tenth woman pilot on Chinooks.

She joined 27 Squadron in the winter of 2004 as a flight lieutenant, immediately spending two months in Iraq. In 2006 she went on an early 1310 Flight detachment to Op Herrick, during 3 Para's eventful deployment. Frankie has now completed three more stints, and like the Boss is preparing for her fifth.

With their needs fully agreed among themselves, the 'C' Flight trio put them to the Helicopter Force Headquarters staff – RAF Regiment Force Protection, Medical, Support Wing, Intelligence and Ops – and a timetable is set out.

A week later, there's an air-gunnery instruction course on the range at Wainfleet, where Minigun and M60 rounds are sprayed into the Wash. Next comes a ten-day Tactical Leadership Training exercise, including three days on 'Frogex' – two Chinooks supporting Sandhurst cadets' final exercise in the forests of Brittany. In the final week of a packed month, a section of 'C' Flight (two Chinooks with eighteen personnel) travels to Scotland for a four-day Tactical Leadership Training Exercise, in which, according to Frankie, 'practically all the types of aircraft in RAF service get involved'. Bad-weather flying in the Highlands occupies the second week of December, and in the third comes Force Protection (FP) ground training: pistol and carbine on the range, hostage and cold-weather survival, forced landing under fire, land-mine awareness – all the skills needed for a combat 'threat environment'. As this training, together with inoculations, remains current for twelve months, nobody should at any time be unqualified for either scheduled or unscheduled call-out to Herrick.

A weekly Intelligence briefing at Odiham keeps them up to date with the latest from Helmand. As Squadron Tactics Instructor, it's Frankie's job to outline developments in combat practice, mission-essential drills, and other air-warfare matters. Throughout PDT, Chinook aircrews maintain a full continuation-training schedule: emergency, air-test and tactical air-warfare drills on the simulator at RAF Benson, heavy lift on the Odiham airfield, and desert-flying techniques in Morocco.

JANUARY 2009
'C' FLIGHT'S COUNTDOWN

From 19 December until 5 January, 'C' Flight take the 'Winterval' with the rest of the nation, before enduring five days of concentrated admin in Week 3 of the new year, undergoing medical tests to check that all are fit to fly and drawing cold-weather kit from stores. A group-counselling session with Air Command psychologists focuses on the Trauma Risk Management (TRIM) procedure – operational in the Marines and the Army, and rolling out in the RAF – which trains individuals to look for signs of over-stress in their colleagues. Ginger has views on this: 'It was developed for civilian use – we query its effectiveness in the tight Chinook group. A change of behaviour in one of the blokes shows up straight away and can be dealt with face-to-face – sympathetically of course.'

Now, in the last two weeks of January, the pressure builds, as the date of embarkation fast approaches. Essential squadron paperwork is tidied up, bags are packed, domestic affairs are put in order, and the Boss, Frankie and

Mister B work on all the administrative details needed to move their people to Helmand.

Mister B is worried about manpower:

> The challenge is to keep this level of activity going. It's a physical job – and after the guys come through the training pipeline, getting them up to Combat Ready status is another matter. It takes nine months to a year to do that.
>
> Me, Ginger and the old hands take the new boys through all the things they need to know in the combat environment – there's a strict syllabus. After that, if they get through a two-day check ride and a three to four-hour ground check – some don't – then, and only then, they're given their substantive Crewman rank, and Combat Ready tag. If they can't manage all that, sometimes I just have to borrow some volunteers from the other flights.

The Boss has a similar challenge:

> It's a question of man-managing the flight at this stage – the whole business of sorting out who exactly is going and when. Four crews are slated to go out next week – a mixture of the most senior and the newest. They'll be training on the job, and it gives them a chance to settle in before German brings the others out the following week. I'll be with the first wave, to overlap and de-brief with 'B' Flight.
>
> That's the plan, but as well as crewmen, we've had to scrounge aircrews from other units. Another headache is making sure they're all issued with desert-camouflage kit. Then there's the not unimportant matter of getting the Airbridge flights finalized with Brize. I'll be glad when we're on the way.

TO THE AIRBRIDGE

Everything comes together, and well before dawn on 29 January, the four 'C' Flight advance crews gather in 27 Squadron Ops ahead of the seventy-mile drive to RAF Brize Norton and the regular Airbridge flight to Kandahar. There's not much chat – thoughts are still on farewells with friends and family the night before. Then they catch the unexpected aroma of hot coffee and bacon sandwiches.

This early breakfast is down to an idea hit on by one of the newer pilots before 'C' Flight's previous detachment. He's a 27-year-old flight lieutenant rejoicing in the nickname 'Chomper':

I went out first in April last year – I should have gone out earlier with the main party, but they had too many pilots and my departure was delayed for a few weeks. One of the guys was going on about no food being laid on at the Squadron before the bus, and I thought, 'I could do something about that.' So I borrowed a barbecue from a mate – just given it to him as a wedding present, handy really – and set it going on the grass outside Squadron Ops at one in the morning. There were a few funny looks from the security patrol, but by two o'clock I had the bacon sarnies on the go. Bloody good they were, though I say it myself – went down well with the lads and the Boss. Made me feel I was one of them after all. Good to see another new recruit getting up early to do the cooking this time round. Another tradition is born.

At 0400, the airmen, laden with kit, clatter onto the bus and are soon immersed again in their own thoughts.

Ginger lives in Basingstoke with his fiancée of three years, a hair stylist whose commitment to her work equals his own:

She's got used to the military way of life, and we don't do long, tearful goodbyes. She has the company of her pals and her family – and anyway, she controls her nerves by keeping her mind on her job. Me? This is my fourth time and I'm resigned to it. No point in getting worked up – nothing to be done about it. And anyway, I like the buzz of going on Ops, and the sense of achievement in doing a demanding job.

Mister B thinks in much the same way. He and his teacher wife, and their two teenage daughters live in a village near Odiham:

It's difficult to maintain community spirit on the base with so many away in theatre at any one time. But when 27 Squadron people are on Herrick, there are good support services and activities for the families. We manage the disruptions of Service life – no dramas.

Frankie enjoys Service life and is motivated by the flying, having completed over 1,800 hours, of which more than a thousand have been as captain. Her parents are proud of what she's doing and she's passed the exams for promotion to squadron leader. She's been a part of the continual round of Herrick detachments for several years, but even so, there's still a sense of excitement at the prospect of another.

She bought her first house while at university, and now has one close to the base at Odiham. She uses the Officers' Mess for lunch, and attends dining-in nights, but when she can get away her weekends are mostly off base:

> I met my feller on flying training in Yorkshire five years ago. He's still up there as an RAF pilot, so I'm quick to get away on a Friday – it's a long commute. I said goodbye again last weekend – found I was holding him at arms' length. Others in the flight say it's the same with their nearest and dearest as detachments get closer. I just hate the hanging around. I'm all prepared now – it'll be a relief to arrive in theatre.

Chomper became hooked on flying when being turned upside down one day in a family friend's open-cockpit biplane over the Longships lighthouse. At grammar school in Kingston-upon-Thames, he won an RAF Sixth Form Scholarship, with a Flying Scholarship into the bargain. All was going well – until he was devastated to be told he was too tall for the RAF's cockpits and ejector seats. But he didn't give up, as he tells Morts:

> I scraped through the anthropometric retest by having a chum sit on my shoulders for half an hour beforehand. Then I made sure I slumped a bit in the measuring chair. It worked, and in February 2000 I was delighted to get an RAF bursary for Exeter University.
>
> After Cranwell I went on a Field Leadership Course in Norfolk, and saw the Cab for the first time, thundering over the tree tops. I was streamed to fast jets, but held at Coltishall with the display team Jaguars, and after a Dartmouth air show I was offered a lift in a Chinook that was going back to Odiham. That was fun – landing in a field to load my motor on board and then riding on the ramp. I was amazed by the machine and what it could do. So when there was another glitch with my height and I was restreamed to rotary, I wasn't too fazed.
>
> It was a bit of a squeeze for me in the Squirrel, but I made it through Shawbury, and got to the Chinook OCF in November '07. At a dining-in night in the Mess I happened to find myself next to the Boss in the Gents. He said, 'We'd like to have you on 'C' Flight, Chomper.' I told him that was more than all right by me.

In December 2007, he flew his Squadron Acceptance Sortie, and within four months was in Helmand.

Currently with no strong emotional ties, apart from his family, Morts is keen to be out there, getting to grips with his first Ops:

> It was good when the PDT round started and we were getting properly ready for the off. We had respirator training, but it was simulated as the

facility was U/S. Then we shot on the 100-metre Army range by day with real bullets and on the electronic range at night. In the second month, up at Lossie, we crewed up, and I'm going to Helmand as NHP to the Boss. That'll be exciting.

Since 1998, the Boss has been almost continuously on Operations. He and his wife, their four children and the dog, live in quarters at Odiham. He is aware of the strain on them all of repeated separations:

I was away for over half of 2007. When I got back, the dog went bananas and wet the floor, and the children said, 'Who are you?' Now I'm excluded from the kitchen for a week before leaving – helps everyone to get used to my not being there.

How does he cope with this almost non-stop action?

What's to cope with? I'm pleased to have been so much in the thick of it – and on helicopters. They can really make a difference.

At Odiham, there's continuous briefing for everyone on developments in Helmand, and Afghanistan generally – the Intelligence Officer made sure he briefed us up at Lossiemouth, to keep us fully in the picture. Some of the guys, and their families, keep on top of this info at all times – others keep it at a distance. But some things can't be ignored. The Chinook's a high-profile machine and a prime target for the Taliban – they shot down an American one near Kabul just last week, and everyone knows that.

The Cabs don't just go to Afghanistan – they've been in action worldwide for years. So the station's always had a twenty-four-hour contact line to the Duty Ops Controller, usually an experienced sergeant. He or she can contact other duty officers and NCOs at any time – and the families know that. The Squadron Commanders are there when needed, and they've put in Internet connections at Kandahar – Bastion too, now. So it's cheerio to the family and the dog, and here we go again.

Time for the off

RAF Brize Norton, twenty miles west of Oxford, is the Airport of Embarkation for UK troops deploying worldwide. But in the winter dark, its main gate offers a downbeat prospect to departing warriors. The last hundred yards of road to the Guard Room are lined with overnight sixteen-wheelers waiting to disgorge their military cargoes. Their drivers give no more than a passing glance to the 0400 bus from Odiham.

The civilian security staff behind the desk in the Control of Entry building process the passes of a dozen contracting staff on their way to join the 600 or so colleagues who, with more than 4,000 Service personnel, make this, in terms of people, the biggest station in the RAF. The sentries wave 'C' Flight through the barrier, and passing the looming hangars of the heavy transport aircraft based here, the bus pulls up outside the Terminal, for the Airbridge flight to Afghanistan.

The daily 216 Squadron Lockheed L-1101 TriStar is standing on the apron. It's a grey-painted wide-bodied airliner, 164 feet long, and 55 feet to the top of its tailfin. Three were acquired from Pan Am in the aftermath of the Falklands war, to bolster the long-range transport capability of the RAF. It makes the flight to Kandahar in one seven-hour hop, and takes off mid-morning in order to arrive overhead its destination after dark.

The Chinook crews troop off the bus and lug their bags into the Air Terminal. Straight ahead are no fewer than five car-hire desks. On the right is the waiting area, and on the left a toddlers' play corner, satellite TV, six games machines, and a cafeteria offering a second breakfast. Afterwards, they can buy books, newspapers and 'nutty' at the shop – and there's a cash-machine, which dispenses US dollars, everyday currency on Herrick bases. Morts is about to withdraw a fistful, but Mister B gives him a word of advice: 'You'll get a far better British Forces rate in Helmand.'

A cross-section of about two hundred Herrick people is travelling today: soldiers, airmen and Marines, journalists and photographers, building contractors and even a junior Defence Minister. The civvies are mostly in jeans and jackets, but the military men and women make a sand-coloured line of desert gear as they shuffle up to the check-in desks. 'C' Flight blends in, in their camouflage combats – they have a couple in lighter-weight cotton for general wear, as now, and two others for flying duties. These are similar to the CS95 kit the soldiers wear, made of fire-retardant material designed to char, but not to melt or burn. Baggage and weapons go in the hold, but heavy body-armour and helmets are to be carried on board. They'll be needed for the landing at Kandahar.

In the departure lounge, after security checks and passport controls, the Hercules and Chinook men meet and greet old chums from previous service, training and deployments. There are 40,000 people in the RAF, but it's still a club in many ways. Then, 'C' Flight settles down to wait for boarding.

Ginger wonders about the name, Herrick. 'It's the usual prosaic codename – it came up next on the randomly generated list at MoD. Americans choose names that they hope will be inspiring, like 'Anaconda' and 'Enduring Freedom'.'

Mister B muses how today's 'low-cost-option' method of operation in the RAF has led to a tripling of the workload on everyone in service. 'We're going to be flying pretty much non-stop this time. This detachment could put me well on the way to 6,000 hours on type.'

Morts is worried about the amount of baggage that he's checked in: 'As well as my rifle and pistol, I've brought two bags – one for winter, one for summer kit. Then there's the Bergen, another hold-all and my laptop. Mister B's got about half that. But there we are – perhaps I'll manage to do with less next time.'

Chomper has been here once before, and murmurs, 'We joined up to serve at the sharp end of the spear, and that's where the Cab is, all right?' – before dozing off.

Frankie remembers her time in Iraq on one of two Chinooks tasked with ferrying the Black Watch out of Baghdad:

> Down there it was mighty cold in the winter. At Christmas we set up a tree in the cabin – lights on it and everything. We did come under tracer fire one night, but it all now seems fairly benign compared with Herrick. Out there, you can come under fire pretty well every mission.

The Boss thinks forward to taking on authority for 1310 Flight next week:

> We'll be supporting the Royal Marines – they're air-minded and they'll keep us busy. 19 Light Brigade takes over the Battle Group at the end of our stint – not so sure about them. Still, it should be a quieter time in Helmand this time of year. The Taliban usually retreat and recuperate in the hills, and there's nothing to do in the poppy fields. Just get through to 13 April, and it'll be our decompression week, hopefully on Ascension Island.

The flight is called, and 'C' Flight and the rest haul themselves to their feet, heave up their body-armour, helmets and laptops, and file over to the departure gate. It's time, at last, for the off.

CHAPTER 3

Afghanistan, Theatre of Conflict

BACKDROP
FROM 1500 BC

As well as following the increasing coverage on radio and TV, and the continuing public debate about the rights and wrongs of the Afghanistan campaign, the Hercules and Chinook crews checking in for the Airbridge have had regular presentations on the state-of-play. And they will have doubtless learnt from history books that they are the latest in a long line of British involved in Afghan internal affairs, and that they're flying into an age-old melting-pot.

The territories of Central Asia that came to be known as Afghanistan have for at least three and a half thousand years been in the path of invasion. Arvan warrior tribes from Asia Minor swarmed into the north of the country around 1,500 BC, and a thousand years later it was the Persians. In 330 BC came Alexander the Great – set on conquering Central Asia, he made his base the town of Balkh. Already considered by its citizens to be one of the oldest settlements in the world, Balkh was to be for four hundred years the centre of the Bactrian Greek Empire. Twenty miles east of Balkh lies the northern Afghan frontier fortress of Mazar-e Sharif, which in 2001 was the launch pad of the American-led assault on the Taliban regime.

In supporting that operation, RAF Chinook mission plans would have featured the exotic names, not only of Kabul, but also Herat, Amritsar and the Hindu Kush. Today, for 1310 Flight these are simply locations mentioned in daily briefings – although they fly hundreds of hours each month, their missions never stray outside the provinces of RC(S). Hercules crews however, are still routed over other parts of the country. Afghanistan covers

RC SOUTH

WORLD BRIEFING MAPS

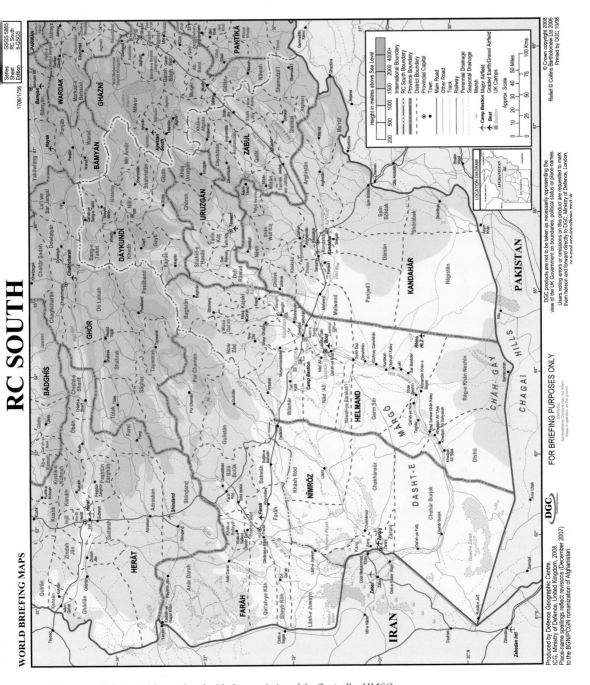

over 250,000 square miles, which makes it larger than France. Its border, close to 3,000 miles long, fronts six countries, including China at the eastern tip. Pakistan lies in the troublesome south, and the other neighbours are Iran to the west, and Turkmenistan, Uzbekistan and Tajikistan along the northern rim. Aside from Iran, formerly Persia, and a dynasty for 2,500 years, these countries' national identities and their borders with Afghanistan have been in flux for centuries.

For 1,700 years from the second century BC, Balkh and Herat were oasis towns on the 4,000-mile Silk Road – the route to Turkey and the markets of Europe for Chinese merchants and their silk-carrying caravans. They returned eastwards with treasure, brides and slaves, and brought prosperity to towns and villages along the route.

Religious beliefs came with the trade. Islam now dominates, but it hasn't always done so. It was through Balkh that Buddhism first spread from India to China. The town then became a centre of Christianity until, in the late fourth century, heathen Huns swarmed in. It was not until four hundred years later that conquering Arabs built some of the world's earliest mosques there. Another four centuries passed before the Mongol Horde of Genghis Khan descended and imposed their hundred years of 'Pax Mongolica' on the region. Then another Mongol invader, Tamerlane of Samarkand, sacked Balkh in 1381 before imposing his Timurid Tartar Empire from the Mediterranean to the borders of India and Russia, and crowning himself among the ruins of the city.

When Tamerlane died in 1405, the centre of power shifted westwards from Balkh to Herat, from where his grandson Ulag Beg ruled over the golden age of Samarkand. For four decades, architecture, art, astronomy and literature flourished, together with religious tolerance. All this at a time when the lands on the other side of the Atlantic, which were to become the United States of America, were the hunting grounds of warring tribes, and the islands which were to become Britain were ruled by superstition and feudal tyranny.

AD 1747
Foundation of the Afghan State

The present Afghan capital, Kabul, lies over on the eastern side of the Hindu Kush mountains, straddling the south-to-north route from Pakistan to Central Asia, always of critical strategic importance over the ages. In 1510, Kabul was seized by Babur, the Pashtun founder of the Mughal Empire. After more than two hundred years of conflict with invading Persians, the Pashtuns, now calling themselves for the first time 'Afghans', were able to acclaim Ahmed Shah Durrani as the new leader. His crowning as Emir in 1747 marked the birth of the Afghan state whose security and governance ISAF is fighting to protect today.

Then, as now, Afghan tribes were many and restless, and Ahmed Shah's control depended on their being given opportunities for booty and occupation of territory. He set out to provide both, leading his warriors first to the east, invading the Mughal territories three times in six years, attacking and seizing Lahore, Sindh and the Punjab. He then turned westwards to take possession of Herat, and sent an army north, to bring the Turkmen, Uzbek, Tajik and Hazara peoples of northern, central and western Afghanistan under control. In 1756 to '57, he made what was his fourth invasion of India. After plundering Delhi he infamously attacked the Golden Temple in Amritsar and filled its sacred pool with the blood of slaughtered cows, warriors and worshippers. Bitterness between Sikhs and Afghans continues to this day. Ahmed Shah, known among Afghans as 'Baba', the father of their country, died in 1773, and was buried in Kandahar under a shimmering turquoise dome, today the town's most important historical monument, and a landmark for ISAF aircrews.

In building the largest Islamic empire of the era, he had been careful to limit his radius of operations on the sub-continent to avoid confrontation with the British East India Company, which was beginning to establish its presence there and for the first of many times showing an interest in Afghan affairs. Nevertheless, the British had been impressed by Ahmed Shah's prowess, and became wary of further Afghan invasions of the Raj. Ahmed Shah's empire became fragmented by warring tribes, and by 1818 his successors held little more than Kabul and its surrounding territory. However, his lineage did endure, and with the exception of nine months in 1929, all of Afghanistan's rulers up to 1978 were in line of descent from Ahmed Shah. The winner in the dynastic conflict that followed his death was Dost Mohammad Khan, who shortly after ascending the throne in 1820 found himself and his country trapped in a power struggle between the Russian Empire to the north and the British to the south – the so-called 'Great Game'.

The nineteenth century
The 'Great Game' and First and Second Afghan wars

Aiming to secure fragmented borders and trade routes, as well as restrict the ambitious British Raj, the Russians were using all their power and influence to control the tribal areas to the north of Afghanistan, while making

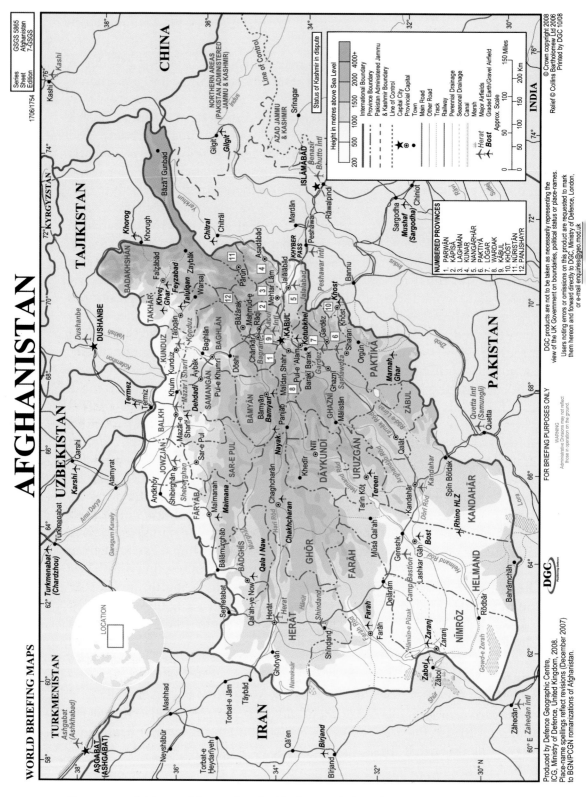

AFGHANISTAN

WORLD BRIEFING MAPS

Crown copyright material reproduced with the permission of the Controller HMSO

diplomatic overtures to Dost Mohammad's court. In reaction, the Emir sought an alliance with Britain, welcoming her ambassador to Kabul in 1837. But His Excellency insisted that the Afghans abandon their ambitions in northern India, and demanded a role in their foreign policy. Affronted, Dost Mohammad reopened the door for the Russians, leading the British in 1838 to mobilize against him, in what became known as the First Anglo-Afghan War.

Imperial troops marched through the Bolan Pass to Kandahar, where they proclaimed a new Emir and escorted him into Kabul. Dost Mohammad sought refuge in the wilds of the Hindu Kush mountains. But after fourteen months, in January 1842, the British, weakened in their isolated camp outside Kabul by the constant attacks of tribal warriors, attempted a retreat to India. The entire column was annihilated, except for one lone horseman. He, a doctor, had been sent by the Afghans to deliver the dreadful news, and was the only survivor to ride out of the Bolan Pass.

A punitive force recaptured Kabul in autumn the same year, but the Raj had by this time learnt its bloody lesson, and resolved to abandon any attempt to intervene in the internal politics of Afghanistan. Dost Mohammad returned in triumph to Kabul, and in 1855, after the reconquest of Balkh and Kandahar, concluded an alliance with the British. Together they wrested control of Herat from the Persians, and by 1863 Afghanistan had been restored as a state.

But within two weeks, the old Emir was dead, and his two sons fought for power. Sher Ali Khan came out on top, but then he too was caught between imperial ambitions. In 1878, after Russia sent an uninvited diplomatic mission to Kabul, the British demanded that their ambassador be accepted instead. The Emir refused, but in September a mission set out none the less from the Raj for Kabul. Its repulse in the Khyber Pass was the trigger for the Second Anglo-Afghan War.

A 40,000-strong British force penetrated the border. Sher Ali appealed in vain to the Tsar for assistance, and retreated to Mazar-e Sharif, where he died in February 1879. Sher Ali's son and successor signed the Treaty of Gandamak in May, giving the occupying British their coveted control of Afghan foreign affairs and the Khyber and Michni passes, and ceding to them the town of Quetta and all the North-West Frontier territories. But after the Imperial Army withdrew, an uprising in Kabul led to the slaughter of the British Resident, his guards and staff. In reprisal, troops the next month again advanced into Afghanistan, defeating the Afghans and occupying Kabul. Uprisings and dynastic struggles rumbled on until the British won a decisive victory in the battle of Kandahar in September 1880. With their previous gains consolidated, the British promised protection and a subsidy, and withdrew.

THE TWENTIETH CENTURY
WORLD WAR ONE AND THE THIRD AFGHAN WAR

Afghans can boast a fabulous if tumultuous history, much of it shared by the ancestors of the Brits flying the Airbridge today. But these latter-day warriors are themselves more directly affected by the recent ravages of the country by Russian invaders and Taliban fighters – the latter are the current enemy, and the former left the Afghan plains seeded with land-mines.

The Russians have been involved in Afghanistan longer than the British. While the First and Second Anglo-Afghan wars were raging, the Tsar's troops and agents were active in the north, and by 1885 had under their control the 'Stans' of the Turkmen, Uzbeks and Kazakhs. But in the early twentieth century, other distractions – for the British the Boer War, and for the Russians war with Japan – took imperial minds off the Great Game. In fact, alarm at Germany's developing ambitions in the Middle East even led to an Anglo-Russian Convention in 1907. The Russians accepted British control of Afghanistan, and the British agreed to actively discourage any attempt by Afghanistan to encroach on Russian territory – in effect they managed the borders of a supposedly subservient state.

Since 1895, the southern border had followed the 'Durand Line' agreed by Sir Mortimer Durand for the Imperial Government with Emir Abdur Rehman. The arbitrary line passed through fiercely defended tribal territories, resulting in continuous conflicts on the North-West Frontier of the Raj. In an effort to transfer responsibility for security to local elders, the British set up a force of locally recruited militias trained and led by British officers. The attempt was partially successful, but then, as now, cross-border incursions, uprisings and murders tested the allegiance of enlisted tribesmen.

During the First World War, Mohammedan Turkey's pro-German leanings buffered Afghanistan from the cataclysms in Europe, but the Anglo-Russian Convention was nullified in 1917 with the seizure of power by the Bolsheviks, who moved to occupy Kyrgiz territory and advanced into Uzbekistan. This emboldened the Afghan Emir Amanullah to march three battalions over the Khyber in May 1919. The Third Anglo-Afghan War had begun. North-West Frontier tribesmen rose in support of the Afghans, and the militias defected. Skirmishes raged for two months, before a British outflanking counter-attack from their stronghold of Quetta led to an armistice in June. Uprisings rumbled on until 1921, when a peace treaty gave Afghanistan full independence and control at last over its foreign affairs.

In this conflict, units of the young RAF were for the first time in action over Afghan territory. Their prime task was to support British ground troops, but the five squadrons of Bristol Fighters and de Havilland bombers were also used to bombard military targets in cities, including Kabul, and in punitive strikes against tribesmen. Historians concluded that the aircraft were most effective when used in ground support, reconnaissance and resupply. They also noted the hazards of flying frail open-cockpit biplanes in precipitous and pitiless terrain, and of facing dust-storms, thin mountain air, and massed ground-fire from tribal rifles. Other problems were shortages of aircraft and spare parts, and hence serviceability.

BETWEEN THE WARS

The years between the World Wars were marked for Afghanistan by the continuing heavy hand of the Russians in the north, with Stalin unilaterally defining the Uzbek and Kyrgiz borders between 1924 and 1927, and of the British in the south. The Raj reorganized the tribal militias into the enlisted Border Scouts and the Khassadar Territorials, to help the Army police the North-West Frontier. Within the country, unrest continued, especially in 1926, when Amanullah declared himself King and sought to introduce social reforms against vigorous opposition from conservative factions. In the turmoil, the British Legation was in December 1928 besieged in Kabul by rebel tribes, and the Royal Air Force, just before Christmas, began the first recorded air evacuation. Vickers Victoria and Handley Page Hinaidi troop carriers diverted from Baghdad operated in severe weather over mountains rising up to 10,000 feet. By the end of February they had airlifted nearly 600 civilians to safety in Peshawar. The next year, Amanullah was forced to flee the country (the only time that the lineage was broken), and four years later, the 19-year-old Zahir Shah became the last in the long line of Pashtun rulers.

WORLD WAR TWO AND AFTER

Apart from a scare in 1939, when the Russo-German pact raised again the old bogey of a Russian invasion of North-West India through Afghanistan, Central Asia was largely unaffected by the Second World War. But when the Germans broke through on the Russian front to the Caucasus, and the threat of invasion became real, the British looked again to their Durand Line defences, erecting 'dragon's teeth' tank-traps in the Khyber Pass. They were hindered in their efforts by the activities of the infamous Faqir of Ipi in Waziristan.

One of the tribal territories arbitrarily bisected by the Durand Line, Waziristan covers an area of close on 4,000 square miles, making it half the size of Wales. To the west, it stretches to the remote and mountainous Afghan districts of Khost and Birmal, some 200 miles north-east of Kandahar. In 1941, it was home to an estimated 50,000 fighting men, well armed since a gun-running boom in the First World War. The men came from the indigenous Wazir and Mahsud tribes who for five years had wielded their weapons in support of the Faqir.

A Muslim cleric from the village of Ipi in the settled Indian border province of Bannu, the Faqir had from 1936 led the British a merry dance throughout Waziristan, in a nerve-war of sniping, ambushing, bridge blowing and wire cutting. The unrest had its roots in Hindu–Muslim tension, which the Faqir turned into a holy campaign against the British. He managed to keep one step ahead of the 40,000 troops sent against him, and melted away into the gorges and caves of the 15,000 ft mountains on the Afghan border, where he survived the best efforts of the RAF to bomb him and his followers into submission. The outbreak of war brought him German and Italian money and ammunition, and he advanced again, tying down British troops much needed elsewhere in India. In 1941, his allegiance shifted as he aligned his movement with Gandhi's civil disobedience campaign and turned his back on the Axis. The Faqir was a thorn in the side of the British Raj right up to Indian Independence and Partition in 1947.

The late Frank Leeson, an eyewitness of the cross-border unrest on the North-West Frontier and the tragedies of Partition, was posted in his early 20s to serve as a British Army lieutenant with the Pathan Khassadar Militia in North Waziristan. In his retirement on the Sussex coast, he published the book he drafted in 1949/50 about his experiences. Throughout *Frontier Legion* are to be found parallels between then and now. The Epilogue concludes:

> Waziristan tribal lands are still bisected by the same border, and some sixty years later, its rugged terrain and hidden caves and fundamentalist inhabitants could afford the same protection to the Al Qaeda leader Osama Bin Laden as they did to the notorious Faqir, and his predecessors.

In 2004, militant Waziri tribesmen, stirred up by the Pakistani Army's search for Al Qaeda supporters in their mountains and caves, joined forces with Taliban fighters and foreign fundamentalists to take up arms again. The militants proclaimed themselves the Islamic Emirate of Waziristan, and the fighting escalated into the undeclared Waziristan War. There was a partial truce in September 2006, but clashes escalated again in 2007, and tension is still high, with Waziristan providing a staging-ground for Taliban operations into both Afghanistan and Pakistan. It could be said that the troops of ISAF and their Afghan allies are still engaged, after sixty years, in the campaign fought by Frank Leeson and his Khassadars.

THE SOVIET DECADE

As post-Partition troubles convulsed the Afghan south, Stalin continued to colonize the 'Stans' in the north, fomenting unrest by laying down more disputed borders. In 1953, the year of the Soviet Dictator's death, General Daud Khan became Prime Minister in Kabul, and as well as introducing a number of democratic reforms, including greater freedom for women, he turned to the Soviet Union for economic and military assistance. In December 1955, Stalin's successor, Nikita Khrushchev, visiting Daud in Kabul, signed an economic agreement and reaffirmed the 1931 Afghan–Soviet neutrality treaty. The Russians enjoyed ten years of relative stability on the borders, but a further decade of power politics led to the exile of King Zahir Shah in Italy. It was not long before Daud himself was overthrown, losing his life in a coup by the leftist People's Democratic Party. Purges and revolt followed, and when the Afghan army faced collapse in December 1979, the Soviet Union sent in its troops.

The Soviets installed first Babrak Karmal and then Mohammad Najibullah as puppet Communist rulers, which was enough to bring warring Afghan tribal warlords together to create the Mujahideen. These freedom-fighters were supplied with money and arms by Pakistan, China, Iran, Saudi Arabia, and the USA – the latter making the key delivery in 1986 of Stinger ground-to-air missiles. Stingers, even in the hands of a semi-trained guerilla, could bring down supposedly invincible Russian helicopter gunships. Chinook crews are well aware that many of those missiles are still in the hands of today's insurgents.

The new Soviet leader, Mikhail Gorbachev, had already announced his intention to pull out his forces, and in 1988 the withdrawal began, following peace accords with the US, Pakistan and the Afghans. On 15 February 1989, Lieutenant General Boris Gromov marched symbolically back into Soviet territory across the Friendship Bridge spanning the Amu-Daria river, over which Russian troops had entered Afghanistan some nine years earlier.

ISAF forces still experience the after-effects of the Soviet occupation. In 1991, the dying Soviet Union granted full independence to the Stans, leaving them with their Russian-imposed statehood and borders, continuing irritants to tribal pride in the north. And of the estimated 450,000 land-mines seeded by the Russians and the Mujahideen, perhaps 250,000 remain – a daily average of four casualties now occurs, mostly to civilians. In addition, half the Afghan population has been displaced – the majority to fundamentalist havens in Iran or Pakistan, where old conflicts continue – and with the added destruction due to the war, the economy has been devastated. Civil war is endemic.

RISE OF THE TALIBAN

Najibullah fell from power and was executed in Kabul on 28 September 1996. The Taliban, who had risen from the chaos as the foremost power group, seized Kabul, introducing a hardline version of Islam, and gaining recognition as legitimate rulers by Pakistan and Saudi Arabia. Opposing warlords regrouped as the Northern Alliance.

The people continued to suffer, finding their towns, villages and farms caught up in ferocious fighting. In 1997 the Taliban seized the Northern Alliance stronghold of Mazar-e Sharif, before themselves being attacked and massacred by Hazara gunmen. The Taliban returned in August the following year, and it was the Hazara who died in appalling brutality. Then came earthquakes that killed whole populations, followed by US missile strikes on what were believed to be Osama bin Laden's bases. In 1999 the UN imposed an air embargo and financial sanctions, which further impoverished the economy.

2001
OPERATION ENDURING FREEDOM

The USA was losing patience with the Taliban for its refusal to hand over Osama bin Laden, and in 2001 the tension snapped. The Northern Alliance lost its legendary leader Ahmad Shah Masood on 9 September, assassinated by Taliban agents. Two days later, devastating attacks on the twin towers of the World Trade Center in New York shook the world. Al Qaeda claimed responsibility, and in direct response, the following month the United States launched Operation Enduring Freedom against the Taliban. Britain mobilized on Op Veritas in support, and its forces were back in Kabul for the first time since the airborne evacuation in 1929.

Al Qaeda had found support and sanctuary in Afghanistan, and the joint objectives of the US–British operation were to capture Osama bin Laden and eject the Taliban from Kabul and the country. The Northern Alliance willingly provided ground troops, while American strike aircraft and cruise missiles bombarded from the air. In support, the RAF contributed reconnaissance, air-to-air refuelling capabilities and resupply. The Taliban beat a tactical retreat, and before the end of the year, the Pashtun royalist Hamid Karzai was sworn in as head of a thirty-member interim power-sharing government. In January 2002 the first contingent of UN-backed foreign peacekeepers arrived, among them the British 16 Air Assault Brigade. British forces, as part of ISAF, have been in Afghanistan continuously ever since.

29 January 2009
On board the TriStar

From the tarmac at Brize Norton, the Boss and his colleagues climb up the RAF-issue metal steps and through the centre passenger door of the TriStar into a standard wide-bodied airliner cabin fitted out in full passenger rig – save for the half-dozen stretcher stanchions in the forward section. Eight RAF air stewards, male and female, are there to take care of the passengers. Overseen by a loadmaster, they all wear desert-camouflage flying-suits. Morts is amused that boarding is by rank, and jokes with Chomper about officers having choice of seats. The aircraft is almost ninety per cent full, but there's comfortable room for everyone – although Chomper, with experience from last time, makes sure he grabs the seats with more legroom. Helmets, body-armour and mission bags are stuffed into overhead storage. The seat pockets have been stripped of non-essentials – a sick-bag has pride of place, together with an emergency drills card, and a single-page brief from 216 Squadron's CO on 'The Op Herrick Airbridge'. There's an in-flight entertainment switch and socket, but it's not connected up. It's a trooping flight, but, the Chinook crews reckon, for all the TriStar's somewhat spartan appearance, not a bad one at that.

'The food's as good as on any other international flight', the Boss tells Morts. 'And this airliner's got a state-of-the-art Defensive Aids Suite that can detect any incoming nasties, and then deal with 'em.'

Unfortunately, this departure turns into a damp squib – two hours into the flight and a technical fault on the aircraft forces the TriStar to turn back for the UK. At Brize there's no crew available to fly them out on a second aircraft today, so the Boss and others who fancy an extra night at home are flown by Chinook back to Odiham. Some decide to stay at Brize, to avoid another emotional farewell, but Chomper is delighted to be reunited with his girlfriend, to enjoy a 'super unexpected evening out at a local pub'. The Boss creeps in late at night and is off again before the kids wake up, to 'avoid saddling them with a second painful farewell'. But for Ginger, going back home is 'a little victory – making it much easier to say cheerio the second time'.

The following day, they try again. Frankie finds she knows the co-pilot, an ex-Chinook man, and 'C' Flight visits to the flight-deck follow, with a can of Coke in the galley as, at 35,000 feet above Azerbaijan, the TriStar whistles past the point of no return and onwards to Kandahar.

'As long as', comments Mister B, 'there isn't a panic and we have to divert. I just want to get to theatre now, and get stuck in.'

SOME SCENE SETTING

Mister B's first Afghan sorties were with the Chinooks in Enduring Freedom, now nearly eight years ago:

> We'd read up about Afghan history before we went, and knew that everyone who'd been there as military had fared pretty badly. I decided there and then to ignore all that, and take whatever came along. Same this time – but it's a sobering thought that so far this winter the Paras have lost six men and the Royal Marines nineteen. It's normally much quieter at this time of year, but now the insurgents are putting down so many more IEDs.
>
> They can rip even armoured vehicles apart if they hit the right place. We see some terrible things in the back of the Cab on a casevac sortie.

Ginger remembers the start of ISAF operations in 2002:

> Of course, that was well before 1310 Flight got going in Afghanistan. We were on Rapid Reaction standby in March when the call came. Seven aircrews flew in via Bahrain. We landed in Kabul, at the airfield outside town, and then moved on to Bagram Base, nearby. Two or three Cabs were flown up non-stop from the Pakistan coast off HMS *Illustrious*. A couple more were airlifted out from Brize. We'd been brought in to support the Royal Marine Commando Mountain Troop, chasing the remnants of Al Qaeda and Taliban forces out of the south-east.
>
> We operated alongside Afghani and American helicopters. We took our Cabs to Bamian, 2,500 metres up in the Hazarajat mountains and 230 kilometres north-west of Kabul. That's where those sixth-century

giant Buddhas used to be before the Taliban blew them up. We went right up to Mazar-e Sharif, the second largest city in the country – 400 kilometres north of Kabul. We operated in the Hindu Kush – mountains to take your breath away. And we came down as far as Kandahar – the base was just a few tents in those days.

At the start, it was cold and wet, and we had just this lightweight kit from Desert Storm in '91. It was pretty flimsy and the buttons kept coming off – the stuff's better now. We were there through July, when it got to forty Celsius. But in the mountains around Khowst, over against the North-West Frontier, it was just twenty, and that felt really chilly. We were often up there – a hotbed of Talibs. The Predator UAVs would spot the targets and we'd insert the Marines to hunt them down. We'd keep the guys resupplied, and extract them when they were ready. Then we'd regroup for the next Op.

It was a real eye-opener. There were old Soviet aircraft all over Bagram, and a lot of the vegetation had been stripped – the Russians used to spray defoliant around to clear the ground cover. It was exciting working with fighting troops – and good not to be loaded down with blunties like we are these days.'

['Blunties' – Anyone not involved first-hand in the fighting.]

Following its takeover of security in Kabul in 2003, NATO nursed the country through to its first presidential election in November 2004. Hamid Karzai was elected Head of State with fifty-five per cent of the vote. He presided over the first parliamentary and provincial elections in more than thirty years, and despite the harshest winter weather for a decade, when several hundred people perished from the cold, the parliament met in December. All was relatively quiet until, in January 2006, the former king, Zahir Shah, returned. He made no claim to the throne, but just his being there was a threat to stability, and in the spring, after riots in Kabul and Taliban resurgence in Helmand, NATO took over leadership of all military operations in the south. Some 3,300 British troops, including 3 Para, moved into Helmand as 16 Air Assault Brigade.

Frankie flew as a captain on the summer 1310 Flight missions that year:

We operated out of KAF and Bastion. Of course they'd briefed us on Afghanistan politics and troubles, and how to behave – impolite to give the thumbs up with the left hand, and all that sort of thing. But when we got there – the culture-shock was something else. And the scenery –

spectacular. Airbridge flights went into Kabul then, and the TriStar landed without its window blinds down. Everywhere you looked there were mountains.

It soon got very nasty in Helmand. The Paras found themselves isolated in their compounds – platoon houses – and we had to get in and out to resupply the poor guys. Musa Qaleh was the worst of the bunch – a one-in-three chance of coming under fire. Best tactic was to dump the load and leg it. Didn't always work – once, at Sangin, the soldiers couldn't get out to the stuff, the groundfire was so hot.

We survived. The Cab's just about the best-protected aircraft in the RAF, with armour, defensive aids and guns. But speed and craftiness are our main defence – and, as they say, night is our friend.

I went out again that winter, October to December. There was frost on the aircraft every morning at Bastion and KAF – no dust, but mud and marshy ground all over. At Sangin, we had to pull some Afghan soldiers out of a swamp. And Helmand river, which just trickles along in summer, was a raging torrent. It got mighty cold in the cabin – the crewmen were frozen stiff and could barely speak, let alone work. The heating system in the Cab's a small jet engine – half the heat goes to the front and half to the back. The cabin's never hot enough, but in the cockpit we need all the windows open. Mind you, the cold weather seemed to quieten the Talibs down.

We've been briefed that they're much more active this winter. We'll see.

The Boss reflects on the business to come, and the stuff he's already done. He was first on Herrick that same October in 2006, when NATO was just assuming responsibility for security across the whole of Afghanistan. He was detached for four months as a staff officer at JHF(A) HQ on Kandahar base:

I turned operational plans into daily tasks for the Chinooks. In command then was a Canadian brigadier, closely followed by a Dutch general. My colleagues were an Army major and a naval commander, and we liaised with Americans and NATO forces – Poles and such. We had to work things out pretty much on the hoof.

The Boss was back in April to May 2007, as a fill-in pilot for 27 Squadron's 'B' Flight, as they took over on 1310. That was the period when NATO and Afghan forces in the south launched Operation Achilles, then the largest offensive so far against the Taliban. There was heavy action in Helmand province:

My first mission went wrong, frankly. We were meant to extract American troops from an area north of Gereshk and bring them back to Bastion. We only had the one Chinook available, so we had to shuttle to the landing-site to get them all out. The tasking called for four sorties, but to reduce the risks – it was a daylight Op – we managed to get it back to three. To avoid setting up a pattern we planned to fly in from a different direction each time. The first run went OK, but as we approached for the second time, we were hit. I felt one impact right below my seat – thank Christ it's armour plated. Another round took out a hydraulic pipe in the cabin. Again, we were lucky. It was a secondary system for the brakes and so forth, and the Cab was still flyable. So we made a hasty departure, with some Wellsing, along the valley. Back at Bastion, the engineers found nine AK47 impact holes in the aircraft. The US troops got themselves on foot to a safer HLS.

By the time the Boss returned to Helmand, this time as OC 'C' Flight in July– September the same year, the former King Zahir Shah had died, and the UN was reporting that opium production had soared to a record high. He was back again for the fourth time in April and May 2008, for a detachment that was 'pretty hectic'. By that time, there were executions, suicide attacks and deaths in action, but the biggest headlines back home had been grabbed by Prince Harry's ten-week service in the Task Force. As 'C' Flight arrived, NATO leaders meeting in Bucharest were pledging a firm and long-term commitment to the campaign in Afghanistan. From that moment, people began to realize that RAF recruits coming out of training could be facing the prospect of serving an entire career in Afghanistan.

By September 2008, disputes on the Afghan–Pakistan border had led to the worst violence there in decades, and President Karzai was threatening to send troops into Pakistan to fight the militants if Islamabad failed to take action against them. There had been a massive jailbreak from Kandahar prison, abetted by the Taliban, which freed at least 350 insurgents. There was also a suicide attack on the Indian embassy in Kabul in which over fifty died, for which the Afghans blamed Pakistani Intelligence. Then, eighty-nine civilians died in a Coalition air-strike in Herat, and ten French soldiers were killed in ambush.

In response to all these events, President Bush announced in September a 'quiet surge' of an extra 4,500 American troops to join the 18,000 already in ISAF, and UK Defence Secretary Des Browne promised 230 more British to bring the force to more than 8,000 by spring 2009. The Germans committed 1,000 to add to their 3,500 ground troops. In the diplomatic background, the

Taliban rejected an offer of peace talks from President Karzai, 'until all foreign troops leave Afghanistan'. In consequence, Karzai and the new Pakistan President Asif Ali Zardari agreed in December to a joint anti-militant strategy for their border on the North-West Frontier.

ISAF TASK 2009

As 'C' Flight and the Hercules men fly in, they are fully briefed on all this background. And they know that the current ISAF task is to secure key areas and keep the ring-road open in an effort to assist in building Afghan-led governance, spearheaded by President Karzai and his ministers. It is hoped that support will come from the Regional Governors, and from the religious leaders, the Mullahs. They've been told that key tasks are to build up the capabilities of the Afghan National Security Force (ANSF), to focus on reconstruction and development (including schools and medical facilities) and to support the Afghan counter-narcotics campaign. They know they'll be in the front-line, working with the military of the forty-four nations making up ISAF. In all that, they very much hope they'll have the support of the British public – and of the media. The Boss has a comment on this:

> The guys and gals are aware of the press, naturally – they also know that a lot of the action goes unreported. What grabs the headlines are the disasters and the apparent hopelessness of the Coalition mission. The media's not so interested in our routine stuff – such as the delivery of water and ammo, insertion of assault troops and evacuation of injured and maimed, under fire, up to four times in a night. All that we RAF aircrews and our team-mates in ground-support can do is get on with the job, and do it well.

DESCENT INTO KANDAHAR

After six hours or more in flight, the TriStar has flown into the dark, pushing eastwards into the three-and-a-half-hour time difference between the UK and Afghanistan. The passengers are dozing, when the loadmaster abruptly commands attention – the aircraft is entering Afghan airspace, it's half an hour to landing and time to get ready for the descent. There's a scrum to retrieve body-armour and helmets from the luggage racks, followed by a struggle to get the clumsy stuff on. With mutual assistance, all the clips and buckles are fastened and everyone's back in their seats. Then, fifty miles out from Kandahar, the captain calls for top-of-descent drills. With window-blinds down and cabin lights switched off, the TriStar begins the downward plunge to its destination.

Because of the confines of Afghan airspace, a rapid descent into Kandahar is required, using air brakes and with landing-gear down. This is a straightforward procedure in airmanship terms, but it's a dramatic difference for first-timer Morts, sitting in the unaccustomed darkness.

'We've had all this spiel about why we're out here in Helmand,' he confides to Chomper, 'but it's been hard to imagine what it's like. Those stretchers up front get to you – and so does this weird max-rate descent in the dark. But the thing's just got to be done, hasn't it? All our training's been for this – I suppose it's a sort of rite of passage.'

'It was the same for me last time', says Chomper. 'I flew out on my own in the freight-cabin of a C-17. The max-rate descent into KAF in that, with body-

'B' Flight 63 (Queen's Colour) Squadron RAF Regiment on patrol – Kandahar GDA. **(Photograph by SAC Neil Chapman, RAF © crown copyright 2010/MoD, image from www.photos.mod.uk)**

armour on, and all lights out except for a few green spots in the ceiling – it made me think, too. Morts, we're going to be up at the sharp end all right.'

Kandahar Airfield is defended by the RAF Regiment at action stations when the Airbridge flies in, and without incident the TriStar sweeps down the instrument landing beams and the tyres thump safely onto the runway. Another plane-load of Chinook and Hercules crews, together with troops, cooks and contractors, has arrived to take up duties on Op Herrick.

CHAPTER 4

Kandahar Base

30 January 2009

Arrival

'Without Kandahar Airfield, there'd be no campaign.' Those words, first heard at an RAF Regiment briefing, echo in Morts's mind at the top of the TriStar steps, in the freezing cold of an Afghan winter night. 'It's big,' he says, 'but that's what you'd expect from an international airport.'

Chomper lifts his nose: 'Still the same old smell – jet exhaust and sewage.'

Kandahar Base is certainly big – twenty kilometres south-east of Kandahar city, it covers some 45 square kilometres. The airfield runway is long – and busy. But it's different from the bases that Morts is used to, starting with the 'goody bag' they're all given as they leave the aircraft, to see them through the first hours.

Under the tented roof of the terminal and shepherded between shoulder-high concrete partitions, passengers are met by movements staff and escorted to their units. Colleagues from Odiham, off 'B' Flight 18(B) Squadron, welcome the Chinook crews – very glad to see them. Their arrival to man 1310 Flight means it will soon be time to go home. Bags and weapons safely collected, buses take the aircrews on through the main camp to the Cambridge Lines, where 'B' Flight has already vacated the accommodation in readiness. It's a drive of a couple of kilometres – on the right-hand side, as is the rule in Afghanistan – through what in the darkness seems to Morts to be a completely built-up area. Just now, there are 8,000 military and 1,500 foreign workers – from thirty-five countries – living on this base.

Mister B reckons that not a lot has changed in the nine months since he was last here – he can see a couple more huts and some extra blast-walls.

The Cambridge Lines are half a dozen rows of American pre-engineered pitched-roof metallic huts, stretching into the distance. Helmets are packed off to the Safety Equipment Section, weapons go to the armoury and bags into the huts. By midnight, the new occupants are settled in, one crew per room. There's no separation of accommodation for officers and NCOs here, neither is there for Frankie. Previously, she's been 'shipped out to the ladies' quarters', but as the Boss has had no direct instruction this time that she should go, she's staying with her crew, which is what everybody wants. Each room has two pairs of bunk-beds, with a wardrobe and a couple of shelves for each individual. Mister B has everything stowed away at once – he has no civvy clothes or books with him: 'You don't get enough time off to need anything other than your working kit. There's plenty of books on the camp, but no time to read those, either.'

It's been a long and tiring twenty hours since the early muster and bacon sarnies at Odiham, and there's not much other to do than settle in and try to grab a few hours' sleep. For the Boss, it already 'seems like we've never been away.'

31 JANUARY

The next morning, the base is up and doing early. A thousand Afghan workers – locally employed civilians (LECs) – commute daily to work here. The new arrivals, each coping as best they can with jet-lag and with varying operational requirements, report at differing times for their first duties.

The RAF Regiment FP men take themselves off early to report to their HQ, in a building down by the runway dubbed 'Taliban's Last Stand'. Once a single storey, it has been modified to two, each floor housing wood-partitioned offices. But there's still a hole in the roof, where a British shell went through back in 2001.

Hercules crews on deployment 'go nocturnal' for a month, and spend their days trying to sleep in their quarters, road-signed 'Albert Square'. They treat their first evening's dinner as breakfast, then get down to EAW Ops for induction and briefing, expecting to be operational as early as their second night.

Hunger pains wake Morts and Chomper, and they just make it in time for breakfast in the cookhouse close by. Morts is impressed by the quality and quantity. Meanwhile, the Boss is having what qualifies as something of a lie-in. 'No kids to disturb. Had good intentions of going to the gym but I'm trapped under the duvet – Egyptian PT.'

Kandahar briefing

In the late afternoon, the Boss and Frankie sign for two Land Rovers from the 1310 Flight transport pool, and drive the crews over to RAF Headquarters to start the arrival administration and briefing. Morts and the other newcomers are given a guided tour of the base on the way. It's busy, noisy and full of building-works. Pedestrians and cyclists have to watch out for the vehicles buzzing about, and the racket on the runway is pretty constant. Over on the right, in the geographic centre of the base, is a 100-metre-square quadrangle of compacted sand, hosting a variety of sports areas and surrounded by the 'Boardwalk' – an unfinished-timber walkway, lined with cafés, shops and limited leisure facilities. Well down to the left lurks the infamous poo-pond, a sewage dump just coping with all the effluent, but far beyond its design limit.

The RAF's HQ building is a long, low block over by the flight-line, alongside the runway. With the green, red and blue Joint Services' flag flying

The 'Broadwalk' – Kandahar Base (The Boss & friends)

from the mast-top, it accommodates the Harrier ground-attack detachment, 904 EAW and the Hercules crews, and Joint Aviation Group. JAG has become operational just a week ago, set up in fourteen days by Group Captain Andy Turner, CO of RAF Odiham. It has taken responsibility for all UK helicopters in Afghanistan, including those of 1310 Flight. It comprises a small command team, focused on wider issues, such as gearing the aircraft up for winter flying, and planning and directing operations, allowing JHF(A) to move forward to Camp Bastion and concentrate on carrying them out.

The Boss and his entourage file into the Operations Room. Group Captain Turner gives the briefing today. The message is that the original aim of securing the Triangle is still pretty much the focus, to create conditions for government departments and aid agencies to pursue development as well as to make things safe for the presidential elections due in August. It's key to ensure that as many Afghans as possible exercise their right to vote. The insurgents' main entrance points to Afghanistan are still in the south of Helmand, near the Pakistan border, over 200 kilometres from Kandahar, but their current strongholds have extended to Marjah and Nad Ali, west of Lashkar Gah. Coalition troops are concentrated around patrol bases in the 'Green Zone', the fertile area bordering the Helmand river, and because of the IED threat most resupply must be by helicopter.

The Boss further notes that 'the Americans are coming in force. Bastion will be able to take a 747, and over a hundred helicopters will be here soon. There's a bunch of civvy contract companies doing increasing resupply work – perhaps the days of our 60-knot Cab freighting transits up to Kajaki Dam are numbered.'

Morts finds it 'similar to the briefings at Odiham but concentrated on Helmand'.

Ginger sums it up: 'The whole place is still basically crazy.'

The Boss, Frankie and Mister B go off to sort out the 1310 Flight tasking programme:

> The master plan for us is for Op Diesel to kick off on Transfer of Authority with an insert to the Upper Sangin Valley in the area where that American Chinook was shot down, followed by a simple insert to the American Marines' patrol base, Dwyer, and then finally into the hornets' nest at Marjah. The Dwyer insert would be a good chance for one of the new captains to cut his teeth – first and third will fall to me. We'll need experienced crews to cover IRT during these first Ops – they'll possibly be eventful.

The remainder of the first day falls to administration – arrival paperwork, motor transport allocation, Intelligence briefings on latest threats, reading of theatre-specific rules and subtle changes to local procedures, and flying-specific briefings, including HLS changes and top tips. All the key maps are studied – they are continuously updated and invaluable for a picture of the combat zones and the latest hazards.

Ammunition is drawn at the armoury – amounts carried are down to individual choice and the level of perceived threat. Mister B as usual draws the minimum for SA80 and SLP Browning. Ammo pouches are sorted out at Safety Equipment.

The critical path for new arrivals during the handover period – a scheduled maximum of five days – is getting hold of body-armour jackets (Mk 60 for crewmen and Mk 61 for pilots), night-vision goggles (NVGs) and Model 112 personal radios. There are only sufficient of these items to kit out one detachment, so it's a question of grabbing a 'B' Flight man and getting them off him. At Kandahar that's difficult enough, but with some of their aircrews up at Bastion at any one time it's a nightmare.

The Boss notices that they're issuing two shots of morphine per person. 'Perhaps they know something we don't.'

By the evening the newcomers have checked out the base for personal and recreational possibilities. There are eighty shower-blocks with hot and cold running water, and an industrial-sized laundry, with each individual allowed two free bags per week. The whole of Kandahar is 'dry', as apart from the social disruption that alcohol abuse could cause in this close-knit community, partner forces are live-armed at all times. The food in the cookhouse is plentiful and good, a lot of it being trucked from Pakistan over the Khyber Pass, and prepared by contracted chefs, mostly Sri-Lankan.

For variety, on the Boardwalk there are separate European, Mediterranean and North American restaurants. Chomper introduces Morts to the excellent coffee at 'Echoes', the Dutch Internet café where network credits can be bought – Chomper is slightly embarrassed when a spot of finger trouble buys him ten times the amount he wanted. Then it's on to the Boston cream donuts and iced cappuccinos at 'Timmy Horton's'. There are three gyms, should they wish to work that lot off – American, Canadian and British. If there's time, they can see what's on at the camp cinema.

No more than a hundred metres from the huts is a row of international phone booths, and an Internet cabin, but those who have brought their laptops from home have tested the new Internet connection, WiFi, installed since the last detachment. On this relatively leisurely first evening they've the time to call home, but for many it's a bit too early in the piece for that. Frankie, however, is one who has already made a Skype connection – she pronounces it very good.

Ginger makes his daily phone call to his fiancée. All personnel are issued with a card to fund half an hour of line time each week – the story goes that it used to be twenty minutes until someone pointed out that that was shorter than the time allowed back home to residents of HM Prisons. More can be bought, and those with higher-maintenance 'other halves' do so, but with the time difference (three and a half hours in winter, four and a half in the summer) it can be difficult to find an opportunity to make the call. But Ginger always makes the time. 'I find it's best to talk when I've finished for the day, after sundown and the evening briefing, when she's still at work. I worry about her. Even if it's just for a few minutes it's good to know all's well.'

But the Boss decides that his face appearing on the computer screen in the living-room just at the children's bed-time would put them in a tizzy, and

'Jingly' Market – after the sound of the merchandise trucks – Kandahar Base (Bob Ruffles)

Main gate – Kandahar Airfield (Bob Ruffles)

leaves Skype until a later day. Enjoying a coffee at Timmy's on the Boardwalk (undisturbed by mobile phones, banned for the military and civilians alike in Helmand), he remarks that 'we've well and truly settled in to KAF, again. And that five-miler on the treadmill this evening makes me feel better about the lazy start to the day.'

Tomorrow he and his colleagues will be in the air.

CHINOOK PEOPLE – SUPPORT ENGINEERS

The engineering manpower on 1310 Flight is sourced from Odiham's ExCES on three-month detachments. At present, some of their men are based at Kandahar, supplying cover for the Chinooks operating from or being serviced at the main base, and manning a rapid-reaction team standing by for emergency deployment out to the field. Others are based forward at Bastion, where twenty-four-hour cover is essential in support of the IRT and the MERT Chinooks on as little as thirty-minute readiness. Under Project Jericho, each aircrew flight is to be shadowed by a specific group of engineers to promote team spirit while at base and out in Helmand. One who at the age of 24 has already been deployed in Afghanistan no fewer than six times is SAC Tech Daniel McComisky. 'Ski' joined the RAF in 2002, and two years later was in Iraq. In 2006, on the NATO take-over, he went out to work on the construction of Camp Bastion – for three and a half months he and his mates lived and worked in two ISO containers and a tent:

> There were three Cabs based there then. In those early days, I didn't get much time at home, and not much notice of deployment. A couple of times there was a piece of paper in my mail slot when I got back, saying I was off again in a fortnight. In the RAF you have to accept the going away, but it was taking a lot of willpower to keep cheerful. Now the new Jericho rotation seems to be bedding in, and the system's far better oiled.

On Ski's team is SAC Phillip West. 'Westy' joined up in August 2007, and has now completed his first Herrick detachment, which ran from the beginning of November to the end of December last:

> It should have come sooner, but I broke my collar-bone and was off work for six weeks. Before going, I quizzed those who had been, and got to know a bit about what to expect, and got really excited about getting some experience in Afghanistan. After all, I chose to work on Chinooks because they're up at the front end.

As with aircrew, the engineers also get a briefing before deployment, as well as refreshing their FP training. The ExCES Warrant Officer, John Edbrooke, has just completed his week of 'soldiery bits', and is ready to leave for Kandahar. He's a senior NCO aged 52, which in a force with so many 20- and 30-year-olds in the front line makes him a true veteran. A craggy six-footer brimming with energy, he's ranked in the top ten in RAF table tennis. He hails from Tiverton in Devon, where the RAF was nowhere in sight:

> I got my three A-levels, and tried a series of jobs. And then I met a pal in a pub who'd joined the RAF as a technician. He sold me on the idea of joining up – which I did, in 1977 when I was 20.

He was a Direct Entry Aircraft Electrician recruit, and did Basic Training at Swinderby. After technical training at Halton, and newly married, his first posting was to RAF Marham, as junior technician on the Victor tankers of 55 Squadron. He was soon abroad, on Ascension Island in 1980/81, just prior to the Falklands War, and a few years later, in Germany, at Laarbruch on the

Tornado GR1s of 16 Squadron, 'The Saints'. This was followed by a posting as sergeant to Brüggen and 31 Squadron, 'The Goldstars', again with Tornadoes. After duties in the First Gulf War, and now a chief technician, in 1994 he arrived at Odiham, and 27 Squadron's OCF for Pumas and Chinooks.

In 2005 John was appointed Warrant Officer Engineering 18(B) Squadron. Within days he was deployed on a four-month detachment in Basra, and by the time he got back, in line with the centralization of Support under Lean Principles practice, 18(B) and 27 Squadron Engineers had been merged to form ExCES. He got the job of managing the combined section, reporting to the Squadron Leader OC.

In September and October 2005, he carried out his first Afghanistan detachment, based at Kandahar and Bastion, with just four Chinooks in operation. Six months later, in '3 Para time', he was back again. He keeps his Herrick kit stacked in the corner of his office – desert camouflage uniform and overalls, a 'Camelbak' water carrier with drinking tube, and over 5 kg of Mk 60 Combat Body Armour. This is bullet-proofed throughout, but reinforced with a plate of DuPont 'Kevlar' carbon-fibre over the heart and belly, and another below the shoulders. 'The standard-issue Meindl boots aren't bad, but I've bought myself a lighter and better pair from the US PX at KAF, with zips down the outside – no faffing about with laces.'

In his CS95 webbing are pouches for magazines for the SA80 automatic rifle always carried at Bastion and further forward. Together with the improved, camouflaged Mk 6a Kevlar helmet, all this is regularly humped about in the heat on the Bastion flight-lines. Finally, John has ready a heavy-duty rucksack with bed-roll. 'That's my "Go-pack" – essential personal kit for nights on forward Ops in theatre. I'm all ready to go.'

CHINOOK GROUND ENGINEERING IN ACTION

Out in Kandahar, ExCES engineers are working through the night to make the Chinooks airworthy for 'C' Flight's first day of action. There are half a dozen machines parked on the helicopter pans on the south-east perimeter of the runway, jostling for space with the fleet of other rotaries operating from Kandahar – other Coalition Chinooks, Royal Navy Sea Kings, and US Army Kiowas and Black Hawks. The Black Hawks are almost constantly in action, day and night. Over the other side of the runway, there's a flight of Russian Mi-8 HiP helicopters – they've been recently chartered by NATO to carry out routine resupply to safer areas, and are manned by Moldovan crews.

The man with the task of allocating space, always at a premium, is the Base Commanding Officer, currently a British air commodore, Andy Fryer. KAF has reached its absolute capacity and there's no room for any more aircraft. With the planned surge of American troops and helicopters, transferring as they wind down in Iraq, something has to be done, and large areas of the camp are building-sites. The United States, which originally built the airfield as a potential Cold War base between 1966 and 1972 at a cost of 15 million USD, is now injecting millions more into further development.

Mister Edbrooke arrives, and doesn't take much time acclimatizing. He finds it difficult to sleep, and is at work by nine o'clock, where he's pleased to find that his predecessor has everything in good order, and ready for an important Internal Quality Audit (IQA) in a week's time. He also notices improvements in the infrastructure for the men. Inside the tented maintenance hangar, which stands alongside the Chinook pans at the westerly end of the runway, four new management cabins with aircon and improved IT equipment have been installed. It's in this office that he carries out his administrative work – scheduling of maintenance, and manpower planning and management:

> We've been waiting for these upgrades for a couple of years. They are a much-needed improvement, to combat the extremes of hot and cold we get working here 24/7, 365 days of the year. But there's still no aircon in the hangar itself. In the summer it really cooks, while now in the winter it's brass monkeys – the electric bar heaters in the roof just can't cope.
>
> After two hours on the flight line, man management can be a bit of a challenge – sometimes it's best left for the tea bar. I like to lead from the front, as it were, and get stuck into electrical engineering repair and maintenance jobs. And I make sure I chip in with the clearing-up ops in camp, perhaps on tea bar duties. I lose a lot of weight on detachment – I find I'm tightening my belt practically every week. In the summer, in the hottest part of the day, if the aircraft are away on tasks we try to get a bit of rest before working through the night. But it's a blessing for us all to be busy – keeps the mind off the dangerous stuff and the discomforts.
>
> On detachment, I work about fourteen to sixteen hours each day, and the ExCES engineers do twelve hours on and twelve off, eighty-four hours a week. They change shifts at midday and midnight, and in their time off it's not much more than sleep, perhaps go to the gym, and eat – they never get more than two meals every twenty-four hours. It gets

ExCES engineers on night-shift – Kandahar (John Edbrooke)

a bit like 'ground-hog day' for the lads, and they're all completely bushed by the end of a three-month tour.

When there's damage to an aircraft in the battle-zone – enemy action, or perhaps transmission or other critical problems, which happens about once a month – then I'll fly out to assess the damage and the tools and manpower needed for repair. For third-line maintenance, other nations' air forces can and do provide a pool of support for us – Americans, Canadians, Aussies and the Dutch all operate, or have operated, Chinooks from here.

But all our careful planning can be thrown into crisis by Talib artillery attacks. The flight-line in particular comes under regular mortar fire, and their accuracy has improved over the years. They were usually pretty random, but twice now the engineers' accommodation has been bombarded by shrapnel from a lucky salvo. Then, last time I was here, a round landed on the pan. It bounced with a hell of a thump before smashing through the fuselage of a Cab and narrowly missing two airmen working on the ramp. Finished up by the wall of the flight-hut. The lads were pretty shocked. Good job it didn't explode – would've been mayhem.

That kind of incident keeps personnel at Kandahar in touch with the dangers beyond the wire. Early in his detachment, fighting against time to get JAG operational, Group Captain Turner experienced such an attack for himself:

We'd jumped into the car at the cookhouse and set off for HQ when the alarm went off. It was everyone out and lying face-down in the dust – for two minutes until the all-clear went. Back into the car, it happened again. It took a quarter of an hour to do that 800-metre drive.

The rockets the Taliban use are basically 107 mm shells mounted on a mortar carrier and fired at 30 degrees elevation, triggered by a car battery. They seldom do much damage, but the random nature of their timing and aim creates fear. The mortar teams are normally caught and removed from the battlefield, and many attacks are stopped before they happen.

That's in large part due to the efforts of the Airfield Defence Force, manned by the RAF Regiment.

Airfield defence

The unit currently in residence is Number 4 Force Protection Wing, of which Squadron Leader Bob Davies is Chief of Staff. Commissioned from the ranks, he joined the regiment from the RAF Police in 1987. He has served in Iraq (twice, in 1996 and 2001) in Northern Ireland and twice in Afghanistan. His first six-month tour was in the first UK deployment in 2001, when he was in Kabul.

One of his flight commanders is Flight Lieutenant Jason Neame, who left his job as a manager at Woolworths to join the regiment in 1998. 'The first six months on IOT at Cranwell were benign compared with the next six of regiment training at Honington, where there was a fifty per cent drop-out rate.'

He has also completed two Afghanistan detachments, the first in Kabul in 2005.

'The RAF Regiment', says Squadron Leader Davies, 'is proud of the Royal Warrant awarded in 1942. We foster air-awareness in our troops, giving them a far greater understanding of air power and its protection than their army counterparts.' But the regiment slots into the Task Force command structure, reporting to its CO, 'the only RAF unit to do so'.

The Wing is one of eight in the regiment, and comprises the HQ at Lyneham, 1 Squadron based at Honington, and 501 Operational Support Squadron Royal Auxiliary Air Force based at Brize Norton. The officers' tours are for two years; on the squadrons, the troops stay for three, perhaps four. No. 501 OS Squadron supplements 1 Squadron on detachment as required – to date no greater than twenty per cent of the force, but that could well increase. The HQ staff provides command and control for the squadrons in the field. Squadron Leader Davies outlines the task:

In providing a high degree of security to the airfield and base at Kandahar, we're a microcosm of the Herrick operation. There are non-kinetic duties, such as Intelligence gathering, local civilian personnel vetting and surveillance, and counter-insurgency measures. Then there's kinetic – patrolling, and holding ground. We have to cover the full range of eventualities, 'from condoms to nuclear bombs', as they say.

The security task sub-divides into 'inside the wire' – within KAF perimeter, and 'outside the wire' – in the 450 square kilometres of Ground Defence Area. The GDA stretches from Highway One and Three Mile Mountain in the north, down to the Red Desert in the south. In it the regiment patrols alongside the Kandahar Task Force – currently manned by Canadian troops – to secure and hold the ground. The multi-national KAF Defence Force is 600-strong and contributed to by thirty-two nations, but it is only the British who go outside the wire. All the others are prevented from that by their national Rules of Engagement – RoE. To date, the regiment has had a number of men incapacitated by often life-changing injuries from IEDs, and has lost three.

Inside the wire, counter-insurgency is half the battle. Aside from vetting and monitoring the hundreds of LEC commuters, there's the headache of having the civilian Kandahar air terminal on the base, with road access from outside the wire. This is a major security problem, especially during the Hajj pilgrimage – last time, in December, 3,500

Charter aircraft base and Three Mile Mountain – KAF (Bob Ruffles)

local nationals used it for travel to Mecca. Saturday market inside the base is also a high risk – locals can make a year's money in a day, and they fight to get a spot. We police all that with the help of the Afghan National Police, the ANP.

There'll be increased tension with voter registration coming up, and then with the elections in August, but the fact there's been no major incident so far is the measure of our success. We're proud of that.

It's a claim supported by Group Captain Turner. 'Given the risks, the regiment does an outstanding job of controlling the civilians who work at KAF.'

1 FEBRUARY
CHINOOK TOUR OF FOBS

Thanks to the security effort, the Boss and his crews can feel relatively safe as, early on a very chilly morning with frost on the Land Rover windscreens, they make their way through the traffic to JAG and the 1310 Flight Office. It's time to go flying over Helmand. There will be AAC Apache attack helicopters from Bastion in support in danger areas, and the highly developed defensive aids of the Chinooks to give protection, but just in case of trouble Mister B has as little kit with him as possible.

'Evacuating the Cab under fire,' he tells Morts, 'you'd have no time to take anything other than what you've got on you.'

All incoming pilots and crewmen must carry out a Theatre Qualification sortie before starting operations, and the drill is that 'C' Flight's training captains get their ticket by flying with 'B' Flight trainers on an operational task, picking up the fine details of the current FOBs and routes before passing on that knowledge to their colleagues. All this must blend with the tasking programme, as there are not sufficient hours to allow special training flights. However, an hour of dust-landing practice can be tacked onto an operational sortie, and those who have not deployed before get an in-depth training package from the flight's Qualified Helicopter Instructors.

Accordingly, at the morning briefing, Mister B finds he is detailed to go with the Boss on an operational task. He is rostered as a supernumerary crewman in the cabin, and the Boss will fly as NHP up front. Frankie and Ginger are similarly deployed in a second aircraft. They bring the newcomer pilots and crewmen along to the briefing and preparation, so that they get to know the drills and begin to understand the general situation.

The first call, at 0800, is to the JAG Operations Briefing Room, where the captains are issued with tasking sheets. Printed on A4, these are an amalgamation of the RAF Support Helicopter and Army briefing formats. The Boss, who did an earlier tour here as Operations Officer, knows that neither Service likes the way the other one briefs, and neither of them likes this version. 'But there we are – the format's constantly changing anyway', he tells Morts.

The task for the Boss and Mister B is largely a routine resupply around the Helmand HLSs in the FOBs. The Boss reminds Morts about the load limits:

The standard maximum load in Afghanistan in the winter is four metric tonnes. In the heat of the summer that drops to three point five – or thirty-six troops, in any combination, according to the mission. The max passenger load is laid down as fifty-four, but the Cab has carried many more than that

– one hundred were lifted from the roof of the US Embassy in the evacuation of Saigon. And the four-tonne load is a Herrick limitation because of the altitude – at sea level, a Chinook can lift a Chinook.

All tasks are scheduled for a maximum of eight hours, with a flex to go to ten with clearance from the CO of JHF(A). This is planned to be the full eight, including a session of dust landings for the Boss. The first leg is a run over to Bastion (BSN), carrying a bunch of Gurkha troops returned from a spell of Rest and Recreation (R and R). From there, there's to be a USL, a 105 mm light gun. This will be carried over to the FOB in Gereshk. Then it will be back to Bastion to take on board a mixture of internal freight – mostly drinking-water, ammunition and medical supplies – for delivery to a series of HLSs south of Lashkar Gah, new to the 'C' Flight men. The mission will give the Boss and Mister B a comprehensive update on their operating environment.

The next stop is at the armoury, where the crews draw their carbines and pistols. There's strict control over weaponry, and a comprehensive set of drills to run through, with muzzles pointing into a sandpit throughout, in case of a 'negligent discharge'. All weapons must be personally signed for by their designated owners – the exception being on IRT duties, when the firearms are held on board in order to keep the aircraft as ready for flight as possible.

Back into the Land Rover for the short run to the Chinook pans, the crew passes helicopters and fixed-wing aircraft lined up along the flight-line as if for an air display. Half-way down the runway stand the bulky Hercules transports, and alongside them is a bay for the American UAVs, the latest high-tech weapons of war. Further on are the powerful RAF Harriers, eight of which have been flying close air-support for NATO's combat troops out here for almost five years.

In the helicopter pans, the 1310 Flight Chinooks stand side by side, each within its protective shield of concrete-block blast-walls. They are all painted in the dark-green paint that gives them, at night, a low infra-red signature. The engineers have prepped the aircraft for flight – they came on shift at midnight, so these lads have been up all night. They keep their body-armour and helmets to hand – rocket attacks are currently a weekly event. A half-dozen of their colleagues are in the flight-hut, clad in full combat kit – they're flying to Bastion for the changeover with the engineers who have come to the end of their week up there.

There's a friendly exchange between air and ground-crews before the pre-flight routines start up. Their living and working accommodation are separated by some distance on this base, and it's the best chance to promote some camaraderie. It's the best chance for the engineers also to meet some of the troops, today a company of determined Gurkhas, who wait patiently in line to board.

The Boss, as the NHP on this trip, clambers into the left-hand seat while the captain checks out the exterior of the aircraft. He ensures there are no cracks in the fuselage skin, and monitors the condition of the tyres and rotor blades for bullet or slingshot damage. Satisfied, he takes the machine over from the crew chief and climbs into the cockpit.

Each member of the crew stows a night-bag holding a sleeping-bag and blanket in the cabin. The pilots fasten their rifles on the seat-backs, and day-bags go down alongside. They contain essential survival kit – dressings, tourniquet, boiled sweets, 1.5 litres of drinking water and extra clips of ammo. Ominously, the bag also carries a mine-clearance kit. This is a simple affair, consisting of a three-inch-square plastic envelope for a short nylon probe, the idea being that you nervelessly use the probe to feel for mines between the fingers of your splayed hand.

There's also a trio of 'Cyalume' light-sticks, translucent narrow plastic tubes which, when 'cracked' with the fingers and shaken, emit a bright chemical luminescence for five minutes to twelve hours, depending on their size. They come in various colours, and are often used by ground troops for identifying a landing-site at night. They are either spun on a string above a soldier's head or laid out in a square on the ground as a 'desert box'. Both give the pilot references when landing in dust.

All the aviators are now wearing their combat body-armour jackets. The Kevlar in the reinforcement is a polymer first produced by Du Pont in 1971 – it can be made into tough, high-melting-point fibres, five times stronger by weight than steel. The pilots don't need it on the back as their seats are armoured, but the crewmen have it fore and aft in their jackets. With an emergency GPS transmitter in one of the pouches, 112 radio in another and with the rest stuffed with ammunition, it's a hefty 5–10 kg to pick up and wear – a burden, but a reassuring one.

Further reassurance comes from the Kevlar armoured sheeting fitted to the cabin walls – a weight penalty of a couple of thousand kilos well worth paying. The anti-noise cladding on the cabin walls and ceiling weighs far less, and brings a little extra comfort for the passengers. They are marshalled into the cabin by the crewmen, with the standard brief in the Chinook of, 'Get in, strap in, shut up, and don't touch anything', delivered, of course, with a friendly smile. The crewmen are also obliged to point out the emergency procedures, but all these men will have been through the 'stage one' training for aircraft familiarity, apart from having heard the brief many times before.

The crewmen's primary duty is to ensure the integrity and safety of the aircraft cabin, and everyone and everything within it. Number One crewman takes up his position at the left rear opposite the maintenance panel, with enough intercom-lead to allow him free movement over and off the ramp, and checks that all's well with the M60 7.62 mm machine-gun mounted there, and that it's all clear outside for start-up. Number Two goes forward to the crew door on the right, where he plugs in his intercom next to the aircraft systems instrument panel and HF radio. He's ready to monitor and confer with the pilots as they run through the drills. He's also ready to man the M134 7.62 mm Minigun mounted in the upper half of the aircrew door (on this flight, Mister B is assigned, as an extra man, to the one on the left, mounted in the escape hatch).

The Boss has his pad of Flight Reference Cards to hand, but he runs through the checks from memory. The APU in the tail pylon runs up, providing the power to wind up the turbines in turn. Number 1 (on the port side) is the first to be fired up – it has the Engine Air Particle Separator (EAPS) installed, to protect it from the worst effects of dust and sand. As soon as it's running, the rotor brake-lever above the captain's head is hauled to the off position (flush with the cockpit roof) the clutches engage, and the six blades start to turn. The helicopter takes on its characteristic syncopated shudder and the transmission starts to scream. With the ECL fully forward, the rotors build to full speed, and when the hydraulics are working and the engine generator providing power, the second turbine is started, under minimum load. The engines are now ready to deliver torque as required.

Crewman Two checks the hydraulics. The Boss confirms that the compass, flight instruments and radar altimeter are set and synchronized, and, at the command of the captain, calls up air-traffic for permission to taxi. It's given, and the crewman on the ramp reports chocks stowed, ramp up, all secure, and they're ready to go.

The captain releases the brakes and eases the collective control upwards, and the natural tilt of the rotors pulls the Chinook forward. Once out of the pan, he checks the brakes with a dab on the foot pedals and swings onto the taxiway with the steerable right rear wheel. With clearance to take off, rotor revolutions are checked at one hundred per cent, temperatures and pressures as normal, and DAS arming on. Crewman One confirms that all's safe and secure down the back, the pilot shifts the cyclic forward and lifts the collective lever, and with the familiar 'wokka-wokka' the whole outfit flies off into the cold Afghan air.

Now, it's every crew member's job to keep a sharp look-out. The pilots scan through the 'chin' windows below their feet, and the 'eyebrow' ones above their heads, as well as the all-round eye-level panels. Crewman Two and Mister B have the open upper halves of the forward doors as viewpoints. Number One crewman keeps watch through the open tongue of the ramp, and through the window ports on both sides at the rear – the bulbous windows themselves are removed for Herrick.

'You can stick your head out and get a good view', says Mister B. 'You get a faceful of dust from time to time, but it's worth it, particularly at night when the curve and the scratches on the window would blot out the NVGs. It's the "five Ss" reconnaissance drill the whole time – size, shape, surrounds, surface and slope – looking to pick up anything out of the ordinary.'

Leaving Kandahar city to the north, the turquoise dome of Ahmed Shah's tomb clearly visible through the winter air, the Chinook sets course along Highway One, which runs roughly east to west for 150 kilometres across Helmand province, the sandy expanses of the Red Desert stretching away to the south. The distance to run to Bastion is eighty-five nautical miles, which will take one hour at cruising altitude, above the danger level for ground fire.

The Boss has selected 'BSN' on the GPS navigation box. The Chinook Integrated Navigation System (CINS) has a numerical display, into which way-points and destinations can be programmed through grid-references. They can then be saved as a route. Pilots can then view a page of numbers showing how far it is to the next point and how far left or right of intended track they are. CINS is a boon for pinpointing IPs in action, and is a great help in the deserts and mountains, where there are fewer good navigational features. But for finding all the routine FOBs and HLSs, the Chinook crews have the landscape programmed into their eyes and brains.

There is no completely automatic pilot on the Chinook. There's an airspeed hold function, which does just that once the pilot has trimmed the collective to the required knots, together with a height hold facility. Working as it does to barometric pressure, this is not accurate enough for use in the hover, but efficient enough at altitude. These holds are used in the cruise, but the pilots are always ready to override them for immediate evasive action.

The Boss listens out on the operational UHF radio and checks the track made good on the map. The Arghandab, a tributary of the Helmand river, snakes along below, its green ribbon clear against the seemingly endless desert. A few miles beyond Highway One rise the foothills that in 300 miles or so become the Hindu Kush mountains. After thirty minutes, Lashkar Gah is clearly seen off to port, on the western edge of the Green Zone. The fields and compounds have a deceptively peaceful look, but the whole crew knows that this is the danger area, which the Taliban make their base for attacks.

Here, the Chinook is in the Triangle. Not more than three dozen miles to the north is Gereshk, where the Boss and so many others have had such close shaves, and the next destination today.

On the descent into Bastion, the captain alters his course to keep the hostiles guessing, and as height reduces, the crewmen are ready at the guns.

CAMP BASTION

Bastion, four miles long by three miles wide, with a concrete runway, comes up ahead. Built from early 2006, it has been the largest British military base construction project since the Second World War. It can be seen clearly today, but when a dust-storm blows up it's a different matter – then the pilots give thanks for its radio beacon and the Chinook's GPS.

The captain brings the helicopter in to land at the 1310 Flight pans. ECLs are set to ground, and as the engines are shut down and the hydraulics turned off, the ramp, closely monitored by Crewman One, drops to the ground. The rotors are still turning – they take a minute to wind down on their own, but as they slow, the captain heaves the rotor brake back to the vertical and brings them to a halt. He's careful with that – it's on a very strong spring and has delivered more than one black eye.

The passengers go their various ways and the crew is off to the 1310 Flight tent for a toilet break. The facilities on the Chinook, as on the Hercules, are primitive, and it's always best to take the opportunity when there is one.

AN UNDERSLUNG LOAD

Before long, the pilots and crewmen are back in their positions and the Chinook is hovering over to the open area to pick up the light gun, alongside the four-metre-high blast-walls. These are constructed using 'HESCO Bastion' blocks, easily transportable and collapsible wire-mesh containers filled with a heavy-duty fabric padding. The inventor, an ex-miner from Sheffield, persuaded the Americans to invest $1 million for development, and now he's a multi-millionaire running a worldwide company. The blocks are to be seen in blast-walls throughout NATO bases in Afghanistan. But near Bastion there are no hills to give easy cover for a Taliban rocket launcher,

Hercules approach to Bastion – runway 01 (Dave Hogg)

and to date the base has incurred just the one attack. However, that was only last month – as 'C' Flight people are well aware.

Waiting with the gun, ready to hook it onto the Chinook, are five men on detachment from the Joint Helicopter Support Unit (JHSU), based at RAF Odiham but reporting to the Royal Logistics Corps (RLC). Mark Evans, the sergeant in charge of the Bastion detachment, is an RAF Movements man.

97

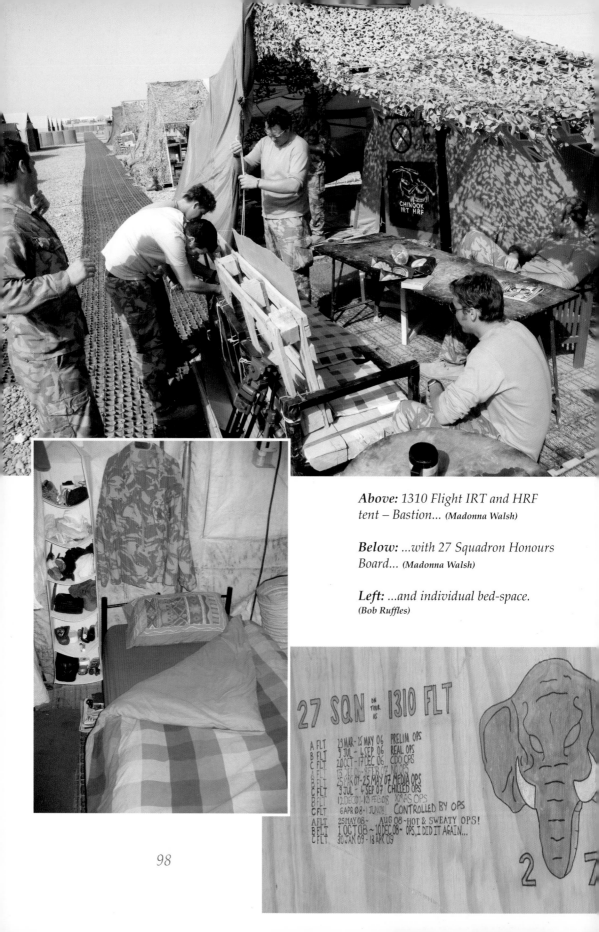

Above: 1310 Flight IRT and HRF
tent – Bastion... (*Madonna Walsh*)

Below: ...with 27 Squadron Honours
Board... (*Madonna Walsh*)

Left: ...and individual bed-space.
(*Bob Ruffles*)

Two of the others are Royal Artillery and two more are also RAF movers. It's their specialist job to deploy and rig USLs. In principle, battle groups out of Bastion should be trained to be self-sufficient in rigging, but many of the troops lack field experience in the job. In any event, in the words of the JHSU Commanding Officer, Major Phil Ritchie, 'We'd rather have the fighting men concentrating on bayonets and bullets.'

JHSU men and women, known to the aircrews as 'hookers' – that gets a wry smile from the girls on the team – have worked with Chinooks on a variety of jobs. Sergeant Evans talks about 'the grounded Lynx helicopter liberated from a hotel park in Devon, the cow stuck in a mud-hole in Wiltshire, and the Army Apache poleaxed after a heavy Helmand landing', but today he's got one of the trickiest loads of the lot, the 105 mm light gun:

> Of course, with all loads you've got to get under the belly of a Cab in the gale of the downwash, grab 50 lb of hook on the end of a swinging five-metre strop, all the time being battered by stones and gravel thrown

Underslung 105mm light gun speeds towards the action. (Bob Ruffles)

up in your face. But with the light gun, the point is, there's a large turning moment on the barrel – you get the 'conker-string effect', big-time.

The team is ready for action alongside the gun, which they've rigged this morning into three separate loads – the ammunition and the support equipment each bundled up in nets, and the gun fitted with a heavy-duty harness sling. The men are dressed for action in helmet, overalls, protective scarf and goggles, heavy gloves and boots, and carrying a side-arm holstered at the thigh with leg-webbing. As the Chinook approaches with three hooks down – forward and aft fixed, and Crewman One at the open hatch above the lowered central – one of the team holds aloft a metal discharging wand,

JHSU 'Hookers' at BSN – eyes fixed on approaching Cab. (Madonna Walsh)

Hooking on (Madonna Walsh)

ready to thrust it against the central hook to relieve the static. The downwash is an icy blast and the noise is terrific.

The hookers brace against the loads as the gale does its best to pluck them from the ground and throw them off the pan, but they're fit for the job and not likely to be bowled over. They've done this many times before, and as the bulk of the Chinook's under-belly moves above them they trust the pilot to keep it there, aware nevertheless that one of their colleagues has a compressed spine from when an ISO container descended onto his helmet.

'The trick is to forget about the helicopter – just concentrate on the job in hand', says Mark Evans.

Even without touching the airframe, the static can be felt crackling in the air. Then the Chinook goes into a steady hover above their heads and the wand does its job. Under the shelter of the broad, flat fuselage, the rotor wash is felt less keenly, but the racket is still such that the troop leader can only communicate by means of hand signals. Two men lift the heavy strop and

In 'brace position' as the load is lifted away. (Madonna Walsh)

heave it over the central hook. Then it's thumbs up to the crewman – that's the gun hooked on. They go forward to attach the ammo, while others, aft, fix the crate of kit. One jumps back involuntarily, with a yelp – he's had an electric shock.

'Happens a lot', says Evans. 'Those jolts are about the same as an electric fence – strong enough to get a cow's full attention. They hurt. You've got to keep that wand working, but you don't always have the time.'

All three loads are fixed now, and the team moves out from under the Chinook, keeping an eye on the load. Once they're clear, the pilot raises the collective, increasing torque. The rotors lift the helicopter away, and the hookers brace against the downwash again. The team leader monitors for a clean lift, and when happy, gives a thumbs-up to Number Two in the starboard door. He tells the captain they've a secure load and the Boss calls for clearance to depart. The aircraft moves away from the USL park and starts on its way.

The JHSU guys, relieved from the noise and the thrashing wind, are off for a cup of tea to recover before the next lift. There's a total of a dozen scheduled for them today.

The Boss and Mister B pick up all the well-known references as their Chinook clatters across to the north-west edge of the Green Zone and the town of Gereshk, just thirty nautical miles to the east on the Helmand river. The Boss knows it well, a frequent destination since that close-run thing on his first mission two years ago.

The town is bisected by Highway One, and because of its strategic position on the main Taliban migration route up from Pakistan it has always been a dangerous spot for ISAF forces. But the FOB, codenamed 'Price' is well west of town and well barricaded. It's relatively safe, but nevertheless the tension

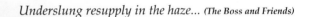

Underslung resupply in the haze... **(The Boss and Friends)**

... and in the dust (Photograph by POA (Phot) Sean Clec, RN © crown copyright 2010/MoD, image from www.photos.mod.uk)

in the cockpit and in the cabin is palpable, and the crewmen man the guns as the pilot brings the aircraft into the HLS.

There on the ground is a detachment of troops who have had good coaching from the JHSU and by now have experienced a fair number of USLs. Despite the hail of stones and mud, the gun, shells and kit are quickly unhooked, and the Chinook can fly away from the danger zone around the HLS. It's been in the hover just a couple of minutes, but time expands when you're in a possible line of fire.

There are no further heavy lifts on the sortie today, but one after another they tick off the northern Helmand landing-sites – Sangin, Kajaki Dam, Musa Qaleh and Now Zad – delivering internal freight, vital supplies for the

Retrieving a wayward Bergen (The Boss and Friends)

military and medical people manning these platoon house outposts of Security and Redevelopment. The Chinook gets back to Bastion by mid-afternoon for refuelling and reloading, and for the crew a welcome mug of tea and a buttie. Frankie's there, and she and the Boss agree that the old-established FOBs to the north are becoming more and more substantial each time they see them – not only that, but there are more of them. The Boss and Mister B continue their mission and see them for themselves.

First stop is in the Nad Ali district, just three minutes' flying time from Bastion, which the captain describes as 'the latest infamous hotspot – the FOBs here can only be supplied from the air'. But all's quiet there this time, and they fly past Marjah to cross the Helmand river to Nawa, which could, according to the Boss, 'become the dustiest of the lot when it dries out'. A site codenamed 'Armadillo' is the final call on this round-trip of the new platoon houses, and with the cabin empty of freight the Chinook wends its way back to the sanctuary of Bastion.

DZ recovery at night (Chris Stuart and friends)

FLYING AT NIGHT

By now it's dark. In theatre the Chinooks fly with the navigation lights switched off, and the retractable searchlights aft of the chin windows are used only in dire necessity. This is not only to reduce the chances of being spotted by hostiles but also to minimize interference with the crews' NVGs. These are battery-powered goggles that clip onto the front of the helmet, above and in front of the eyes, with a counterweight fixed by Velcro onto the rear – the whole assembly weighs 2–3 lb, and makes an extra load on a tired head and neck. But the kit is more than a godsend on night operations – it's an essential. With it, any light source, including infra-red, shows up almost as clearly as day. There's even a data-lead that, plugged into a socket in the cockpit, shows the state of the instrumentation in the eye-piece, allowing complete head-up operation.

There's been much development with NVGs – so much so that they now cost £15,000 a set. Improvements continue, but they still have their limitations. The Boss explains:

The goggles work like binoculars – no magnifying effect, but the same tunnel-vision and limited-field image – and that takes some getting used to. Levels of illumination are measured in millilux. When they're above a certain level, it's 'green illume', and you get a good picture. But if the light source is too bright, like a full moon, the picture will 'back down', and 'blooming' fuzzes the image. On the other hand, if it's absolutely pitch-dark, it's 'red illume', and you'll see practically nothing. In Afghanistan it's often at red. Outside the NATO bases, there's little or no background lighting, and for most of the month the moon sets early

Sunrise – nocturnal Hercules crew lands back at KAF. (Dan Wilkinson)

and there's just no light for the goggles to pick up. Then in theory it's too dark to fly. But if we have to, especially on casevac calls, or on specific missions where the risk has been justified, we'll operate on red.

Tonight he is glad to see the lights of Bastion coming up ahead. Together with Mister B, and Frankie and Ginger, he's now Theatre Qualified (TQ'd). They debrief together on the Hercules shuttle back to Kandahar, deciding that apart from the changes in the landing-sites, it all looks pretty much the same.

They arrive back for a late supper, before flopping on their bunks for a fitful sleep. Tomorrow there'll be more work to be done and more risks to face.

CHAPTER 5

Hercules into Action

HERCULES PEOPLE

The Chinook air and ground-crews share the camaraderie of flight life, working closely on base and serving all together on Herrick. But it's of necessity different at Lyneham. There, the aircrews of 24 and 30 Squadrons, flying the 'J' Model Hercules, share a building, a pool of aircraft, and centralized servicing. Separate squadron identities are maintained to foster squadron spirit, though with up to a fifth of personnel away at any one time down the routes or on detachment, that's not easy. But they do crew up for Afghanistan.

The engineers are organized independently of the flying squadrons and work to their own deployment rota. But there are opportunities for teamwork, as at least one from the group of air/ground engineers, cross-trained in all technical areas, fly on all Hercules missions – apart from air-drops, in order to minimize the number of crew at risk. In addition, they share with aircrews the same cycles of PDT: Survival, Evasion, Resistance and Extraction (SERE) techniques, together with a dedicated Force Protection week (general FP training is continuous over the year). Practice operational air-drops are flown over Salisbury Plain and elsewhere, while Pendine Sands in South Wales and West Freugh in Stranraer are used for tactical landings. In addition, there's a major bi-annual training exercise in the USA. Squadron Leader Pete Cochrane of 30 Squadron explains:

> Before they go on Herrick detachment, crews and engineers will normally have operated in Iraq, where the weather and the terrain are relatively benign. To give them a taste of what to expect in Afghanistan, we send them for 'Hot and High' pre-deployment training at China

Lake in the Sierra Nevada, on Exercise Crown Pinnacle. China Lake's the premier weapons development lab and range for the US Department of the Navy. Our people are well looked after at the Naval Air Weapons Station.

The thing about the place is that the mountains go up to 14,000 feet and the desert goes down below sea-level. So there's hot and high, and flat and dusty – not a bad simulation of Herrick. Multiple crews and engineers take one, sometimes two Hercs, for two weeks, to practise air-land and air-drop techniques in a far more representative environment

Hercules tracks edge of Red Desert – KAF-BSN Shuttle. (Dave Hogg)

Above: *Hercules view of Hindu Kush barrier...* (Dave Hogg)

Left: *... and the snows beyond.* (Dave Hogg)

than at home. When our crews arrive in theatre, they're better trained for the job.

Pete Cochrane joined up in 1994 aged 21. He had no family background in the Service, but he spent formative years living under the Heathrow approach at Windsor. He won an RAF Sixth Form Scholarship, and flying started at school, on Cessnas over Bodmin Moor. It continued at Oxford UAS, where he held a commission as acting pilot officer.

At destination – a busy day at Kabul (Dave Hogg)

After IOT at Cranwell, he was selected for multi-engine training on the Jetstream. 'Although initially disappointed, when I realized I was happiest working with a crew I didn't mind it at all.' He was posted to Hercules at Lyneham in September 1998 as a 30 Squadron co-pilot.

He had a two-and-a-half-year break from route flying and Afghanistan deployments in 2005, when he was promoted to squadron leader for a staff job at Air Command. Back at 30 Squadron in the winter of October 2007, he was deployed again to Kandahar for the first two months of 2008 as Hercules Detachment Commander within 904 EAW. At the end of the year, he was back there as a captain, and carried out seven air-drop missions, including a resupply to FOBs on Christmas Day. And he's in post as Detachment Commander again from February to April this year. Among his Hercules crews are two newly qualified captains from 24 Squadron.

Stu Patton won a Flying Scholarship at grammar school, aged just 16, and then, at Southampton University, studying Aeronautical Engineering, he joined the UAS. Once in the RAF he was initially streamed for fast jets, and the Tucano course. The Tucano is a powerful aeroplane, with a speed of 240 knots, ceiling of 25,000 feet and 'g' limit of 5.5. Stu was proud to complete the course and gain his wings, but a backlog on the AFT Hawks at Valley led to a reduction in the fast-jet stream, and he missed the cut. After fifty hours of multi-engine 'cross-over' on the King Air, in 2005 he arrived at the Hercules Operational Conversion Unit at Lyneham.

Dave Hogg went from school to Loughborough, where he joined the East Midlands UAS and flew Bulldogs out of RAF Newton. Like Stu, he was originally destined for fast jets, but after seventy hours on the Tucano, was also restreamed for multi-engine. He was awarded his wings on the King Air at Cranwell, and, within a few weeks of Stu, was posted to the Hercules.

As with the Chinooks, most of the OCU 'flying', including all instrument training, was on the simulator – actual time in the air was restricted to three flights, one of which was the Final Handling Test. But the flight-deck on the 'J' Model is heavily computerized, and the two pilots reckon their systems experience was just as well gained in the simulator as in the sky.

Three years of co-pilot tours then followed for both. Once on the squadrons, training continued on the job – working with the loadmasters, and flying the routes. Stu did a great deal of that in 2006 – all around the world, including across the United States. Dave, on the other hand, who became Combat Ready after less than five months, was soon on detachments – to Basra and Afghanistan. A planned four weeks at Kandahar became six, as the crew, operating the first 'J' Model in theatre, were pitched into a series of tasks, leading to night-stops in Kabul and sorties to up-country natural-surface landing sites. 'We must have flown into all the strips in Afghanistan.'

Following that, Dave did four or five more month-long stints in Kandahar, with a similar number in Iraq. As yet, neither he nor Stu had done any supply dropping, but when four co-pilots were required on a nine-week course for tactical flying, they both volunteered. They soon found themselves on air-drop missions in Afghanistan, up to four each week, delivering to mobile units and all the FOBs.

'It was good to make contact with the ground forces,' says Stu, 'even if from an altitude of a couple of thousand feet. It's one of the most direct human connections we have in theatre, and we can see we're making a difference.'

Dave says that the power and technology of the 'J' give them the edge needed in the conditions. 'The Herc is well protected by its warning systems, but we still maintain more traditional techniques, such as positioning look-outs in the doors. Our chief enemies are terrain, weather and other aircraft – the GCAS, radar and TCAS help us with each of those. The FLIR's a godsend too. Then there's the tedium of repetition – you have to work at keeping focused.'

[GCAS – Ground Collision Avoidance System.]

[FLIR – Foward-Looking Infra-Red.]

Both pilots have now completed a three-month conversion course and are on deployment as captain. 'It's not been a great step up', says Dave. 'As co-pilot on the "J", you have to stand on your own in most areas – there's no nav or engineer as there is on the "K". Of course, you don't have as much responsibility in the right-hand seat as you do in the left, but you have to be able to operate all the knobs and switches.'

TQ'd for their first missions, and now 'fully nocturnal', in addition to air-drop sorties three to four times a week, they fly regular resupply shuttles to Kabul and Bastion. To the latter, it's to up to four each night – two sorties with engines-running turnaround. The flight takes thirty-five minutes one way on average, but often they fly longer, varied routes, south over uninhabited terrain, to confuse hostile observers on the ground. And for added safety, they fly high.

At Bastion they stay on the ground for as short a time as possible, parking and loading on the crescent-shaped dispersal alongside the runway. On these, and all other non-air-drop trips in theatre, the Hercules carry two pilots, a loadmaster and that air/ground engineer, who provides an extra pair of eyes for look-out.

Mission to Kabul

Tonight, Dave is detailed to skipper a shuttle to Kabul, and at 1800, two hours before scheduled departure, he and his crew are driven down to the EAW Ops Room for flight planning. For an air-drop, tasking is issued three to four days beforehand, but for tonight's freighting trip they received it yesterday. This evening they get an Intelligence brief, before getting final authorization from, the Hercules Detachment Commander.

Squadron Leader Cochrane reports to the CO of 904 EAW, whose boss is the 1-star CO of 83 EA Group at Al Udeid, the Coalition forward HQ base at Qatar in the Gulf. Routine tasking in support of Task Force Helmand comes from Joint Force Support – another 1-star appointment (air commodore or tri-Service equivalent), but based at KAF – while a certain amount of flying hours are allocated to NATO theatre-wide Ops, and others to RC(S). Pete Cochrane explains his job:

> I attend the morning round-table briefings, negotiate priorities and liaise with the Air Movements Cell, which generates the detachment's routine tasking. If we are resupplying an Op for the resident (UK) Kandahar Battle Group I also make sure I attend the ground troops' operational meetings, to find out exactly what they reckon they need in the way of air-supply – and where and when they'd like it delivered.
>
> Reporting to me is the Junior Engineering Officer, a flight lieutenant or warrant officer running the Hercules engineers out here – small groups on an eight-week tour. He's right down there behind the Herc pans, but we keep in close touch. He's on the other end of the phone, and we make sure we meet face-to-face at least once a day.
>
> It's my Ops Officer who compiles the flying programme. He comes into work later in the morning so as to stay up at night until all the Hercs have landed. I come into work a couple of hours before him, and might get to bed earlier.
>
> 904 EAW provides the IT systems we need for monitoring Ops, Intelligence and the other generic support functions. Their people are on a four-month stint, and because of the Detachment Commander's extended working days, he's supposed to be on six weeks – but that can stretch to eight.

Dave and his crew pick up their tasking sheet and, wearing CS95 combats and heavy-duty flying-boots, hump body-armour, helmet and NVGs to the aircraft. It's in full-freight rig, as for a routine shuttle, but tonight the load is more than unusual. There's normally advance warning of special cargo, but it seems the authorities have wanted to keep quiet about it this time. The freight cabins are full of Afghani coffins. There has been a mass suffocation of refugees in a transit container lorry, and a request for assistance has come

NVDs pick out lights of Kabul dead ahead – from Hercules flight-deck. (Dave Hogg)

from a high Afghan political level. ISAF has responded in a spirit of co-operation, and the Hercules is flying the dead back to Kabul:

Generally we undertake 'home nation' tasking, flying our own troops and kit around. Our own RAF Movements team organizes these loads, within a ten-tonne limit. But when it's an ISAF call – about twenty per cent of our work – the load's processed by their Combined Air Transport Officer. He's got a multi-national set-up in the big hangar by the main ramp at KAF. Tonight, we'll be flying with an ISAF callsign.

The distance to Kabul is close to 600 km, and the trip will be about an hour each way, flying at 25,000 feet, but this load will take careful and probably lengthy unloading, and total sortie time is unspecified. They calculate the fuel required – this is always a trade-off with payload, especially from the hot and high airstrips of Afghanistan. With maximum fuel, for maximum range, the limit on the payload the 'J' can carry is about 10,000 kg – on the other hand, maximum load is around 15,000, but that entails a drastic reduction in fuel and therefore range.

Pete Cochrane comes into Flight Planning to meet his men – he takes care to do this every day, as it's often his only opportunity to see his night-owl aircrews. He makes sure to watch for signs of fatigue. The RAF monitors 'harmony figures', making sure there's a sustainable limit on days away in theatre over a certain period. The fatigue that comes with repetition is the main danger – in one particularly busy week on his last deployment, Dave Hogg flew twenty-six Bastion shuttles off the reel.

Between flight planning and take-off the crews must find time to eat, collect rations for the night ahead and draw weapons and ammo from the armoury. Half an hour before take-off, they call for transport to the flight-line, where they sign the Form 700 and make their way to their machine, seemingly even more massive under the brilliant arc-lights. The 'J' Model is immediately distinguishable from the 'K' by the six-bladed propellers on its Rolls-Royce turboprop engines. From the ramp, the yawning cargo bay stretches away for a hundred feet – its floor stacked with plain wooden caskets.

The aircraft has been loaded by a ten-man team of specialist handlers from Air Mobility Wing. These guys – many of them reservists – are part of a thirty-strong section deployed from their base at Lyneham, where part of their job is to receive and despatch the Hercules freight and run the cargo-hangar operations. Out here for up to sixteen weeks at a time, their task is to receive and batch goods from the airlift aircraft on arrival at Kandahar, before

Hercules 1-tonne air-drop over the desert (Chris Stuart and friends)

transferring them to pallet-loads for the Hercules and helicopters for onward transport, or to the men of 47AD Squadron for air-drop. They do the same in reverse for outgoing consignments. In addition, it's down to them to calculate the all-up weight (AUW) and balance of the aircraft, and ensure the load is properly distributed and secure. Then, when the occasion demands extra hands, and Movements expertise, one or more of them accompanies the freight to its destination – as on tonight's solemn duty.

The captain runs through the external check of the airframe, making sure that nothing is loose, leaking or missing. Up on the flight-deck, the layout's nothing like in the 'K' Model, except for the same array of cockpit windows. There are banks of computers and circuit-breakers, state-of-the-art avionics

Above: *Loading the CDS on Hercules at KAF...*
(Chris Stuart and Friends)

Left: *...and making the delivery to the troops.*
(Chris Stuart and Friends)

screens on the instrument panel and head-up-display panels on the pilots' windscreens. There's no navigator and no flight engineer, and the loadmaster and crew chief sit downstairs with the passengers and freight. Although Dave is the qualified captain and has overall responsibility for the aircraft and its safety, on the 'J' the pilots alternate between being at the controls and handling the radios and navigation, turn and turn about. They use the terms 'pilot flying' (PF) and 'pilot non-flying' (PNF).

With doors closed and all checks completed, the captain guides the heavy freighter out to the ever-active runway. As those who can are settling down for another night on Kandahar Air Base, the Hercules with its sombre load soars into the dark Afghan skies, the crew peering through heavy goggles for rocket trails – heading yet again for the forbidding peaks, and onwards to Kabul.

CHAPTER 6

Forward to Camp Bastion

3/4 FEBRUARY
BAPTISMS OF FIRE

On Tuesday, Morts completes his first full day's tasking with the Boss, eight hours and forty minutes around Helmand:

> I confess that it's all gone by in a bit of a blur. The navigation was a breeze – all done on the CINS. The most difficult things were the radios, and the control radars. It was hard to keep up – but the Boss knew what was going on. And the biggest surprise was the beauty of the place – striking.
>
> At first I was conscious of the carbine by my seat and the pistol in my jacket, and I couldn't get it out of my mind that everyone around Lashkar Gah was trying to shoot at us. Mind you, ten minutes later at 'Gibraltar' – that's a patrol base just north-east of Gereshk – they actually were. We'd just dropped off the load when the Apache up above reports seeing the Taliban. In the Boss's words, 'We leave, sharpish.'
>
> Then, our defensive flares deployed several times. The first time it happened I jumped out of my skin – and got rubbished for it. And there was plenty of hostile tracer out there – at night you could see it spraying up all round.
>
> But by the end I began to get the hang of it.

The first groundfire of the detachment mercifully did not find its target, and back in Cambridge Lines, Morts takes comfort from the fact that his two first-tour mates have also found the pace leaving them behind. And he would be

Smoke marks the spot at a riverside FOB. (Bob Ruffles)

pleased to know that, at the end of the day's work, the Boss writes in his journal:

First day's tasking with Morts. He was on good form and wide-eyed throughout but refreshingly honest about being behind the aircraft. Departed in a three-ship and I effectively had to do left- and right-hand seats. But mid-way across the Red Desert it was, 'Right I'm back with you – what have I missed?' He got better and better through the day and will do well on Ops, although the first one will be a tall order for him.

Chomper has to wait until Wednesday for his update on operating in Helmand, crewed with 'Smithy', an experienced captain, and crewmen Mister B and 'Richie', a flight sergeant who has also put in many hours on Ops. On his first mission of the det, Chomper is served up with a speedy reminder of the hazards of Herrick:

One of the Cabs had gone U/S, so we picked up an extra tasking – some pax from Bastion to HQ RC(S) at Lashkar Gah. Turns out they've built two concreted helo landing-spots since I was last here – up by the Governor's house on the eastern side of a low ridge. We're coming in quite fast and spot it late. Smithy kicks the tail left and the rotor RPM pushes us upwards. He counters, and we sink like a stone –seems we'd got into some bad air. Richie down the back yells, 'Up five, up five!' as we're about to land heavily on three guys right under us. Smithy pulls through on the collective but feels some restriction in the lever and levels us out with a huge power input. Helmets blowing all over down below. We move slightly further forward to avoid troops and a HESCO blast-wall, and land on with no further issues. Good show, Smithy – phew!

After all that, the Marine Lynx escort calls us up to say we've landed at the wrong HLS – I check it out and Smithy's able to tell the chap quite firmly it isn't so, or words to that effect.

Later on was Sangin – quite dusty there – and Delhi, where we turn in from the north after crossing the wadi and Richie sees something on the ground that tells him, 'We're being dicked!'

Saw troops in combat in the Green Zone near 'Inkerman' – lots of flashes and smoke, very unpleasant – and a massive explosion north of Sangin. Picked up pax from Nolay – had to wait a nervous fifteen minutes for them on the ground – and then we collect a USL, two quad-bikes. By now it's dark, but the load's lit up with red cyalumes and the hookers get it attached in the murk. As we're flying off, the radio squawks – there's been some confusion over times and have we got the CO on board? We have, and it's back to BSN, where Smithy reports the collective issue. After some engineering assistance we make it back to KAF via Lashkar Gah, escorted by a Sea King – just in case.

We land at 2100. I reckon I've got fully TQ'd today, so it's off for some pizza action, and to spend some of the hundred quid of Internet credit I accidentally bought on Monday ...'

['Helo' – Military abbreviation for helicopter.]

[Wadi – Dried-up river bed.]

['Dicked' – Coalition aircraft are monitored by local 'dickers' on the ground, who pass information through the 'dicker-screen' to the Taliban.]

FINAL ARRIVALS

By Wednesday, all the 'C' Flight people have arrived, German travelling with the last of them. Yesterday, the dawn bus collected him from the Odiham Officers' Mess:

It's a good Mess, and I've got a comfortable suite in the newer wing. My girlfriend lives nearby, and she and I take my detachments in our stride. But I can't say I'm really looking forward to this one. With the weather and the workload, not to mention the Taliban, it's going to be a challenge. But I never know which of my old Cranwell mates I'll run across in Helmand. Over the years I've met one on the Harriers, others on the TriStar and Hercules crews, and another on Air Traffic at Bastion.

The TriStar was not quite full and we all got some sleep. But after a diversion, we didn't arrive until daylight this morning. It gave me time to think about earlier deployments. When I first came out here – it was with 'A' Flight in April '06 – I'd been out of training less than a year. But I'd seen some action already, with the G8 Conference task in Scotland and a go down in the Falklands – I'd got my Combat Ready tag. We were in Helmand before the main build-up of British forces, just as 1310 Flight got going again. We'd read up on the history of the place, but there was little perception of the threat – the senior guys who'd done Iraq found it pretty easy going.

The TriStar didn't fly direct to Kandahar in those days – it was into Kabul and onwards by Herc. Most of our flying was shuttles between Bastion and Lashkar Gah, but we did work with the Pathfinder recce platoons, and once with French troops on an Op to Kajaki Dam. We also flew some of the first IRT sorties. The worst danger, like now, was the dust, particularly at Bastion. There was a brown-out practically every landing. Sand storms and dust devils would sweep in and fill the camp with muck. Didn't help that living conditions were rougher then – the engineers worked out of an ISO container, poor bastards.

But it was less crowded then at KAF. The AAC with their Apache attack helicopters were only just moving in, and the sum total of Ops staff was five, with a wing commander boss. Happy days.

We arrived in time for the briefing today. They've figured out that if all Afghan opium production stopped right now, there'd be enough of the stuff in the pipeline to keep the customers supplied for twenty-three years. There's a thought.

We've all drawn our kit, so now it's off for a bit of shut-eye. Tomorrow we fly, and get qualified for Ops.

By this time in the first week, most of the outgoing crews have high-tailed it for the UK, and just one crew remains to familiarize German and his group. However, it all dovetails, and late on Thursday, the Boss is able to assure CO JHF(A) that 'C' Flight is ready, and assumes authority and responsibility for 1310 Flight.

6 FEBRUARY

Friday finds Frankie up at Camp Bastion, in the 12 × 24 ft tented accommodation for the two IRT and Helmand Reaction Force (HRF) crews.

'Up here, I'm one of the lads', says Frankie. 'We eat, sleep and fly together – and shower, but in separate cubicles, of course. That's the routine. And at BSN, we're operating next-door to the ground-crew – we're much more of a team.'

Chomper is up at Bastion too, on the second crew. He got up early this morning for a lift on the 0800 Sea King. 'But it all got changed, and we finally took off at midday. We "borrowed" half a dozen mattresses and stowed them surreptitiously on board. Fell asleep on one for half an hour – nice flight.'

In the afternoon, he and the others start to construct a new flagpole for the IRT tent: 'We need to make it taller so that the RAF ensign flies higher than the Navy ensign on the Sea King HRF tent next door.'

They get it up in a quiet few minutes the next day, to a full 36 feet, where it 'billows beautifully in the wind'.

BASTION FROM 2006

Chomper's mate Baz, NHP on Frankie's crew, is a new boy, on the squadron just three months and not yet Combat Ready. He's learning on the job, and has a good teacher in his captain. Last year, she took a month away from the usual round of detachments and PDT for a course at RAF Benson, qualifying as a Helicopter Tactics Instructor. And she's been up here on IRT many a time before. Her first stint was in the summer of 2006, when 3 Para were the Battle Group:

> The Standard Operating Procedure was for two crews with two aircraft to be permanently at BSN, and four at KAF. For certain Ops, those four would 'surge forward' as well – it was from Bastion that UK troops

mounted their ops, and still is. It gets crowded here then. In '06, there were no helicopter landing-pads and it was dusty as hell. The ExCES lads' set-up was in an ISO container and their office was a tent. And I had to sleep on the floor of our tent for three nights. I was up here most of the eight weeks, although I did squeeze in a few days at Kandahar – after Bastion it felt like R and R. We came under fire a lot but were lucky – they never managed to hit us.

In the years since 2006, there has been heavy and continuing investment in the whole base. The north–south runway, built in late 2007, handles up to 5,000 movements each month. There are blast-walls between the aircraft dispersal stations, to protect against hostile rockets. The sand and gravel in the helicopter pans have been covered with a layer of compacted large stones, each about four inches in diameter and big enough not to be thrown up by the rotor downwash.

The perimeter of the 20-square-kilometre encampment is protected by continuous razor-wire, an earth bank and a ditch. Inside the barrier is a maze of 20-foot-high HESCO blast-walls and anti-Rocket-Propelled Grenade (RPG) nets. It is home to 6,000 men and women, and as at Kandahar, these include LECs serving as tanker drivers, cleaners, domestic staff and interpreters – or on the fuel dumps, and even on casevac duties. A good deal of accommodation has been built, and there's more going up, but still here and there are stacked ISO containers, pressed into use as workshops and emergency billets. The military field hospital cost £10 million to construct. In it, casualties brought in from the battle zone are treated first in A&E, where five ER doctors are on duty at any one time, and then where necessary in the two state-of-the-art operating theatres, staffed by surgeons, anaesthetists and nurses.

FRONT-LINE MEDICS

Robin Berry has worked in those theatres. He is a consultant anaesthetist and a serving RAF wing commander. He's based at the Ministry of Defence Hospital Unit (MDHU) at Derriford in Plymouth, but serves regularly on UK-based and deployed operational tours on the Critical Care Air Support Team (CCAST) within the Tactical Medical Wing at RAF Lyneham. While a mature student in Nottingham University Medical School, Robin was offered a Medical Cadetship by the RAF. On graduating, after twelve months of house jobs, he found the Officer Training course at Cranwell 'somewhat therapeutic'.

When, after 250 years, the Conservative Government in the '90s took the axe to the Armed Services' secondary-care hospitals and introduced the MDHU programme, Robin was posted to Peterborough, and then, in 2000, to Derriford. Since then, he has deployed on four operational tours – Oman, Iraq, and twice in Afghanistan. On Herrick, CCAST is based at the Bastion hospital, sharing quarters with the MERT. He explains where CCAST fits in:

> The MERT job, retrieving the injured from the point of wounding by helicopter, is in effect the front entrance to the hospital – CCAST, providing intensive care at Bastion and on the airlift home to the UK, is the back door. But in theatre, the role of a consultant like me is less clear-cut. I've done several MERT shouts, and also spent time in ER and theatre. It has to be like that to make the Bastion operation work.
>
> It would be misleading to use the word 'enjoyment' in respect of being out here, but it certainly makes a change from the NHS. The camaraderie is strong and there's an attraction in meeting challenges, including those that test you, yourself. And it's a chance to roll out your whole range of medical skills – we get all sorts of casualties with all kinds of trauma. Rewarding is the right word for this work.

MERT delivers casualty to TA medics and Bastion Hospital.
(Photograph by Cpl John Bevan, RLC © crown copyright 2010/MoD, image from www.photos.mod.uk)

CCAST nurses stand by for patient-escort duties on UK-bound TriStar. (Photograph by Sgt Pete Mobbs, RAF © crown copyright 2010/MoD, image from www.photos.mod.uk)

We're bolted on to the hospital unit. That's run by the resident Task Force – in 2006, when we were in tents, it was the Paras, and in 2007, when the permanent building was still under development, it was the Territorials from Cardiff.

The primary role of the hospital is to treat ISAF combat troops, but care is also afforded to the ANSF (who are entitled), to Afghan civilians caught in the cross-fire (for humanitarian reasons) and on occasion to wounded Taliban (with caution). However, it's only British troops who are entitled to evacuation by CCAST to the UK – Afghan nationals cannot be taken out of the country, and they have to find treatment within its boundaries:

Offering care to civilians is a sensitive issue. Being seen to be in contact with ISAF forces and medics puts them at risk of retribution from the Taliban, for supposed collaboration. But they often come onto the Chinook. I remember a brigadier visiting the unit when two Afghan adults and two children were in the ER. That opened his eyes.

Another medic who's had her fair share of the front line is Squadron Leader Charlie Thompson. She hails from Bedfordshire, and after A-levels at eighteen, she trained as an A&E nurse. She had been in the ATC, where the first-aid interested her, but confesses that it was *Casualty* on the telly that got her hooked on nursing – that, and the fact that her mother was herself a nurse. After nearly five years at Addenbrooke's, where alongside her medical qualifications she gained a BA honours degree, she was looking for more excitement. On an Air Training Corps visit to Coningsby she'd seen a visiting Chinook and learnt about its aeromedical evacuation role – so one day she walked into an RAF Careers Office. She took the tests at the Nursing Service Liaison Centre at Cranwell and was offered a four-year deal. But after IOT, now aged 27, she signed on for eighteen.

She spent a year at the MDHU at Peterborough, on the orthopaedic ward, before beginning her round of deployments. She has now completed four. The first two were on Telic, in 2003/4 and 2005, in Aeromedical Evacuation Liaison and Flight Nursing roles. From November 2007 to February 2008, a winter when the weather was particularly bad, she deployed for the first time on Herrick, promoted to squadron leader in command of the Bastion MERT. She was back there again from July to November. 'Missions took us over the whole combat zone, and the Chinooks came under fire many times. I remember that when Ant and Dec came out to present the "Pride of Britain" award, they showed them the bullet holes.'

Now, she's there at the same time as the Boss and 'C' Flight, but she particularly remembers her first, when she took over the team from Matt Haslam for the three months over Christmas 2007:

> I was very apprehensive going out in the TriStar on that first detachment – travelling on my own, away from the unit into a hostile environment. It was very cold. We made an effort with a bit of tinsel around the place, but there wasn't much Christmas spirit. There had been a call-out on a particularly nasty job. A Marine had been blown up by a double land-mine, and had suffered severe injuries. He was lying at the bottom of the mine crater, losing a lot of blood and in deep shock. We had a very experienced paramedic on the team, Sergeant Mills. He took over and

we got our casualty back to Bastion. The whole hospital was involved in his treatment, and he survived. That first experience still haunts me.

On IRT standby

One of the two crews on the 1310 Flight four-day detail at Bastion spends two days on IRT, while the other mans the HRF. For the second two days they swap over. Each crew can expect to spend thirty per cent of the detachment forward at Bastion and see a lot of action, on both IRT and HRF. Frankie has had her fair share of both:

> Last time we were here on HRF we were called out on emergency water resupply for the Gurkhas – they were down to their last day's rations. Then there was vehicle recovery for the Task Force, and extraction of prisoners from the Triangle. The HRF does all sorts of stuff like that.
>
> Today, we're on IRT. This is when we're at our most focused and most driven – massive adrenalin, especially when the casualty is a Brit. In 2006, with the Paras, we were very, very busy, and again that winter. We flew a lot at night, often under fire – machine-guns, rifles, mortars, RPGs, the lot.
>
> We also bring out injured Afghans – Talibs, army and police, as well as victims of road traffic and domestic accidents. We once had a year-old baby who'd been scalded in the kitchen. It's the kids that affect us the most – we've been told that one in five Afghan children doesn't live to see their fifth birthday. Of course, mostly they're innocent victims of the Talib IEDs.
>
> It'll all be much the same this time, I suppose.

This morning, after early breakfast ('the food's just as good as you get at KAF') and briefing in the JHF(A) HQ, the crews are waiting in the tent, resting when they can. There's a hand-held short-wave radio to alert them at mealtimes, but in the three tents, a field phone stands in the corner, wired up from Ops. A single ring is targeted at the Apache VHR team, three rings alert the Chinook HRF, and four the Naval Sea King crew. If it stops after two, it's an IRT 'shout'. 'The first ring gets you on your marks', says Frankie. 'More than one gets you going.'

An IRT 'shout'

In the tent, some of the aircrew are reading and others writing. A couple of the younger men are putting in some desultory work on weights in the compound outside. There's a wide-screen satellite television recently installed, showing the channels of British Forces Broadcasting Service (BFBS), and that can be good for settling nerves – it depends what's on. The guys are already weighed down with body-armour and ammo, but all their operating kit – flight-bags, maps, helmets, NVGs and weapons – are ready in the aircraft.

The phone rings – and stops after the second pulse.

There's a short run to the Land Rover and a dash to JHF(A) HQ, with Number Two crewman Richie at the wheel. Frankie jumps off for briefing from the Medical Liaison Officer and release authority from Ops, while Baz and Mister B are driven on to the Chinook stands. There, the ExCES engineers are waiting in strength, having prepped the aircraft for flight in

Left: *Chinook lifts for Deliberate Op – with Apache escorts.* (The Boss and Friends)

Below: *Chinook launches defensive flares.* (The Boss and Friends)

the early hours. The engineering book lists one or two things to note, but none of them safety critical. The allocated machine has been rigged by the medics in standard casevac role, with the cabin floor cleared for stretchers. As the Land Rover speeds off to collect the captain, Baz scrambles into his seat, ready with Mister B to start the engines. Adrenalin pumps, but the air and ground-crews move with practised efficiency through familiar drills. Within five minutes the transmission howls and the rotors fly.

The Land Rover speeds back into the pan. Frankie signs the Form 700, then leaps up the ramp and across the cabin floor, dodging the medical kit and the half-dozen stretchers. Those will be exchanged at the destination for any they bring back with casualties on them. The MERT people have arrived. A team of four are strapped into the canvas seats alongside the fuselage walls, forward of six armed men from 16 Close Support Regiment.

Frankie hands Baz the tasking brief. There's been a fire-fight at the Gereshk FOB. The ground forces have come into contact with the Taliban to the west of the old Soviet camp buildings, on the edge of the desert. There are at least two casualties, both British. Baz keys an eight-digit grid into the navigation computer and marks the track on his chart. All the crew know that it's no more than a ten-minute flight to Gereshk – that's twenty for the round trip. But already they're ten minutes into the golden hour, and counting.

This is the worst time for Frankie.

'Sitting with engines running, waiting for launch authority from Ops – just one minute can seem like a lifetime.'

'Chewbakka – clear for immediate take-off', crackles over the radio, and Frankie lifts the collective lever at last.

As the Chinook rattles at top speed across Highway One and eastwards to Gereshk, there's an AAC Apache escort overhead. The Apaches and Chinooks work closely together. Neither has overall command of the mission – the Apache is there to warn of incoming fire and on occasion will advise the Chinook to hold off from the HLS.

On an IRT mission the normally jovial banter is subdued, and everyone concentrates on getting the most out of the machine. On the intercom, Frankie is addressed as 'Captain' and Mister B becomes 'Number One'. Callsigns like 'Chewbakka' and 'Princess Leila' for the casevac missions are not concessions to informality – they're to give a unique identity to the IRT aircraft. Casevac flights take airspace and radio priority.

Baz has his hands full operating the radios, keeping a look-out and handling the navigation and map reading. Although his captain knows the way to Gereshk by heart, the weather could turn any time, and it's vital to have a double check on what the GPS is saying. Frankie concentrates on the controls, and she as well as the crewmen manning the guns all keep their eyes skinned for signs of insurgents. There's always the chance that their attack at Gereshk has been specifically set up to lure a Chinook into the open.

'At night, we tend to spot any incoming fire all at the same time', says Mister B. 'You can see the tracer, and RPGs let off a big doughnut-shaped flash as they're launched. But most times in daylight you don't see anything, and just get reports from the ground or the escorting Apache that you've been under fire.'

For the medics in the cabin, it's the flight out that's the most nerve-wracking part of the mission. 'It's the tension', says Charlie Thompson. 'You tell yourself it's going to fall away once you're in action, but that doesn't help. It's the same no matter how many times you do it. On the flight back, you're too busy to be aware of any turbulence, heat, cold, groundfire or even the darkness if it's a night Op – you're wholly focused on your medical duties.'

The usual gale is roaring through the cabin this morning, and it's freezing cold, putting an extra strain on the extremities. Frayed nerves are at breaking-point when, just over half-way to the destination, there's a loud explosion on each side of the helicopter, and a 'whoosh' that can be heard even over the racket of the transmission. The newcomers among the nurses are visibly shaken – even the old-timers shift in their seats. But it's not the Taliban, it's the Chinook's own anti-missile flares being automatically launched.

Mister B reckons, 'The Cab is the best-defended aircraft in the RAF. With the various wars it's been in, more and more has been developed and bolted on – there's now scarcely enough room in the cockpit for all the switches.'

Minutes later, the helicopter is running in low over the desert to Gereshk. The Apache up above reports on the secure radio that it's all clear for Chewbacca to approach the pick-up site. To save those precious seconds Frankie takes them straight in without evasive weaving, and lines up on the green flare laid by the troops for an aiming-point. This is the key time for the crewmen to be ready at the guns, reporting any hazards below to the captain.

Then, as the Chinook sinks below ten feet, Mister B moves away from the M60 on the ramp and grabs a secure hand-hold – he's learned from experience that any ruts in the surface could bring the aircraft to a shuddering stop and throw him down the cabin.

They're on the ground. Mister B drops the ramp, and focuses on getting people on and off the aircraft as quickly and as safely as possible. But as the riflemen run out to do their stuff, he's never far from the M60, ready to protect the stretcher bearers. The men at the FOB have sought to secure the

HLS with the utmost diligence, but you never know. The field medics have the casualties ready-strapped to two stretchers, and hand them over to the MERT people on the ramp, shouting a medical report to the lead consultant. All this goes on in the downwash of the Chinooks' windmilling rotors.

It's all over in seconds, but to the pilots up front it seems an age. They know that they're at their most vulnerable sat here on the ground, in the open. Frankie herself has been under AK47 fire before – and mortars: 'You can see the puffs of dust where they explode, and feel the shock-waves. And I've seen the damage where a Cab's taken an RPG shell in the rear pylon.'

She and Baz are poised and tense, ready to make the critical decision to lift off. Lifting without confirmation from the back could result in people being flung off the ramp and suffering serious injury, or FP troops being left behind on the ground, isolated and vulnerable to attack.

The pilots can judge how the loading's going from the patter of the crewmen, and in their rear-view mirrors see the stretchers being lifted on board, and the exchange stretchers shoved out. Mister B remains in the aircraft and on intercom at all times, 'except *in extremis*', and counts the MERT and the riflemen off and back up the ramp.

With practised self-control Frankie waits patiently for his 'All on board – ramp up!' before lifting the helicopter and its critical cargo from the landing-zone. Down below, the soldiers turn their backs and shelter as best they can as mud and stones are flung in all directions – before the chop of the rotors fades away and they can retreat with their replacement stretchers to the relative safety of their lines.

In the departing Chinook, the medics are working on the injured soldiers. First, they must establish the exact nature and state of their wounds. There are four levels of Triage, T1 to T4, which can be communicated by hand signals between the medics. For example, a nurse holding up one finger over a patient would indicate that the situation is critical.

Crewman Two comes on the intercom to tell the captain what she's already suspected – it's to be Bastion, with all speed. A call to the Apache, and then the Chinook's accelerating off for base, leaving the slower machine in its wake.

Frankie has asked Richie to close the dust-curtain behind the cockpit – she doesn't want Baz, or herself, distracted by the scenes down the back. Expert hands in blue rubber gloves staunch bleeding, tighten tourniquets and set up morphine drips and blood transfusions. A splint is applied to a shattered leg and a wound is cleared of blast debris. At this critical stage, although Frankie is in overall charge of the aircraft she will consult with the doctor on

RAF AMW personnel load ammunition into a Cab... (The Boss and friends)

what's best for the patients: 'Sometimes what he wants – like which hospital would be better – conflicts with what I'm told on the radio. We go with the doctor.'

Approaching Bastion, the medics prepare the stretchers for immediate transfer to an ambulance. With priority clearance, the Chinook settles straight onto an IRT landing-spot built close by the hospital. With rotors still turning, Mister B drops the ramp and the medics are away and running. Within minutes, the casualties are in ER, under the care of trauma doctors and nurses.

The MERT medics give a full medical handover to the trauma team, under the MIST format: Mechanism of injury, Injuries sustained, Signs and symptoms and Treatment given to date. Vital signs and symptoms, and details of drugs given are often written onto the patient with a marker before transfer.

The drill is that the MERT people make sure to distance themselves emotionally and physically from that group of cases. There is nothing more they can do for them, and they themselves are in need of a clean-up and a coffee – eyes and ears already open for the next call-out. Frankie and crew do the same.

The next shout is not long in coming. This time, the casualty is a soldier from the Afghan National Army (ANA) who's been shot in the buttocks. It's no more than a flesh wound, and a few days later he's back on duty, with no lasting injuries bar a dent to his pride.

CHAPTER 7

Operation Diesel

5 FEBRUARY

THE PLANNING CYCLE

With all his aircrews now in theatre, the Boss, in his room in the Cambridge Lines, discusses with his senior captains the tasks to come:

> It seems we've still the same three categories of mission. First, the responsive – casevac and reaction sorties out of BSN. We need to sort out a rota for that soonest, as Frankie's due back here from Bastion at the weekend. Then there's the routine resupply – we've got a full range of those, with all the new FOBs open around Lashkar Gah, so the guys can start in on their mission planning right away. And added to all that is the string of Deliberate Ops the CO warned us about yesterday – half a dozen at least scheduled already. We're going to keep busy.

Preparing for a routine Chinook resupply task starts not much more than an hour before scheduled departure, but Deliberate Operations are something else. The Boss briefs the first-tourists about them:

> They usually involve the insertion of large numbers of troops in hostile territory – each one takes a week or more of planning. We work in concert with the ground troops, finding out their preferred options and just how they can best be met. On occasion, to maximize the contribution of our Cabs, we'll suggest modifying the assault plan, such as: 'We could, if you like, land you closer to that compound and minimize your foot-slog over open ground', or 'How about moving the HLS a hundred yards further from that known Taliban firing-point?' With the basics agreed, then we get on with setting up the flight-paths

and GPS navigation points, and rehearsing with the ground troops alongside the Apache and other helicopter crews. Meantime, the engineers make sure we've got enough Chinooks ready and rigged for troop carrying. Then it's the business of waiting for the action to start.

He tells them that planning for the first Deliberate Op, codenamed Diesel, starts on Thursday:

It's a two-day affair scheduled for the nights of Monday and Tuesday next, involving the insertion of soldiers of the first Battalion Princess of Wales's Royal Regiment, and Royal Marine Commandos. The target list has been built over a period of twelve months. We and other helos are going to demonstrate our ability to insert a large force of troops – more than six hundred altogether – at a place of our choosing, at will. It's called 'sustaining the footprint' – we want to let the Taliban know there are no safe havens.

The main target is a village south of Kajaki Lake, some fifty nautical miles up the Helmand river, where the hills of the Helmand Plateau start their rise out of the desert. Intelligence surveillance has identified it as a narcotics centre and insurgent stronghold. Now, a Predator has spotted the senior Taliban commander for Helmand moving among buildings there, and a force is to be inserted, at night, to try and ferret him out.

Another, larger body of troops will be landed to the west, ready to be moved further into the Green Zone on command. The rotaries to be used for the insertion are three 1310 Flight Chinooks, two Royal Navy Sea Kings and two US Marine CH-53 Sea Stallions. The Predator will be overhead as well as two AAC Apaches as top-cover.

Detailed planning continues on Saturday in the JHF(A) Ops Room. The Boss and his crews study detailed imagery of the landing-sites, trying to strike a balance between landing the troops as close to the target as possible and the risk to the Chinooks. The airmen are able to view real-time pictures of the target compounds, fed in from the Predator overhead. These have shown them occupied each evening, but no obvious enemy activity has been spotted. Today, smoke can be seen rising from narcotics processing fires.

'It's surreal', says the Boss, 'to stand here watching live feed of the target from a UAV flown by a pilot in Las Vegas – and being analysed by someone at KAF, eighty miles away.'

The target village is 300–400 metres from the probable troop insertion area. The CO JHF(A) has asked the Boss to work up the HLS options:

Rolling delivery to troops in combat. (Bob Ruffles)

I told him there and then that it's simple – we'll put the troops in wherever they'd like us to, based on the threat that the live feed's giving us. We could move further south along the wadi and increase our safety, but that would put the troops at more risk. I'm happy to take the aircraft further north. But anyway, he's the one who signs off the Op so ultimately it's his choice.

I'm more concerned about the weather – a deep trough is forecast to move over the area on the first night. But there'll not be any early decision to rolex – forecasting is notoriously difficult in Helmand.

Although a delay would be a pain, it'd give more time to sort out the aircraft. They all have minor niggles, and three have more serious issues. Mister Edbrooke has the job of dealing with those.

['Rolex' – Postponement of an operation.]

139

Above: *Resupply continues all year round.* (Photograph by Sgt Anthony Boocock, RLC © crown copyright 2010/MoD, image from www.photos.mod.uk)

Right: *Cabs deliver Land Rovers, complete with driver...* (Bob Ruffles)

Left: *...and troops, with full kit and equipment.* (Bob Ruffles)

140

ENGINEERING CHALLENGES

John Edbrooke is pleased with the results of the IQA:

> The check was done by the new JAG. That seems to us to be an improvement – it's allowed the majority of JHF(A) to move forward, nearer the action, while JAG concentrates on support issues. They gave us a big tick in the box – that's helped in fuelling the 1310 Flight 'morale tank' for the challenges over the next ten weeks.
>
> Our main challenge is to meet the serviceability target for the Chinooks. An above-target performance has now been achieved for four consecutive months – something for us to live up to. As well as the schedule of routine maintenance – there's one in the maintenance hangar here at any one time – three aircraft have sustained Category 3 cracks needing repair. Fuselage skin cracks happen all the time, usually around the ramp hinges – there's a lot of strain there. Others are behind the cockpit. When it's carrying a heavy load the Chinook flexes and flies somewhat in the shape of a banana – bent up slightly at both ends. It's designed to do that, of course, but after a while you get these fatigue cracks. Two of these Cabs can be repaired at KAF, by the Navy's team in the MASU facility, but one will have to be shipped back to the UK in a C-17. We won't get a replacement for that one until early March. We're expecting a spare aircraft to be air-lifted out next week, but it'll take us four days to rebuild it once it arrives.
>
> SAC West will have been working on that shipment back at Odiham.
>
> We can get a whole Cab on board the C-17 – take the blades off and stow them inside the fuselage, and the same with the forward transmission and aft pylon, too. Very neat.

[MASU – Mobile Aircraft Support Unit.]

When on deployment, his job as aircraft maintenance mechanic would be to provide a spare hand on the team, getting involved in routine servicing, changing engines and carrying out all the fixes needed to keep the Chinooks in the air.

'It was young Westy', says his boss, 'who found one of those earlier fatigue cracks, up front by the avionics cupboard. Good work, that was.'

Mister Edbrooke's headaches are not helped by those 'minor niggles' mentioned by the 1310 Flight Commander. The Chinooks are regularly hit by small-arms fire, and one has been struck in the aft pylon, sustaining just minor damage. Another two have taken bullets in the rotor-blades, and that requires the best efforts of the Odiham Blade-Bay representatives:

> There's always one of our blade-bay men out at KAF. The blades are taken off for maintenance at every 200-hour service, but there are regular daily and weekly husbandry tasks to carry out. The titanium leading edges are susceptible to erosion and damage from Helmand dust and gravel, so sacrificial tape is applied to the leading edges as a preventative measure. When that gets damaged as well, the blades whistle in flight – only regular husbandry of the tape will stop the big bird singing. They do good work, those guys. One of the rotor-damaged Cabs landed back here one evening at 1900 – the blade was quickly removed and the specialist worked his magic through the night. He had the repair completed and the blade refitted in time for an 0600 lift the next morning.

'IT'S ALL BEEN CHANGED'

Late on the Saturday evening, the Boss has an announcement for his crews:

> Based on the weather forecast, it's been decided to rolex Op Diesel twenty-four hours to Tuesday. Time will tell whether this is a good move or not – at least it gives Mister Edbrooke that extra day's grace with the aircraft.

MORE SHOUTS

Not that the Chinooks are inactive meantime. Sunday turns out to be a busy day for the IRT, with first of all a bomb at an FOB named 'Argyll' with one Category B casualty, and three men killed in action (one of those from the ANP). Next, a Marine at Sangin takes a lump of shrapnel. No sooner back from that, the crew takes off again for Nawa.

At the Nawa HLS, the muddy one by the Helmand river, the Chinook comes under indirect fire from a skirmish on the ground. JHF(A) Ops are keen that the IRT presses on – the casualties are apparently civilian victims of Coalition bombs – and the troops mark out an offset landing site in a hurry. The decision is taken to fly the injured – an elderly Afghan couple, looking understandably terrified by the whole experience – direct to the local hospital at Lashkar Gah.

Further missions are flown – one to pick up ANA and civilian casualties from a Taliban IED, and another to collect two girls reportedly injured by the bomb dropped from a Coalition aircraft in retaliation.

Chinook formation lifts at KAF, positioning forward to BSN for Operation Diesel... **(The Boss and friends)**

...and approaches Chinook pans alongside the HALS. **(Bob Ruffles)**

RUN-THROUGH

On the Monday morning, three Chinooks are flown up to Bastion to position for Operation Diesel. Frankie hands over the IRT duty and joins the Boss, German and their crews in more planning at JHF(A) HQ. They've put in hours of effort to prepare a PowerPoint presentation of the Joint Mission Brief (JMB) – it only takes minutes to give. It's followed by a Rehearsal of Concept drill in the Lynx hangar. The Boss explains the RoC procedure to the first-tourists:

> A junior pilot has been tasked to make a ten-by-ten-metre model of the area for the Op. Each of the captains of the aircraft involved then adopts the right start position and moves about the model in the manner that has just been briefed. While these moving parts are demonstrating their understanding of how the Op will unfold, questions are fired into the players as to what they will do in the light of different events. These can be such things as an aircraft unserviceable prior to launch, the HLS being attacked prior to or during landing, an aircraft being shot down on the target, and so on. While this square-dance can be a somewhat comical sight for those watching, there's a very real purpose to the drills. They serve to highlight potential areas of conflict and provide a safety check.

That's what they do, and Morts takes the exercise seriously, noting in particular the Boss's moves around the conflict zone. After the run-through the crews go off to their tent to get some rest before Diesel kicks off at midnight. Meanwhile, up in the area planned for the operation, the Brigade Recce Force has motored in armoured vehicles up to the Ghorak Pass area in the west of the target zone. It seems the Taliban must have been monitoring the column, and planting a daisy-chain of bombs along its route, for a vehicle strikes one, and is wrecked. The IRT is called out from Bastion. No one is killed, but a soldier recovered on the Chinook has multiple broken bones.

THE LONG WAIT

News of the Ghorak incident gives the Boss something to think about as he tries for an hour or two of sleep in the 1310 Flight surge tent – the one used by crews positioned forward at Bastion for a Deliberate Op:

> How the boys cope with the constant pressure that any second their vehicle may hit an IED I do not know. I would imagine that the constant

vigilance and heightened alertness must be absolutely draining. Evidently, the HRF were tasked to see if they could lift the remains of the vehicle out. But at six tonnes this was just not an option, so in the end the vehicle was denied with Hellfire missiles from an Apache. The first didn't do the job, so a second was launched. Then it needed a burst of 30 mm cannon to finish the job. All in all an expensive day out – particularly for one young soldier.

No one finds it easy to drop off, and soon the Nintendo Wii is brought into play for an extended Mario Kart tournament. For this they have four wireless steering-wheels, funded by a whip-round of the whole flight. Eventually, one by one they flop onto cot-beds and sleeping-bags – some manage to doze, others gaze at the tent roof. Frankie fills Baz in on some of her past Ops:

> We did these inserts weekly with the Paras in 2006 – and about the same in the spring last year. On that det, I flew on fifty-four missions in seven weeks – including half a dozen casevac call-outs, one of them needing three shuttles in a row, right into the Green Zone.
>
> But you don't have to wait for an IRT shout or an Op for excitement. I was Number One in formation on a routine tasking sortie – it was to an HLS just about a kilometre from Lashkar Gah city, after a dust-storm had gone through. Visibility was minimal but the imperative was high as we had a brigadier on board. He was needed back at his HQ for an assault being launched that day, so we pressed on. We could just about see the ground if we looked straight down through the murk. My NHP talked the other aircraft in – left, right and ranges to go. The rotors carved a wake in the haze – looked more like a boat than an aircraft – and I could get in behind him. We delivered the brigadier in one piece.

Mister B ponders the difficulty of finding a convenient time to call home:

> I'm either just finishing, or off to work at 10 p.m., at the time when it's coming up to 6 p.m. at home, and she's not back from work. Then, in the morning I'm either off to work again at dawn, or just finishing – and it's the middle of the night at Odiham. It's not easy.

Morts considers the risks on the coming Op:

> They'll know we're coming – but we're told the Cab's omni-directional noise makes it difficult to tell exactly where it's coming from. And the varied-approach tactic keeps them guessing. Anyway, it's going to be

quite a show – the largest movement of Royal Marines since the Second World War, apparently.

To Morts, and the other first-timers, it's the waiting that's daunting. There's been a lot of hype on the flight about Operation Oqab Sterga ('Eagle's Eye') in June 2008. It was the last Op the Boss and his guys did at the end of their previous tour – a major ten-day Task Force Helmand insertion of the Paras into the Upper Sangin valley. That night, no fewer than nine RPGs passed through the formation of four Chinooks. Everyone involved then is half-expecting a rerun of that scare. It's a considerable relief when it's finally time for the off and the adrenalin's free to flow.

THE OFF

On the helicopter pans, there's a crowd of Marines, loaded down with kit and armament. Apart from occasionally in the cookhouse queue, this is the only time the Chinook pilots have close contact with the mass of ground troops, when they're waiting to board. The crewmen meet them in the cabin of course, and look after them for the flight out, but the men mostly sit hunched impassively on the floor, focused entirely on the job ahead.

Diesel involves an airlift into three drop-zones. The 1310 Flight three-ship formation is tasked to deliver over a hundred Marines to 'Willow', the site nearest to the target village. One by one the engines wind up and the unique beat of the Chinook rotors builds up the suspense. The blast-walls at Bastion hide adjoining aircraft from sight of each other – all that's visible is the uppermost pylon strobe-light, switched on to show that the aircraft is ready for action.

There's a delay as the Apaches run up, and then taxi out to the 500-metre-long Hardened Aircraft Landing Strip (HALS) they use for take-off – they're too heavy to lift vertically. Then they get away, and the Chinooks lift off in turn.

Maintaining radio silence, the Boss sets course to the north-east and the Helmand river valley, snaking in a 'conga' to confuse the dickers. Numbers Two and Three keep their NVGs focused on the leader's infra-red formation lights as he swoops the three-ship down to low level along a sheltering wadi that leads them to the Green Zone. All eyes are alert for incoming fire – but Morts forces himself to focus on the run to the IP. 'The implications of making a mistake here are huge. In training, I'd just get a bad report – but this is for real.'

Air delivery to FOBs... (Bob Ruffles)

...reduces the need for vulnerable convoys. (Bob Ruffles)

Each Chinook has a different target, within half a mile of each other. The NHP's job is to get his aircraft to the IP and then on to the target. If it's missed by a hundred yards or so ('a couple of seconds in a Cab, minutes on the ground', says the Boss), then the troops will have to make it to the right spot on foot, weighed down with kit and exposed to hostile fire.

In the goggles, Morts can see the river bending to the right and the village further over. The computer confirms they've made it to the IP – now it's a

147

mile to their target, a village compound. As yet, there is no hostile fire. At 1,400 yards the Boss starts the flare, bringing the airspeed down while maintaining height. Still no fire. Morts has done his job well, for at half a mile the Boss spots the landing site – but they've still to find the target compound. It looms up in the gloom, over to the left. And still there's no fire. At the last moment before landing, the Boss picks out a deep ditch down below, and with a touch of torque extends the flight-path further forward. Out of the darkness, a barking dog comes charging at the helicopter – then thinks better of it and scampers away. The Chinook settles onto the ground, with the ramp no more than ten yards from the compound walls. Almost before it drops open the troops are on the move – all forty of them, off and running in seconds.

The Boss has been careful to set the Chinook down pointing in the direction of the egress wadi, and as soon as the call comes from Mister B that the troops have gone, he lifts off to twenty feet, before accelerating down the wadi and away. The crewmen are back on the guns, but there's been none of

One of the more challenging locations. (Bob Ruffles)

148

the expected heavy fire from the defenders of the Taliban commander. The formation reforms at the RV point and congas its way back to Bastion.

THE DEBRIEF

The hours of preparation have paid off. At the debrief all crews claim to have reached their targets and delivered their loads. Frankie reports losing her intercom on the insertion. 'With forty blokes in the back it was a bit of a facer. But we made it – Baz did a fine job.'

At breakfast, the Diesel crews meet up with Ginger, who's been on IRT standby all through the operation:

They briefed us to expect a load of casualties, but so far there's been none. The grapevine must have tipped the Talibs off that the Task Force was coming – seems they'd melted away from the action.

It turns out that Ginger had it spot on. The assault force finds a drug factory and arms dump, but very few Taliban and no commander. They find no heroin but they do destroy several hundred thousand dollars' worth of opium and a large quantity of the chemicals used to produce the white powder itself. They also make safe a motorbike lethally primed as a suicide bomb. And it's been a copy-book operation involving all Coalition assets that's certainly met the objective of extending the footprint. It gets good coverage in the Western media, and, above all, the aircraft are safe, and no NATO troops or civilians are injured, or worse.

For Morts it's been a good baptism of action: 'All that preparation – days of it – built up the tension almost to breaking point. But once in the Cab and into the air, it all came together.'

CHAPTER 8

Air Resupply

THE WORLD'S FIRST AIR-DROP

In December 1915, troops of the British Mesopotamian Expeditionary Force found themselves under siege. Commanded by General Sir Charles Townshend, they had marched in September a hundred miles north from Basra, and after three days of fighting had driven Ottoman forces out of the fortress town of Kut-al-Amara.

Kut, known to Telic forces as Wasit, lies on the left bank of the Tigris, in a bend in the river so sharp that entry and exit to the fortifications in 1915 was only possible across one narrow spit of land. General Townshend waited at Kut for nine months before marching up-river to re-engage the Turks in battle. He and his forces came off second best and retreated to the fortress. The Turks laid siege on 7 December. It was to last until April the following year, and become a most humiliating disaster for the British. An estimated total of 23,000 British and Indian soldiers died, and just 8,000 were alive when Townshend was finally forced to accept unconditional surrender. That any were alive at all was something of a miracle, given the privations that the troops suffered – totally inadequate medical facilities, and an almost complete lack of provisions. The little relief that they enjoyed came from the air.

On 4 January 1916, 30 Squadron (then of the Royal Flying Corps) began an attempt to supply the besieged force. Flying from Basra in BE2c biplanes (max speed 62 knots, gross AUW 972 kg), they flew 140 sorties in six days. The Lewis machine-guns and ammunition had been removed, and food and supplies stowed in their place, and as the pilots flew low over the Kut fortress, braving the Turkish rifles, the observers in the rear cockpits heaved the bundles over the side. Their fall was only partially cushioned by elementary parachutes, fashioned by the seamstresses of Basra out of Army blankets. The ingenuity of the attempt and the courage of the aircrews were in the end to no avail, but the missions did bring some comfort to the besieged. According to the Historical Log of 30 Squadron (now of the Royal Air Force) at Lyneham, it was 'believed to be the first recorded air-drop operation in British military aviation history'.

AIR-DROP IN WORLD WAR TWO AND AFTER

In 1942, three years into the Second World War, British and Indian forces again suffered a humiliating defeat, when mobile Japanese columns drove the once proud Burma Corps out of the country it was defending. From the fall on 9 March of Rangoon, the capital at the mouth of the Irrawaddy river on the Bay of Bengal, it took the invaders just to the end of May to chase the defenders the 900 miles up to and over the north-west border into Indian Assam. Only the arrival of the unforgiving south-west monsoon rains prevented the Japanese from fighting their way through to India.

The Allied commander, Lieutenant General Bill Slim, and his men licked their wounds and regrouped. They had lost 13,000 soldiers killed and wounded. Yet in this almost unmitigated disaster, Bill Slim and his staff had seen the first small glimmer of the means of turning the defeat into eventual victory – air-supply.

In the retreat, the Douglas DC-2 and DC-3 Dakota transports of 31 Squadron RAF mounted a lone shuttle-service between Assam and Burma, taking in supplies and evacuating wounded. When the air-strips had fallen to the enemy, they dropped supplies and medicines by parachute to the columns of troops, enabling a force of 8,000 to make it back to India, and under arms.

In the subsequent reconquest of 1944 and '45, a formidable British and American air-supply operation succeeded in keeping an army of over 600,000 Allied troops in the field for what became the longest campaign of the war. Transportation and air-drop of munitions, food and medical supplies, and a multitude of casevac missions, were undertaken in the most extreme conditions. Mountains and monsoon weather, enemy fighters and ground fire were hazards faced by aviators, daily. Over one hundred British and Indian Dakotas, and many of their crews, became casualties by the end.

The Japanese had no air-supply. They overstretched their lines of communication, ran out of food and ammunition, and never reached Assam.

By May 1945, the Allies had retaken Rangoon, and the atomic bombs on Japan in August sealed the invaders' fate.

Bill Slim went on record that the campaign itself, let alone the ultimate success, would not have been possible without air-supply. When supply-drop parachutes became scarce, he and his staff experimented with using material woven from jute. Unfortunately the performance of these 'parajutes', especially in the drenching rain, was no better than those made out of blankets in Mesopotamia, but the attempt says much about the determination of the air-supply organization.

That determination continued to be tested later in the twentieth century, notably in the Far East Air Force, where air-supply brought two campaigns to a successful conclusion.

In the struggle against the estimated 20,000 Chinese Communist guerillas in the jungles of Malaya, RAF Dakota and Valetta squadrons, supported by RNZAF Bristol Freighters, kept British and Allied combatants supplied from the air for the twelve years from 1948 to 1960.

In the Malayan Emergency, as the campaign came to be known, aircrews operated at 300 feet or below in steaming heat, losing up to 3 lb of body-weight per man per sortie. In one record month, March 1955, 218 supply-dropping sorties were flown delivering 808,000 lb, from just seventeen useable airfields. Payloads were varied: not only food, boots and bullets but also assault boats, marine engines, water pumps, tractors, earth-moving equipment, furniture and livestock (including rat-catching cats). They were delivered into the smallest of jungle clearings, but for all that, not much more than one per cent of supplies dropped were lost.

Notable in the campaign was the arrival of the helicopter. The first RAF Casevac Flight was formed in April 1950 at Changi Hospital on Singapore Island, operating three Westland Dragonflies, which flew at just 70 knots over a range of no more than 225 miles. They were upgraded to Sycamores in 1954. The Army generals reported that casevac, reinforcement and resupply with the rotaries contributed massively to troop morale and effectiveness.

The Communist cause was fatally damaged when in 1957 the Malay States were granted independence within the British Commonwealth. The courage, dedication and sacrifice of British soldiers and their allies won the day, supported by Intelligence and internment on the ground and strike and supply from the air. Success came at a price for the supply-dropping crews – their casualty rate in the campaign was four times that of the infantry they were supporting.

With their own plans for throwing off the colonial yoke, Communists and Nationalists in Indonesia had watched the Malayan struggle for inspiration and example. When in 1962 the British and their forces were still in Malaya, Singapore and Borneo, the Indonesian President, Dr Achmed Sukarno, who had seized power from the Dutch colonialists after the Japanese surrender in 1946, determined to see them off through a policy of armed 'Confrontation'. An undeclared war was waged along the 800-mile border on the island of Borneo, lasting into 1966.

In this campaign, the British and their allies applied many of the lessons learnt in the Malayan Emergency: the winning of hearts and minds (not a bomb was dropped in the whole campaign), strong points (a fort was constructed every 100,000 yards along the border), Intelligence gathering (by the SAS, Paras, Gurkhas and local scouts) and air-supply. By this means, six infantry battalions held down a frontier where they were at times outnumbered ten to one.

Navy and merchant vessels carried goods in bulk to the ports on Labuan Island and at Kuching, capital of Sarawak, and the men of the Royal Army Service Corps broke them down into crates and packs for air-drop to the forts. RAF Valettas continued the work with harness-packs that they'd done in Malaya, joined in the task by Hastings. One squadron each of Beverleys and Argosies dropped 42-gallon drums of fuel, several dozen at a time, for the Single and Twin Pioneers, and helicopters of the RAF and the Royal Navy (there were seventy-five rotaries at the peak) that carried the stuff forward to jungle clearings, keeping the patrols in action for weeks at a time.

In August 1966, three months after President Sukarno had been ousted by his generals, a peace treaty was signed. The whole exercise had been a triumph of logistics. An army of 16,000 men was supplied in the field, in the most aircraft-unfriendly terrain and weather, for over three years. The Federation of Malaysia had been proclaimed, to survive and become a Tiger Economy of South-East Asia.

In 1968, when the last of the ground troops had been withdrawn from Borneo, and Indonesia was a friend and ally once more, the Rt Hon. Denis Healey, by now Secretary of State for Defence in Harold Wilson's Government, rose to his feet in the Commons to declare:

> When the House thinks of the tragedy that could have fallen on a whole corner of a continent if we had not been able to hold the situation and bring it to a successful termination, it will appreciate that in the history books it will be recorded as one of the most efficient uses of military force in the twentieth century.

The Borneo Confrontation was Britain's last campaign in Asia – up until now within ISAF in Afghanistan, where air-supply is once more well to the fore.

Delivery method of choice in Afghanistan

Staff officers at the MoD's PJHQ spend their working days in a multi-storey underground bunker built for the Cold War. One of those in January 2009 is Brigadier Mike Hickson OBE, a man of action who has served in most theatres. His most recent command was of 29 Regiment, the parent unit of 47AD, the air-drop squadron, and at Northwood he is now responsible for, among other vital areas, the whole of the British forces' air-supply:

> In the twenty years since the Falklands flotilla was supplied by the Hercules in the South Atlantic, air-drop was very little used for routine resupply – the accuracy of the delivery left too much to be desired. But then, in 1999 and 2000, there were experiments with satellite-guided 'chutes, and as technology has improved so has precision. Ever since our troops went into Afghanistan in 2002, air-drop has been one of the Task Force commanders' methods of supplying the FOBs. As the threat from mines and IEDs has escalated, Combat Logistic Patrols in theatre have become even more dangerous and challenging – and, especially for the more remote and dangerous FOBs, Air Despatch is often the delivery method of choice.

Major Chris Stuart concurs with the judgment of his boss. Major Stuart is an SO2 at Air Command HQ in High Wycombe, responsible for the MoD's entire inventory of air-drop equipment. He came to the job in June 2007, from a tour as Operations Officer at 47AD:

> Air-drop is ideal for the bulk delivery of staples of campaigning – food, water, clothing and ammunition. It saves convoys, just one of which could be a hundred vehicles long and stretch over ten vulnerable kilometres. And they take time. A journey by road from Kandahar up to Kajaki Dam takes two days – a Hercules can do it, there and back, in an hour.
>
> There have been some remarkable achievements already in Afghanistan. Air-drop has been delivering twenty-five per cent of resupply to troops in the field. In some places it's less – the Chinooks deliver three-quarters to some outposts – but in one month in 2001, a record 229 containers were dropped by the RAF Hercules crews, delivering everything from fresh food, water, ration packs, ammunition and HESCO panels.

The Americans drive the development of advanced air-delivery system – their forces are currently dropping over 400,000 kilos a month around the world. The MoD is looking to develop inter-operability with them through standardization. I'm tasked to work on that.

Both US and British forces operate Hercules for air-drop and Chinooks for land-on capability. They complement each other, of course – it's all air-supply. We're taught that logistics are the key to the successful prosecution of a campaign – on Herrick, that still means the air.

The air-drop inventory is extensive: parachutes, door bundles, harness packs, 'torpedo tube' cases, one-tonne container base-boards and netting and the CDS kit for despatching them. Larger platforms – medium and heavy, and those that carry the range of air-dropped boats – make up the list. Repair and replenishment are major tasks – and that includes the parachutes, which cost £5,000 each:

Mixed freight and 'fuel bollocks' move forward from Tarin Kowt. (The boss and friends)

We lose twenty-five per cent of 'chutes used. Most of those have been abandoned – soldiers on mobile patrol already hump seventy-two kilos of kit, and just can't carry all of them away from the drop. Others are recycled into windproof clothing, and hats, bags and sunshades. Those we do get back are air-lifted to the UK – not just from Afghanistan but from all over the world – and sent to a private firm up at Letchworth, Armed Forces Parachute Services, that's got the contract for cleaning and refurbishment. Quite a few will have fallen into the sea – salt is corrosive – and others get covered in dust and mud. So they have to wash them all. But before they can do that, they have to hang them up in this tall tower in their workshops to see what falls out. They get all sorts. From Herrick, they get scorpions and camel-back spiders – some of those finish up in London Zoo.

Air-drop 2001–6

Warrant Officer Scott Johnson, 'Geordie' to his friends, works as a Project Officer at the Joint Air Delivery Test and Evaluation Unit (JADTEU) located in a hangar on the southern perimeter of RAF Brize Norton. In his 30s, he started in post in January, responsible for ensuring the airworthiness of all light air-drop rigs, up to and including Rigid Inflatable Boat platforms. Testing of new delivery systems is carried out on gantries in the hangar before they can be cleared for dropping from the air. The unit is very 'joint' – REME look after the MSP systems, and one of the senior NCOs in the rotary section is a naval chief petty officer.

Behind Geordie's desk is a cabinet full of job-specification folders, and on the wall a series of posters with the JADTEU operational methodology – military work systems are necessarily organized and formal. Before this job, for two years Geordie was on the Standards and Examination (STANEVAL) team at Lyneham, and before that, he was with 47AD as a despatcher, 'from the day I became operational'.

His first action in Afghanistan was in 2001 on the 'K' Model Hercules:

In October, the squadron was given just twelve hours' notice to leave. We flew out on one of the new C-17s and were positioned in the Arabian Peninsula. When we asked where we were staying, they showed us these tents – still in their bags. We got ourselves together, and by December were on an eight-hour sortie in a 30 Squadron Herc for an air-drop south of Kandahar.

There, we were tasked to land in the middle of the night on this rough strip, in an area they call the Fishhook – it's where there's a big bend in the Helmand river. We sat there refuelling Chinooks with kerosene from our tanks – you can do that by using a series of hoses and either a portable generator or the number one engine fuel pump, running in reverse.

On that trip, we were the first to land on over the border. I had a bet with the Despatch Crew Commander, the DCC, on who'd be the first air despatcher to set foot on Afghan soil. He takes me on, reckoning it's a no-brainer, him being team-leader. But, as he's waiting for the ramp to drop, I jump off the side as it's still going down. Bet won. He's now the 47AD Squadron Ops Warrant Officer, and he's never forgiven me.

47AD's been operating out there ever since, dropping all sorts, and into difficult DZs, like the one at Kajaki Dam, just a couple of hundred metres square. Our Hercs have been in demand – our blokes will come in as low as they need to make a good delivery.

Of course the 'K' was great for the job – it can drop anything. The 'J' can't be beaten for accuracy – it's got computer-aided aiming. But a major difficulty is that it's got this 108-inch-wide drop-delivery system – it can only really drop CDS, none of the other stuff, yet. We're working it up for fuller capability, and it's all looking good.

The air-drop section has worked with standard 105-litre fuel drums, which are fine for despatch by parachute but leave the burden of disposal on the receiving ground troops. The answer has been the development of a spherical rubber 1,800-litre Air Portable Fuel Container (APFC), collapsible and returnable after delivery. Two of these can be slung in a net under a Chinook – where they rejoice in the name of 'fuel bollocks'. They are recovered in the cabin after use. The work that made such systems airworthy was done by the USL team in the rotary section.

Corporal Ioan Roberts has been in post there for two years, and he also is on detachment from 47AD. He has responsibility for assessing the airworthiness of systems for lifting twenty- and forty-foot ISO containers, Land Rovers, light guns – the whole spectrum. He works with the Chinook – the 'king of the lift', being able to shift the equivalent of ten family saloon cars – as well as the other helos in British service:

The Chinook has the flexibility of three hooks, the Merlin just the one. Sea Kings have just the one, too, but it's a very reliable platform. We also do a bit with the Puma, and with the Lynx – but that's very limited for

USL, although it's managed very well lifting one-tonne bags of stones for path repair up in the Lake District. We test the systems on the gantries – there's an Air Portability Section responsible for internal loads.

Ioan has also done his time on Herrick as a despatcher, from May to August 2006, based at Kandahar:

That was when 3 Para were deployed. We dropped to them at all the FOBs – Sangin, Robinson and Gibraltar, hairy places like that. The DZ at Sangin was just 250 feet long – the first load we dropped there missed, but the next two were spot on. Those Paras found out what an air-drop can deliver. Once, in a 'K', we lobbed in fourteen one-tonners in a single pass. Another time, we added a couple of fuel drums in a harness-pack under twin 'chutes, just to make up the load. It's always good for the air-drop operators when the ground troops understand what they can do. Some are better than others – but 16 Brigade's air minded, all right.

Geordie goes along with that. He was on Herrick in April to July 2008 as the Air Despatch Liaison Officer (ADLO) to 16 Brigade when it was commanded by Brigadier Mark Carlton-Smith:

Brigade HQ was at Lashkar Gah – mostly tents, some hardened buildings. My job, reporting to G4 Logistics, was to issue tasking for drops to the Battle Groups – North, North-West and South. We used Harrier GR9s to recce new DZs, one of which was for a delivery of engineers' supplies for the construction of two new patrol bases. That pressed all my buttons – getting really into things in a multi-national HQ, and at the hub of operations.

There were conflicts of priority to deal with – 47AD reported within Command South and was not strictly a 16 Brigade asset. It was a theatre asset and could be tasked to support ISAF anywhere. But we worked it out.

A CLIENT'S VIEW, 2009

The Royal Marines, in the opinion of Pete Cochrane, are 'definitely air-minded'. The Commanding Officer of 42 Commando on its current deployment, Lieutenant Colonel Charlie Stickland, confirms that view:

I was first deployed on Herrick in September 2006, for seven months as Chief of Staff to the UK Task Force – we commanded all the British forces in Helmand, together with the Danes and Estonians. We took over

Operation Aabi Toorah – 42 Commando Royal Marines disembark in the Fishhook.
(Photograph by LA (Phot) Gaz Faulkner, RN © crown copyright 2010/MoD, image from www.photos.mod.uk)

from 16 Air Assault Brigade as the main Helmand Battle Group. My team and I were intimately concerned with the tasking of air assets, with the Deployed Air Integration Team becoming part of my staff. The operational theatre was extremely immature, and a key early focus was understanding the dynamics and actors fuelling the insurgency. There were fewer IEDs then, direct and indirect fire were the principal threats. Air-drops were not really on – the country was too restrictive around the FOBs, with no room for DZs – so we relied heavily on the Chinooks for resupply. It was a frenetic period – consolidating in Gereshk and Lashkar Gah, holding Garmsir and then pushing the enemy line further south before seizing Sangin on 7 April 2007 in the final bold action of the tour. In relation to this deployment the use of air assault was limited.

This time, as Regional Battle Group (South), southern Afghanistan's manoeuvre force, we've been involved in half a dozen aviation assaults already, with more to come. We're not tied to FOBs, choosing where and when to insert and exploit our targets. Crucial is agile resupply from a desert leaguer, and the air-supply assets can now certainly make a difference. The shock effect and rapidity of the actions change the dynamic in an area, giving my Marines a distinct psychological and physical advantage.

We run my main HQ from Kandahar, with the Commando Group deployed away at significant reach. We gather together and integrate all the core expertise that will enable these complex and imaginative manoeuvres. A key piece of this jigsaw is Pete Cochrane and the Boss of 1310 Flight playing a full part in this planning process.

[Leaguer – Defensive formation, as in a circle of wagons.]

Major Morton agrees:

In return, I've taken the opportunity to fly on an air-drop to see for myself. I now understand the amount of time and effort that goes into planning and executing a sortie, and from that we have decided only to use this method of delivery when the situation clearly requires it, as a last resort. I've also been up in the Chinooks. We reckon that British crews and aircraft are our helicopter delivery platform of choice – they understand our need to get as many men as possible on board each aircraft.

We run the logistic operation as we would a seaborne Op – the Marines' original operating environment. My team co-ordinates from the equivalent of a sea-base while the Logistic Hub goes, as it were, ashore with the assault force. The hub takes input from the field companies, noting and consolidating their daily requirements, and radios these to KAF, where we work with the various sources of supply to specify and build the loads. We radio the drop or helicopter schedules back to the hub, which then sends out the team to set up the DZ or HLS.

Scheduling loads for both helicopter and air-drop routine resupply is a matter of finessing the required thirty-two-hour lead-time for load preparation with the make-up of the loads and their priority. Some can go to the DZ – some need to go by Cab direct to the blokes. It's also horses for courses. The CDS system on the Hercs is fine for bulk supplies, but inflexible – for small loads, such as batteries, which are vital for NVGs and all the electronic kit, we tend to use Chinook resupply flights. Urgently required material gets sent on the Herc shuttle to BSN, where a team of half a dozen of our chaps work with 47AD to build a pallet for inclusion on the next helo drop. Then there's the weather forecast – which will tell us if storms are on the way. Above all, there's the priority of the delivery – without food and water the Op can't continue.

The relationship with the Herc and Chinook commanders is crucial in all this. If Pete Cochrane says, 'Do you really need this, Justin?' and I say yes, then the vital stuff gets fitted in somehow. At times, we need additional help, and it's surprising what extra NATO air-assets can be drummed up in exchange for a 42 Commando T-shirt ...

One who confirms the need to bargain for assets is Captain Chris Trinick, a Devonian with twenty-three years of service in the Blues and Royals, a regiment of the Household Cavalry. He joined up as a boy soldier, and was commissioned from warrant officer in April 2008. Trained on Chieftain and Challenger tanks, and operating more recently on the Scimitar, he describes himself as an 'armoured-recce man'. He was deployed for a six-month tour on Herrick in November last year, and spent the first three in the Lashkar Gah HQ of Task Force Helmand (TFH) as the Battle Group (South) Liaison Officer. Working as a staff officer within the Joint Tasking Group, he has formed his own views on the allocation of air assets:

The air-assaults of the RBG(S) get essential priority, but for routine resupply to the FOBs it's more often than not a question of who shouts the loudest as to who gets the air-hours. It's not ideal, but there we are – Guards Regiments have been in Afghanistan before, and it was probably the same back then, bargaining for resources. Actually, I find that bullying doesn't work – a polite chat over a cup of coffee is more likely to do the trick. The trouble is that giving a concession to one outfit's demands usually means taking away from somebody else just as needy. And it's an efficient supply-train that's the key to sustaining front-line Ops.

Both in the rear and out in the field, the ground commanders get to know the capabilities and appetite of the air-supply crews, through contact at briefings, and operational communication on planning-forms and in emails, and over VHF and UHF radio nets. Of course, as the Chinook and Hercules crews are constantly remanned, this is something of a continual re-education process. But 42 Commando get to know which crews have been on multiple deployments and know all the wrinkles – such as Pete Cochrane, and the Boss of 1310 Flight and his veterans. They're now in their fourth week, and having, especially for the winter, a more than usually busy time.

CHAPTER 9

Joint Operations

1310 FLIGHT TWO WEEKS IN

Fourteen days of tasking and call-outs, lack of sleep and isolation on the NATO bases have presented the Boss and his team with a challenge – how to remain focused on the job and at the same time keep in touch with their human side. Some take on the 'Iron Man' challenge, a running and weight-lifting test of strength and endurance in the dusty Boardwalk enclosure. Others treat themselves to a regular shampoo and shave in the barber's shop, while yet others indulge in extreme comfort eating. And phone and laptop networks give valuable access to the world back home. They are always humming – the more so as Saturday 14 February approaches and thoughts turn especially to loved ones.

The Boss plans to find time every day for keeping in shape for the London Marathon after Easter, but his good intentions far outrun the miles he's managing in practice. Today, he flies back to Kandahar after a morning's tasking on HRF at Bastion:

> I'm off down to the laundry with the world's supply of dirty washing. Then, back at Cambridge Lines I find a pile of birthday presents waiting and ready to be opened – absolutely great to get, but not Marathon friendly.

Mister B has noticed more improvements on Kandahar base, and outside:

> The French have built a large new patisserie on the Boardwalk, and other shops and eateries have opened too. More accommodation's going up – a lot of that's for senior officers, but the new American gym is open to all. There's more tarmac going down on the roads – and on the

Chinook pans as well, thankfully. Out in the field, they're enlarging some of the FOBs, and laying matting at some of the landing-sites to keep the dust down. Even over at BSN the pans have been cleared a bit – probably swept clean by the downwash of our Cabs, as much as anything.

He takes comfort from the work rate:

Judging by the hours we've managed so far, we're going to be putting in three to four months' worth of tasking in the next two. And even when we do get stood down for a bit, we don't exactly sit around drinking coffee. There's always accumulated admin to clear up. I'm not complaining. It all makes the time fly by, so you don't end up counting the days.

Frankie confirms that it's been a more than usually hectic start, especially for the winter. Her crew has already flown a batch of casevac missions:

We've done ten already – over two a day. Still, just about now the Americans are moving their casevac unit into BSN. That'll help – their HH60 Pavehawk helos have a better night capability than our Cabs.

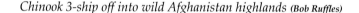

Chinook 3-ship off into wild Afghanistan highlands **(Bob Ruffles)**

Up in the Green Zone, the Talibs seem to be showing their hand more. Previously they were just parading their heavier weapons around – not firing them in case they get a bomb in their back garden. Now they are actually firing them – most often a ground-to-air World-War-Two-style Russian heavy machine-gun. We've not been hit yet – but we've seen too many blokes down the back who have.

While on HRF, Smithy and crew were called out to Lashkar Gah to pick up the Regional Governor. Chomper reports:

It was pitch-dark and the Lynx escort managed to shine its laser at us on the run-in. Not helpful – scrambled the night goggles. We had to fly a figure-of-eight till we got some vision back.

There was more action for them the following day on a three-ship resupply sortie around the FOBs:

Not good to begin with. We were late getting off, the radio reception was garbled, smoke signals got let off too soon and the aircraft picked up various niggles, including a low rotor-rpm call at Nolay. It got better by the time we arrived at Sangin, and then it was on up to Kajaki Dam.

While we were on the ground there, right by the lake, dickers popped up on the cliff tops – like in a cowboy film. And as we left, we saw one of those giant Russian helicopters coming in with an underslung ISO container – looked pretty small under that massive airframe. On the next leg, we spotted a Poppy Eradication Force convoy of trucks – with all those people hanging on and bristling with guns, that was more like a scene from *Mad Max*.

When we got back to base after Inkerman and Gibraltar, they stood us down for a quick dinner. But not before I contrived to hit myself in the face with the goggles, struggling with the NVGs. Now I've got a war wound – on the bridge of my nose.

After dinner, it was another three-ship night tasking to Gereshk, and on the way back, two of the Cabs test-fired their Miniguns. The fire-power is awesome – an almost unbelievable 3,000 rounds a minute. They sound like a jack-hammer going off.

Chomper got a rare free day on Wednesday. He enjoyed a late breakfast, then went off to the gym for a first attempt at the Half Iron Man challenge. In the evening, it was dinner on the Boardwalk and an early night.

Operation Pakula

The next morning, Saint Valentine's Eve, planning starts at HQ for the next day's Deliberate Operation. Pakula is to be a two-ship insertion of Australian and American troops in the mountains to the north of Tarin Kowt, the capital of Oruzgan province, forty miles up the Helmand river from Kajaki Dam. The assault is tasked with capturing an IED factory that's been spotted by a Predator.

Tarin Kowt is an isolated market town of about 10,000 people. It has only small-scale economic enterprises, but there are more than a couple of hundred shops in the bazaar – the Provincial Governor lives and works in a compound close by. There are some 2,000 Arabs in the town, mainly of Iraqi origin. In autumn 2001, the region was the last stronghold of the Taliban regime. The one road out, south down to Kandahar, is still subject to attack. In May 2004, the Americans began to construct a patrol base on the outskirts, naming it 'Ripley', in honour of a US Marine hero of the Vietnam conflict.

Tasking Chinook takes over resupply to Australian troops north-west of Tarin Kowt.
(Bob Ruffles)

Two-ship Chinook formation leaves KAF for Tarin Kowt and Operation Pakula. **(Bob Ruffles)**

The route lies directly over abandoned Russian Camp...
(Bob Ruffles)

As NATO took over responsibility in August 2006, nearly 2,000 Dutch troops moved in, and it became 'Kamp Holland'. Now, several hundred Australian soldiers have joined them there, and it's the Aussies that the Chinooks will be inserting into the target area tomorrow night. The base has a dusty airstrip that's often used by the Hercules, so the Chinook pilots seek out 30 Squadron to get details of the place.

On the briefing map, they're shown Tarin Kowt on the south bank of the river, and the mountain escarpment rising to the north. The green country

...over mountain crags...
(Bob Ruffles)

...and up to Green Zone and highlands towards 'Kamp Holland'. **(Bob Ruffles)**

along the flood-plain gives good sight-lines on the approach from Kajaki, but mud banks and farmers' *qalats* (rural compounds) provide a haven for insurgents. They are the Taliban's hunting-grounds – they seldom these days engage ISAF forces outside their cover. A twin-towered mosque is a distinctive landmark, right in the town centre. Kamp Holland lies a couple of kilometres to the south-west, with a natural-surface airstrip – hardened by US engineers for their own Hercules – and thirteen helicopter pads.

For 1310 Flight people not on the mission-sheet, much of the rest of Friday is taken up with an Orderly Officer's armoury check. It takes three hours and ends up showing that a dozen weapons are unaccounted for – and an inquisition begins. Chomper's mood is improved when he spots a holster just right for his side-arm, and in the confusion grabs it quickly.

Saint Valentine's Day dawns, and for those on Pakula there's a lie-in, as the Op is scheduled for late tonight. Before reporting for an hour of final briefing at 1400, Chomper is one who finds a moment to telephone Odiham – he greets his girlfriend and lets her know where to find the present that he hid in the bedroom before he left.

Take-off for the hour's transit from KAF to Tarin Kowt is to be at 1530. The weather's good as the two Chinooks, the Boss leading, with Smithy as Number Two, lift off. The afternoon light picks out the landmarks below, the turquoise dome of Ahmed Shah's tomb standing proud amid the sprawl of Kandahar to the left of track. As the aircraft cross the green line of the river to the north of the town, the lines of an abandoned Russian camp appear below, barrack blocks still discernible in the engulfing Afghan sand.

After half-an-hour, the Chinooks climb to thread their way through the first foothills of the Hindu Kush mountains, their dark-brown flanks rising sheer out of the desert, before reaching the flood-plain and approaching their destination. The pilots welcome those promised sight-lines of the Green Zone as the CINS leads the helicopters to Kamp Holland. The formation settles noisily onto the ground, facing north across the perimeter barricade and in sight of the peaks across the river, as a Hercules raises dust on the runway, taking off for another nocturnal mission.

As they trudge across the heavy gravel of the pans to the drab grey-brown camp – a series of Portakabins bolted together – there's just enough light for the crews to see the Coalition flags flying from the main gate: orange, white and blue for the Netherlands, black, red and green for the Afghans, and the familiar 'Southern Cross' of Australia.

It's five o'clock as the final briefing for Pakula gets under way. The AAC Apache escorts are here, and their pilots join the party. It turns out the ISAF bosses have scaled the operation down to 'cordon and search', which the Boss reckons means that the troops are 'not allowed to kick in the doors of dwellings, but instead have to shout and hope that any suspects respond, and come out'. The troop commander asks about the IP grid that's been given – he's not happy that it's in the right spot. The Boss asks him where exactly he'd like it to be, and they choose one that's a lot closer to the target compound. The Aussies declare themselves 'well chuffed'.

The Boss has decided that Smithy should lead the formation on this Op, 'a chance to bring him on'. He works out a plan to leave Tarin Kowt on a north-westerly heading into the hills, circle round to the north and then come in down the slopes – a direction that will, it's hoped, deceive the dickers.

The troops tramp on board and the sun is dropping behind the mountains as the Chinooks lift off at 1815, with a time-on-target of 1830. For night formation the pilots have the aid of their Tactical Air Navigation (TACAN) box, which can be programmed to keep track of the distance from another aircraft. On a moonless night like tonight, it could be invaluable.

As the formation flies off into the threatening badlands north of the river, jaws tighten and the usual mission nerves kick in. These steepling crags are a lonely place to be by day, let alone at night, and even the sturdy Chinook seems frail in the cavernous darkening sky. Banter dies away and minds focus on the job.

It seems to the Boss that the leader is flying too high on the circle to the north and is running the risk of being spotted by dickers against the glow still beyond the mountain tops. He's about to get on the radio when he spots the Apache sitting high up above, 'marking our presence to anyone down below like a diver's balloon'. He takes his thumb off the transmit button.

Chomper peers through the gloom in the valley for the target as Smithy flies in low, the Boss and Morts behind them tracking the TACAN screen and the leader's IR lights shining like beacons in the NVGs. All's well. Chomper and the CINS have done their job and Smithy has flown straight in to the IP, and on to the target. As the Chinooks land on, the 'Ramp down – troops off' drill works like clockwork, and the men are disgorged from the helos right alongside the compound they'd targeted. As the last man goes, the formation lifts off for Tarin Kowt. No tracer rises up to meet them, and gradually the crews relax their muscles and the banter returns.

They land back at Kamp Holland at 1915. The insertion was just the one hour of adrenalin-fuelled effort – now it's time for rest and relaxation before setting off for the extraction in the small hours. First, there's a great meal, courtesy of the Australian cookhouse. As Chomper puts it in his diary:

'Aussies host us in their feeder. Chilli fest ensues and lots of food is consumed. The hosts' rations store is depleted and people walk out of the Mess hall like Michelin men.'

They sit and work some of it off with a little vicarious action in front of the satellite TV – thousands of miles away, the England rugby team is struggling to keep the rampant Welsh at bay. Then it's over to the Chinooks to doss down for a few hours, awaiting the call for the extraction. It's cold in the cabin, but they're snug enough in quilted sleeping bags.

The call comes at 0215. They're to pick up the Aussies from two locations in an hour. The grids are still programmed in the CINS, and Smithy leads the formation around a different route this time to keep any hostiles on the ground guessing. But on the way, the leader's GPS fails, so the Boss surges forward and takes over control. All goes well to make the time-on-target, and as before, the Boss is able to go straight in.

But close to the ground, he flares hard, loses speed fast and drops the Chinook to the ground. It seems that he and Morts have spotted the HLS just at the last moment, and Smithy, with little or no time to react to the Boss's manoeuvre, finds himself out of position and with no option but to overshoot. In the pitch black, he goes round again – above a suspected hotbed of Taliban. But he makes it safely in the second time around, and all the troops are picked up, together with the five prisoners they've taken. All objectives made.

There's no further trouble, and the Boss is pleased to receive the heartfelt appreciation of the Australian commander for a service well provided. He leads the two-ship formation of 1310 Flight night-owls back to Kandahar. By 0615 they're in Cambridge Lines, and Chomper is reading the Valentine card just arrived from Odiham.

15 FEBRUARY

The Pakula crews get some sleep in the morning before debriefing with Australian staff officers in the afternoon. They are pleased with the results, and are planning follow-up operations with RAF Chinooks.

The Boss calls a Flight Meeting for 2015, which goes on for an hour. There's a discussion about the Smithy overshoot of the previous night, and the lessons learnt. The main point is that any apparently smooth-running operation can turn sour in a flash, and they should always be ready for the unexpected. There's talk about the weather. As yet, there's been no snow and no icing, and up at Kajaki, the river's not near being in full spate. In fact, the temperature's rising by the day, and the Boss warns that dust will soon

Cab approaches Kajaki HLS...
(The Boss and friends)

...lands on at river level... **(Bob Ruffles)**

*...and lifts off
over the dam.*
(Bob Ruffles)

become a problem. As well as that, the Met men are predicting thunderstorms before very long, with those dangerous down-draughts and strong winds that could make flying tricky.

Everyone who's been on Herrick before remarks how unlike previous winters this one is. No one's getting time off from flying more than once in every eight to ten days. Casevacs are a daily event. The insurgents haven't packed up and gone home and the Task Force hasn't gone to sleep either. Deliberate Ops are coming thick and fast, many at short notice, so there's no routine. The norm for previous troop insertions has been every ten days – this time there's a 'surge' up to Bastion about every four days.

According to the Boss, that's likely to continue, and he's right – by the weekend, 1310 Flight will be on a four-ship shuttle to insert 42 Commando into action down south.

16 FEBRUARY

Meanwhile, routine tasking continues, and the next day it's an early start for Smithy and crew. Lift-off for positioning to Bastion is at 0400, after just a couple of hours' sleep – and the Kandahar Station Commander is coming along with them, too. By 0800, they're carrying a four-tonne load up the river to Sangin, reckoned by many to be the most volatile area in Helmand. Then, it's on to Musa Qal'eh, which not long ago certainly was. During 3 Para's time in 2006, it was an area of much bloodshed and destruction, until a fragile truce was brokered by the town's elders that saw both Taliban and troops draw in their horns. For a year, the insurgents kept away, allowing the townspeople a chance to rebuild their shattered community. But now they are back in the area, and when Coalition forces are up there, no one can relax.

It's on flights into such zones that the reliability of the Chinooks' turboshafts is critical, both for the safety of the aircraft and for the nerves. The drive between the turbines and the rotors is synchronized through a gearbox with which, in the event of one engine failing, all the power of the other gets delivered to both sets of blades. But the crews know that with an engine out, especially in high and hot air, the Chinook is pushed to fly at anything near operational AUW.

Today, Smithy's aircraft suffers nothing worse than a bird-strike, which caves in the front of the external hoist. Mister Edbrooke's men get that fixed, and the crew is gearing itself for a 1700 round-trip to Gereshk, Nolay, and Sangin again, when the machine is collared for an IRT launch, and they're stood down, with the chance of some rest.

OPERATION AABI TOORAH

Back at Kandahar, planning is under way for a Deliberate Op, Aabi Toorah. Translating from the Pashto as 'Blue Sword', it's to be an insertion of 42 Commando Royal Marines, reinforced by Royal Canadian Regiment troops, into the Fishhook, the long bend down south on the Helmand river. It's an area previously unexplored by ISAF forces, but a known Taliban transit route. The 42 Commando Royal Marines are due for relief in a few weeks, and they are keen to cover the ground before the planned US reinforcements take over down there.

The Fishhook area is in the region of Helmand allocated to the British Task Force, but this is to be an RC(S) operation. It's planned to last for three weeks, and the objective is to get Coalition troops into an as yet untouched area, and secure it. For 1310 Flight, it will involve a four-ship, two-day troop insertion, at the limits of the Chinook's operating radius. No. 904 EAW Hercules will resupply with air-drops every two to three days.

Return to base – Chinook pilot's view of Kandahar Airfield. (The Boss and friends)

It's planned that 42 Commando advance parties will position forward to Bastion and to the US Marines' Patrol Base Dwyer in the desert of Southern Helmand, to be used as a staging-post during the insertion by air. A convoy will then link up for a two-day run down to the Fishhook, fifty to sixty vehicles in three segments. Jackals and Ford Pick-ups will be up front carrying the Commando Recce Force. Next will come the Vikings, loaded with stores – later in the Op, during manoeuvres, these vehicles will serve as troop transports. Third will be the Echelon vehicles, moving independently and with WMIK armed Land Rovers out front, Sergeant Eames in the lead vehicle. Mister Mallinson will be at the rear with the heavy stuff, including three fuel tankers – the fuel requirement is expected to peak at 2,100 litres a day.

The convoy will be carrying three days' worth of food and water, the latter in the plastic bottles that can be seen in any supermarket. They can usually take stores for between seven and ten days in the trucks, but because they're not sure of the terrain, they will be travelling light, planning an early resupply when they've confirmed the ground can hold their heavy vehicles.

Rehearsal of Concept for Aabi Toorah 2 **(Bob Ruffles)**

The Echelon will set up the hub and reconnoitre the HLSs and DZs, ready for troop insertion and later resupply. In this they will be supported by men of the Mobile Air Operations Teams (MAOTS) from RAF Benson, specialists in selecting, marking, supervising and controlling landing-sites for support helicopters.

Justin Morton will be stationed back at Brigade Headquarters at Kandahar, handling the logistics.

On Saturday 21 February, the Chinook crews are preparing for their four-ship insert in three waves. A JMB at Bastion gives an opportunity to iron out differences and snags. The Operations Officer, an Apache pilot, queries whether the Chinook people have done sufficient planning – the Boss responds that for this operation, a PowerPoint presentation of the plan would have been excessive, and would have 'burgled time'. The same officer is not happy with the number of planned refuellings – the Boss insists that they are necessary and can be fitted in between the waves of troop insertions. Lieutenant Colonel Stickland needs to know that the refuelling will not delay

42 Commando Defensive 'Leaguer' **(Bob Ruffles)**

the arrival of each wave. The Boss gives an assurance, and Charlie Stickland declares himself content. He will lead his men on the Op, as he does on all air assaults:

> The Chinooks are essential as the main stay of our aviation assaults, so my team and I go out of our way to make contact with JHF(A) and JAG HQs, and our planning is always joint. Changeovers in Chinook crews can lead to a need for some 're-education' and some variations. We work through these niggles as there just has to be a high degree of co-operation and rehearsals at every stage.
>
> For this Op, as with all the others, the Marines carry an average 'Patrol Order' of 55 kilos – some specialists, such as Signallers, will be carrying 70 kilos plus. Our procedures are very clear. We walk off the ramp of a Chinook when delivered to an HLS – running can lead to mishaps and lower leg injuries. Then the drill will be to clinically remove insurgents, and search in detail. We're looking for bomb factories, arms dumps, opium, that sort of thing. We'll only detain people where there's probable cause. All the while we're aiming to gather Intelligence, and most importantly, to seek engagement with local nationals, operating as 'honourable warriors' – robust, fair and culturally sensitive. Winning the trust of the Afghans is hugely important.

The 1310 Flight contingent and the other support helicopters position forward to Dwyer, and there the crews meet to discuss the air assault part of the plan, which is to insert the Marines' L Company at designated targets down in the Fishhook. They work out action required on unexpected events, not forgetting the possibility of aircraft unserviceabilities. By the evening, the plan's agreed, and the Boss finds himself in the surge tent with a dozen others, looking for some sleep before the off in the early hours.

SUNDAY 22 FEBRUARY

The 1310 Flight Commander recalls how things turned out on the day of the Op. He'd had a bad night, and was feeling sorry for himself. 'I'm getting too old for this. Had a bloke snoring his head off in the next bunk for what was left of the night – a Canadian Liaison Officer who was on the team.'

By five o'clock, he was sitting at Number Four in a formation launch that didn't go all that smoothly:

> We had a rolex of five minutes – the first Apache was U/S. Three out of four Cabs got their lights flashing on time, so Numbers One and Two lifted while Three was still loading – I waited for Three. We finally got

off at 0525 – still dark in red illume, and at 150 feet couldn't see the ground. Number One gets a bird-strike on lift – slows them up but they carry on. The IR lights have a snag so we've all turned them off, which means the formation lights are off as well — only things we can see clearly in front through the goggles are engine exhaust bins. Just three spans away we can barely see the shape of the next aircraft. It seems Numbers One to Three are not flying the same speed, and are closing too quickly. As they correct, the formation ripples, and at the back we have to come to the hover twice. I get cross. I tell them to close up, go to the same level and speed and get a move on. Then it gets light and we descend to low level. A four-ship at fifty feet, cresting the ridge to the Green Zone, is quite a sight and I get a bit more cheerful – this is the stuff.

Just four minutes late, all our Cabs made their positions as planned – dropped in on target within feet of the crosses placed on the imagery. We retracked to Dwyer to collect the rest of L Company. There was a kind of aerial ballet as we refuelled and reloaded, and afterwards the second insert went OK, but the formation flying could have been better.

Then Number Three's central hook goes U/S, so we slot in as briefed to take over the underslung load task – a net of the Marines' Bergens full of kit. As we transit, the crewman reports one falling out – he did well to spot it. It bursts as it hits the ground, and the stuff inside's all over the place. Morts marks the position and I call Number One to land on and get the contents back in the bag, which his crewman does. We can't land as we've got the USL – we'd have to dump the whole net and there'd be no one to hook it back up. So we get the crewman to stand there with the Bergen on his head like a native porter, and in a low hover I bring the Cab in over him. Our man leans down through the centre hatch and somehow they get the bag passed up. The crewman almost disappears in the dust-storm, but we've got all the Bergens. We deliver the lot as planned and transit back to BSN for a couple of hours' debrief.

None of us was totally happy with the performance this time. We managed most of it in radio silence and close to plan, but we felt we'd let ourselves down. The formation lift-offs were loose. Frankie pointed out that some of the boys were new to all this and not trained for maximum AUW four-ship Deliberate Assaults in red illume. I said perhaps I'd been harsh, but we are professional and need to learn. We agreed that perhaps a few new loading instructions needed to be disseminated to tighten up the departures.

Cab crewman and gun in combat zone. (**The Boss and friends**)

42 Commando Royal Marines set off on a mission.
(**Photograph by LA (Phot) Gaz Faulkner, RN © crown copyright 2010/MoD, image from www.photos.mod.uk**)

We had a short while to regroup and were then back on routine tasking until 1830. Knackered.

The 1310 Flight dissatisfaction with themselves is not shared by the Commandos. According to Sergeant Eames, everything's gone fine with the first day's insert. 'A hoofing job', he reckons.

Aabi Toorah continues to go well. The Chinooks fly resupply sorties carrying up to 5,000 kg at a time, every two to three days, in what are now becoming seriously dusty conditions, and the Hercules fleet makes nine air-drops over twenty-three nights. Pete Cochrane remembers one in particular:

> It was a close-run thing. The Marines were down to their last twenty-four hours' rations, but the Chinooks couldn't get in as the Met men's promised storms had arrived. So it had to be an air-drop. But the winds were gusting strongly and would have scattered the load from normal dropping height. The risks were assessed, and as the captain was very experienced, CO 904 authorized a low-level drop. The Herc got in just

Bastion return – the Boss in a hurry. **(Bob Ruffles)**

before the main weather front, and at that level the wind turned out just right – blew all the containers smack into the middle of the DZ.

For this operation, all supplies other than those carried in the trucks of the forward Echelon are delivered by air-drop or helo. The distances involved are too great for ground resupply, which in any event would monopolize convoy resources needed elsewhere in the province.

Throughout Aabi Toorah, Captain Trinick is at Dwyer, the key Logistic FOB for Garmsir over the Helmand river. He has moved down from Lashkar Gah to take post for three months out in the field with 1st The Queen's Dragoon Guards (QDG), the Battle Group (South) unit. As OC FOB Dwyer, he's making input to all tasking of routine aviation resupply for the Battle Group, as well as to that for this Deliberate Op:

> The air-hours available from the RAF Chinooks have been of necessity mostly dedicated to Assault Group troop movements. They've done that very well – crews flying all hours, and never any dramas. And often they've loaded up with cargo all along the centre-line of the Cab, before filling up the rest of the space with Marines. But for routine freight resupply we've been relying on Russian Mi27 helicopters, and. they're awesome. They're known as 'Halos', and they can lift two WMIKs at one go, or carry eight water containers underslung. There are enough of them to come in daily if needed. The airframes are immaculate – of course they haven't yet taken the punishment the British Chinooks have soaked up.

After four weeks, the Chinooks and other helos extract the Marines back to Dwyer and Bastion. Lieutenant Colonel Stickland says that the Commandos have had one or two intense engagements, principally with groups of foreign fighters, but much of the time has been spent searching, patrolling vast distances, drinking tea with the locals and understanding the dynamics of a complex and unknown area:

> We've clinically removed those who wished to fight us, with minimum collateral damage and sustaining only minor casualties. But importantly we now know a lot about this key insurgent staging area, and this knowledge will be fundamental to inform how we deal with the location in the future.

INSERT AT BAHRAM CHAH

The following day, 23 February, 1310 Flight starts its preparations for the next in this series of Deliberate Ops. Early tomorrow, the Chinooks will be providing a two-ship formation out of Bastion for a challenging insert in the Bahram Chah area, on the mountainous frontier with Baluchistan. This has proved to be ideal fighting country for the Taliban ever since October 2005, when, on one of the desolate dirt roads along the wadis, they launched a devastating attack on an Afghan Police convoy. The area is also a hotbed of cross-border smugglers and narcotics production.

The Boss briefs on the background to the Op:

> They tell me the target area is not unlike the Wild West – a lawless place where insurgents meet to compare notes and trade drugs and arms. We're taking in the ANA to have a look-see as to what they can find. It'll be challenging for us – we'll be flying to the extreme limits of our range, and our calculation on weights and fuel loads will have to be down to the last few kilos. We'll be landing at unprepared sites and will have to take the line from the Intel brief as to which are safe and which benign. But COM JAG believes we're a force that can handle this kind of Op,

Down south towards Bahram Chah. (Bob Ruffles)

and it's all part of making sure we deliver more than just the routine tasking in our allocated flying hours each month.

The plan is outlined at a Mission Brief. A strike force is to be inserted on pre-determined targets triggered by Intelligence sources. The force will have driven their vehicles south from the habitation at the Fishhook and will be roaming the desert to remain concealed. At the appointed time, they will position at a lying-up point (LUP) closer to the target, but far enough away to avoid being compromised. After the insertion, the Chinooks are to loiter in the area for as long as possible within their fuel constraints to ensure that the troops are within the golden hour for casevac extraction at all times. The lead aircraft will be carrying a doctor. The formation will then return to Dwyer to refuel, and if the action, fuel and time allow, Aabi Toorah resupply will be blended with the Op. Radio communications will be relayed through an aircraft on station at altitude. Should the ANA find any high-value Taliban assets, close air-support jets can be called in with bombs. The 1310 Chinooks will then return and extract the troops back to the desert LUP.

The briefing, and the day's tasking over, the Boss, Smithy and their crews find their way to Bastion, for another night on the surge tent cots. Many are so tired that they sleep like babies despite the assorted noises of restless men, and the relentless racket of twenty-four-hour helo Ops.

Next morning, the lift is scheduled for 0815. The two Chinooks transit the hundred miles down to Dwyer, and top up their fuel tanks. Then it's on to the LUP to pick up the ANA. The Boss remembers clearly the sequence of events:

Once across the Green Zone, we drop to low level for the routeing to the rendezvous. Not many aircraft come this far south, and it's new territory, for us at least. Over the desert plateau, the GPS shows that we're not far away, but there's nothing to be seen in the distance – it's completely arid down here and the dust's already thick on the horizon. Then, at half a mile out on the CINS, a circle of vehicles looms up ahead. Closer, we can see an orange marker panel in the centre – we're at the LUP. Morts calls them up on the UHF and we land in a mushroom cloud of talcum-powder dust that whirls up hundreds of feet. The ANA battle through the brown-out and climb aboard – the commander on Smithy's aircraft and the 2I/C with me. Full of troops and muck, we lift and rattle on south, blowing the worst of the dust out of the cabin. We tweak our speed to make the time on target – don't want to arrive before the jets come on station.

Approaching the target compounds. (Bob Ruffles)

Evasion in the sand.
(Bob Ruffles)

It's flat, bare rock below, with just these crescent-shaped mounds of sand breaking the monotony. They're all lined up across the prevailing wind, rolling over the desert towards the mountains. All at once, the first peak – about 1,500 feet according to Morts – rises up through the windscreen. Then there's another behind it, and then another. 'It's the Chah Gay hills,' says Morts, 'not unlike Mordor in Lord of The Rings.' It's time to call the air-support jets – they're on their way and will be here as fragged. All proceeding as planned.

['Fragged' – Scheduled, from FRAGO, a truncation of 'Fragmentary Order'.]

As they press further south, the Boss and Morts run through the plans and back-ups outlined at the briefing and get themselves into 'target mode'. Then, the CINS shows they've reached the pre-IP way-point and they start to pick out the landmarks they're expecting. The Boss threads the formation low along the wadi leading to the target – all eyes peeled and the crewmen ready at the guns:

The drill is to move the Number Two crewman between left and right Miniguns depending on what we see coming up – but there's just the odd vehicle here and there and not much else. Speed is good, timing spot on. I haul the Cab 90 degrees left for the final run-in and the troops come to action stations in the back. The jets come on the radio – all looks OK on the target. No movement of hostiles to firing positions, so we'll proceed to the IP.

I've watched the fly-through with Morts countless times, and we talk through the features as they come up – like a rally driving team. It's, 'Re-entrant on the left, small ridge on the right', and 'Compound round this bend', until there's just one nautical mile to run. I brief Number Two crewman to go to the right-hand gun, as that's the likely contact side, and at fifty feet above the ground and still some 120 knots, we climb to crest the ridge fronting the target, flaring now to kill the speed. Smithy is bang in on our left-hand side. We crest the ridge – and down in front, there's pandemonium.

Two Cabs, erupting over the ridge with rotors slapping and guns at the ready, is like nothing the locals down here have seen before. Panic breaks out. A sea of people is on the move, making for the hills left and right – some on motorbikes. But I can just make out the target in the mayhem, and go on in to land on.

This is where hours of formation-landing practice prove their worth. As I slow, Smithy comes up level on my left, so that my dust cloud doesn't brown him out. Speed is back and I hit my gate – the aircraft starts to sink and he drops with me. Morts tells me I'm running straight – speed and height, speed and height, all in a calm patter. Then, as we slow, the dust blows forward and we're blind. I catch a glimpse of the ground, which tells me I'm slow and straight. I can feel our position and know that the back wheels are about to hit. Back wheels on, no speed and lower the front wheels down. Hold on the brakes and it's, 'Ramp down!' Fifteen seconds later the ANA force is off and into its business. The dust begins to thin a bit as they leave, and there's Smithy, sat there serenely alongside as if he could see through the muck all the time, so why wouldn't he be in perfect position?

From the back it's, 'Troops gone – ramp up – clear above and behind!' Power in and off we go. The radios light up as the troops check in with the jets. We clear to the north along the planned route, and well away from the target we loiter, just in case there's a problem in the first few minutes, when the troops are most vulnerable. I move around the area to prevent the opportunity for insurgents to set up a hasty ambush. We recalculate the figures with the wind and distance to go, and tell the jets how long we can hang about – they pass that on to the troops. As loiter time ends, it's a message to the jets and we're off up north, climbing to height, and then spot on best-range speed to make sure we make it to the refuel. We track over some nomads and their camel train down in the desert and veer away – don't want to panic the beasts.

The wind drops en route and we're better placed – we'll land with an extra fifty kilos. But any problems now and we couldn't get any casualty back to the medics. We worked out with JHF(A) before the mission that we could go in and extract, but then we'd have to sit in the desert until a refuel bollock got ferried south to us by the HRF Cab. They'd bring in a few troops to protect us while we pumped the fuel, and they would have to take the casualty back. But there's no emergency call from the ANA, and we make it to the refuel at Dwyer.

Chomper picks up the narrative:

While we're filling up the tanks, I tell the Boss that down in the wadis I'd spotted a couple of pretty smart cars and some sharp-looking characters with them. Looked like smugglers to me. He said we'd keep an eye open for them on the way back.

After a couple of hours, we're off again. There's been some delay down at the target, so the Boss has suggested to Ops that we bring forward a resupply to the Aabi Toorah Commandos originally scheduled for later. He and Smithy have done the maths and agreed that we can just fit it in, get refuelled again, do the extraction and get back to KAF. All that – just about – without exceeding our maximum flying-hours limit of ten in the day. It's normally eight, but CO JHF(A) can flex it up by a couple. It has taken some explaining and cajoling from the Boss, as he's working between the conflicting requirements of RC(S) and Task Force Helmand. Long story short, we're soon back down south over the Green Zone, high, and at best-range speed to make the Fishhook area on time with the maximum fuel for return. The Cabs are full of fuel, water and ammo for the Commandos, and we roll it all off at a LUP very close to two Jackals where the lads are firing off mortars. All's going well – so far.

On the way to the Fishhook from Dwyer, the Boss had contacted the Apache on patrol down there for a sitrep on the action:

'All quiet,' he said, 'nothing to report.' The bloke must be bored – he'd been hoping for a fight.

As planned, we load a bunch of Marines due for extraction, take them back to Dwyer, and refuel. It's reported that the ANA troops at Bahram Chah will be ready on their rebriefed timings, and we head south again. Twenty miles out we're down at low level, over the crescent dunes and looking for our valley entrance to Mordor, when we get a call from the jets. The troops won't be ready on time. Some more quick maths – how is the fuel burn and how long can we wait? We bring back the speed and start a meandering route towards the pick-up point, killing time. The radio's alive with chat between air and ground, but we can only hear the jets' side of it. Tense times for them, waiting – we leave them to it, as fuel is running low if we are to make it back to Dwyer. Time to redo the sums – if we cut a corner we can find five minutes extra. Time passes – still no bombs, still no call forward. I find a bit of cover and land on – no questions from Number Two, he trusts me.

We've been too long on the ground, so I lift and move somewhere else – would be hard to explain if we were downed by indirect fire here. Even sitting on the ground we're not saving enough fuel – we have to go now or we'll all be in the desert for the night. I brief the jets that we're running in – they tell me the troops need another fifteen minutes. I tell them we can't wait, we'll be there in five – no duff! I don't know if the US pilot understood 'no duff' or even passed it on, but he tells me it's been acknowledged from the ground.

As we crest the ridge within sight of the target, we can see smoke billowing from buildings and our men running for the LS. We land on and wait. A quick look at the fuel shows that we'll be just below our minimum on landing back at Dwyer. Troops and some prisoners on, and we're off – straight to range speed and whizz-wheel reviewing the fuel every few minutes.

We see Chomper's cars and a pick-up truck down below, and some FAMs sat next to it apparently drinking tea. The 2I/C says they're probably smugglers, and could we land on and check them out? We've no fuel for that. But luckily, a southerly wind picks up and we make it back to Dwyer on the right side of empty, landing on with ten kilos of fuel to spare.

['Whizz-wheel' – Circular slide-rule for navigational calculations.]

The prisoners are handed over to the authorities at Dwyer, and the Chinooks refuel for the transit back to Kandahar. The Boss reckons it's just as well that he has got permission for that two-hour extension, as the crews have been in the air just over nine already:

> After all that adrenalin-fuelled action comes the low. We're all tired, and the forty minutes of the final leg seem an eternity. There's none of the usual banter and any attempt at chat dries up. The sun has set, and the crewmen are slowly freezing in the cabin – we just want to be back at base. Then, we call air-traffic at KAF and get a bit of entertainment.
>
> One of the Russian charter helos is in the circuit, and former Soviet Bloc air-traffic procedures are idiosyncratic, to say the least. Added to that, the controller's an American with a slow Southern drawl. So with clipped English and thick European accents on the airwaves, he's got a problem. Honestly, it's straight out of Monty Python. What with random calls and misunderstandings it's a somewhat protracted recovery to the airfield – but it's all highly amusing and cheers everyone up.
>
> Finally we get back in and shut down. Ten hours twenty flying in all, and a full twelve sat in the cockpit.

The JAG Commander, Group Captain Turner, is waiting to debrief them. He can report that everyone's very pleased with the action. But the ANA will be going back for more, and they want 1310 Flight to be the ones to take them in. The Boss says they could do it again, but the attempt to dovetail in a resupply task to the Fishhook would have to be dropped – it would be unfair to other crews to have them forced to tussle with various task owners like he's had to. Then he's off to the gym – and afterwards bed. Chomper gets a take-away pizza and watches his new DVD, his Valentine's Day present.

The ANA go in again five times. On the next runs, the locals are ready for them, dicking from the hilltops and letting off their weapons at the troops and aircraft. But the assaults have turned up a clutch of narcotics factories. Conservative estimates place the value of the heroin destroyed at £100 million plus. The RAF Chinooks get the repeat order and complete the inserts.

CHAPTER 10

Links with Home Base

CHAIN OF COMMAND

The day after launching the Bahram Chah inserts, the Boss debriefs further with the JAG Commander. He expresses to Andy Turner his concern that the Chinooks are being squeezed between Regional Command requirements and those of TFH. That would lead to his crews being forced to obey two masters, as happened this time, when the twin aims of inserting the ANA and resupplying the Marines had come into conflict. The CO counters that the dynamic of Regional Ops avoids the Chinook force getting stuck in the rut of Task Force operations and compounding the risk that regional commanders might not be so ready to use them. The Boss remarks that when 1310 Flight does work with assault forces such as the Marines of RC(S), the crews get rave reviews – so they must still be pretty agile.

'I suspect', says the Boss, 'that the problem is that the regional guys find it difficult to get hold of us if Task Force Helmand keeps us close and do not share. The answer is to be even more efficient – complete our Task Force tasks in fewer hours and free up time for the Region.'

It's been an objective discussion between a deployed Flight Commander and his Operational Commander, responsible for strategy and tactics in the combat zone. But back in the UK at Odiham, Andy Turner is the Boss's Station Commander, and responsible for every one of the myriad matters affecting his life, as well as his work. This is the man who has a significant input when his annual report is written and his career prospects are reviewed. He also knows his family well. So the personal concerns of the home base can hover in the background even when they are sorting out the life-or-death matters of combat.

RAF men and women can never forget that the military machine that is tasked to control their affairs, and at the same time to support them and ensure they can do their job, stretches its tentacles worldwide – right out here to Afghanistan. These are ties that bind – made possible by modern communications.

TELECOMMUNICATIONS

When the Boss finished debriefing, he took a call from Odiham. It was his Squadron Commander, Wing Commander Dom Toriati, to say that 'Frenchie', Flight Lieutenant Alex Duncan, one of the squadron pilots, was to be awarded the DFC.

The DFC, Distinguished Flying Cross, is the equivalent of the Army's Military Cross and is one of the highest awards for bravery – it's the medal the Boss received from the Queen after the rescue in Sierra Leone. On Frenchie's last 1310 Flight detachment, he kept his Chinook flying even after a Taliban RPG had taken out part of the rotor blade, and in the process saved the life of the Afghan Governor of Helmand, who was on board.

Dom said that the announcement would be made in the UK on the sixth of the following month, and Frenchie would be paraded at Colchester with 16 Air Assault Brigade award winners. The Boss told Dom that he was very pleased for Frenchie, but he'd have to be careful when he eventually told the flight – they'd be disappointed on behalf of other colleagues who'd been cited but not favoured by the awards committee this time:

> Then Dom said, 'Congratulations, by the way!' I said, 'On what?' He said, 'Hasn't the Station Commander told you? You're being promoted wing commander in the 2010 New Year's list.' Good news, of course, but it gives me something else to worry about – what should I be aiming for now, career-wise?

When the Boss gets back to Cambridge Lines, he tunes in to Skype on the laptop, and there on the screen in sharp focus is his wife and all the family – sitting in the living room, the children ready for bed. 'Seeing them there – the dog and all – makes me almost unbearably homesick. The younger boy asks me to come home. Would love to – hard to say no.'

THE AIRBRIDGE

Aside from the telephone and Internet, the most common link with the UK for everyone in Helmand is the Airbridge. The aircraft that land at Kandahar daily carry reinforcements, spares (even spare aircraft) , armoured vehicles, winter clothing and mail. Then, as they take off again, the flow is reversed. And there are not many serving on Op Herrick who don't count the days to their end-date and a seat on the TriStar.

There are other routes that they could take. The Senior Air Movements Officer (SAMO) at Brize Norton, Squadron Leader Ruth Harris, explains:

> We have more than one way of getting people out to Afghanistan. One route is to take a charter flight to a forward location outside the war zone from which a C-17 can fly directly to Bastion – that's being done more and more to save RAF airframe and aircrew hours, and reduce the pressure on Kandahar. Then again, we can give people a ride on a C-17 with the freight.

The Boeing C-17 Globemasters at Brize are operated by 99 Squadron. They position forward to Al Udeid in Qatar on the southern route, and to Incirlik in Turkey on the northern, to make the flight into Afghanistan as short as possible – two and a half hours from Al Udeid and four and a half from Incirlik. It's a purpose-built freighter – huge, powerful and fast, and more passenger-friendly than a Hercules, but it's no airliner. Andy Turner has personal experience of the trip:

> I flew out to KAF in a C-17 that was carrying a Sea King destined for JAG. It was a long journey via Turkey, starting with the 0300 bus from Odiham followed by 0600 take-off. After three hours on the ground in Turkey, arrival at KAF was 0300 the next morning. We'd all brought sleeping-bags, and we just dossed down wherever we could find a flat surface – even on top of the cargo. The crew did their best to make us comfortable – the loadmaster did a heroic job in the galley, and the crew plugged a CD into the public address and piped music to us on the ground. But basically, unless everything goes like clockwork down the route, going that way to Helmand can result in up to thirty-six hours without sleep, when seven days are needed to re-orientate properly to normal business. But for me, like so many others, it was no more than three hours dozing before getting down to work.

A 99 Squadron captain, Flight Lieutenant Marcus Eyers, fills in the details:

> The C-17 – we call it 'the Jet' – is designed to carry freight. The spec grew out of what the US military needed to be carried – like 70,000 lb of Abrams tank – and how the loadmasters wanted the cabin designed. The aircraft was then built around that. It was the same for the cockpit – they asked the pilots. It's got superbly pilot-friendly instrumentation

– all-electronic and screen based. It can do low-level flying, air-to-air refuelling, air-drop, paratroop dropping, NVG and semi-prepared strip operation – but we don't do any of that. The release to service which the RAF operates under doesn't yet allow it, and anyway the training burden on our crews would be massive, so we leave all the tactical stuff to the Hercs.

But we carry the full spectrum of freight, from a Tornado or a Chinook, to a Bulldog or Mastiff, or a 65,000 lb truck. Recently, we managed a 143,000 lb tank – from Denmark to Kandahar in two hops. We take mixed freight on 10,000 lb pallets. But what the Jet isn't is an airliner.

It doesn't do too badly, for all that. For large troop moves we go into 'pax-rig', when we can carry 130, with fifty-four individual fold-down seats down the sides and the rest palletized in central rows. We add a comfort pallet of two additional toilets and extra tea- and coffee-making facilities. But when the pax are travelling with the freight, there's none of that, just the one toilet and a small galley – and nothing but sandwiches. There aren't any windows and the noise-level's terrific, but we get the people there – at 500 mph all the way, and reliably. We can fix most issues with the electronics down the route by 'blacking the Jet' – switching it all off, and back on again. With all those benefits, and the high probability they can stretch their legs out on the floor in a sleeping-bag and get some sleep, it's becoming the Airbridge aircraft of choice for a lot of the guys in theatre.

There's a C-17 in Afghanistan four or five days each week. Crews go out to Al Udeid and Incirlik on a nine-day slip deployment – pax and freight go on both routes, but bullets and bombs are taken on the southern. A charter aircraft brings in 130 passengers and we take them onwards to theatre – same on the way home.

In between all that, by the way, we service the other hotspots around the globe. And we still find time for the odd air show.

The Lockheed TriStar C2 that transported 'C' Flight to Kandahar is, together with the rest of the fleet, operated by 216 Squadron. One of captains, Flight Lieutenant Tim Rushworth, flies that trip regularly:

It's a comfortable enough aircraft to operate. It's got a roomy cockpit, but the seats are designed for short-haul – there was no money left for an upgrade. Most of the instrumentation is 1980s vintage, but it's been refurbished and well serviced. And they've bolted on the GPS and warning systems – legally required now as airspace around the world is becoming more and more congested.

My mates who have made the trip as passengers tell me they're well looked after in the cabin. But we get stick for any delays – I suppose we're the face of the RAF for the Army and the Navy, and they tend to hold us personally responsible. We make a habit of going back and explaining the reasons – all for their safety and such – which deflects the flak somewhat. The seat-pocket brief was written by the Squadron Commander to try to do the same.

We can boast that we've never technically lost any passenger baggage. It's hand-loaded into baggage tins and stowed in the hold – if anything should go astray, at the worst it would be back at one of our three stop-offs en route. The cargo we carry is made up into palletized loads, and brought to the aircraft on flat-bed loaders that can take three at a time – the Air Movements people like that.

Rocket attacks have occurred while TriStars have been on the ground at Kandahar, so we keep our body-armour and helmets handy during the turnaround. Thankfully, no TriStar has yet been damaged by enemy action.

47 AIR DESPATCH (AD) SQUADRON RLC

The Hercules transports on deployment in Herrick have delivered over 600 tonnes of air-dropped supplies to waiting troops in the field in the first three months of this year. October last was their record month to date, when they delivered 347 tonnes. That's taking the equivalent of one and a half convoys off the perilous roads of Afghanistan each month. None of that could have been done without 47AD.

Of the 138 men and women on the Squadron, seventy-two are qualified as Air Despatchers by trade, and are on a rolling roster to deploy on Herrick. A large proportion of the people in their home base outside the Lyneham perimeter bring combat experience to their job. One of those is the current Operations Officer, Captain Ross Edwards:

We're the only AD squadron in the Army and we've been in Afghanistan since 2001. Although the normal length of tour is three years, there's a high retention rate, and some of the men spend their entire twenty-two-year career here. The work's tough. The Op Herrick drops are often at low level, and always at night, and weighed down with body-armour,

our lads really earn their specialist pay allowance. For all that, there's no lack of recruits.

It takes a year to get a new guy up to speed for operations, and six to eight years to develop a Despatch Crew Commander. A crew is three men plus the commander, and we've two of those in Helmand at any one time. There's no specific PDT. Combat skills get refreshed on an annual basis – survival techniques too, on Dartmoor and in the Welsh hills. The teams go out to Helmand at least once a year for three months. With that continual rotation, there's always a cast-iron connection between the base here and the action there.

Captain Edwards has a new boss-elect. Major Chris Stuart is coming to the end of his time at High Wycombe and is due to take over command of 47AD in August. He has served here before, as Operations Officer and as Troop Commander, but is taking a tour of the base with Captain Edwards to get up to speed.

Inside the main entrance stands a Dakota, in full Arnhem markings, a static reminder of a long air-supply heritage. Beyond it is the rigging hangar. Here, loads are prepared for practice drops on Salisbury Plain and Keevil Airfield, and for live drops elsewhere – the squadron supports theatres other than Afghanistan. The hangar is manned all day, every day of the year, and is humming with activity. Heavy-duty fork-lifts pick up heavy containers and haul five-ton 'Mexi' trailers. They steer around stacks of empty ammo boxes (filled with stones for practice drops) and four-foot-square base-boards (made of laminated resilient marine ply, and reused again and again until written off). Wire cages as tall as a man hold scores of parachutes, new, recycled or ready for scrapping. There are sturdy cardboard boxes full of leaflets – known as 'kicks', as that's the way they're propelled out of the aircraft doors. Seventy thousand leaflets were delivered from the Helmand Hercs in the Kajaki area in January, aimed at highlighting the benefits of hydro-electricity – afterwards, a vital turbine was carted by road up to the dam without incident. Ration packs stand ready for delivery – 'American Operational' being the ones of choice, as they're self-heating.

'MRE is the acronym,' says Major Stuart, "Meals Ready to Eat". American troops call them "Meals Rejected by Ethiopians" – but the Brits think they're wonderful.' HESCO bundles are wired up for air-drop, later to be filled in theatre for building FOBs and blast-walls. Ranks of one-tonne containers, some with 'chutes attached ready for use, rest on lines of rollers. Everywhere in the hangar men are getting on with the job. Ross Edwards is proud of them all:

Every member of 47AD serves time in this hangar. We know the buzz of the place motivates them. Air-drop at its peak has delivered a quarter of all the resupply to troops at outer Herrick FOBs, and they know they're making that sort of result possible. We've no problem with morale. It's after they leave here that they might need some looking after – anything else can seem an anti-climax.

Out in Helmand the men of 47AD report for welfare and discipline to the resident Task Force commander, and for operational purposes to 904 EAW. But they have their own hangar at KAF, with a constant link to this one in Wiltshire. It makes for a powerful operation.

JOINT HELICOPTER SUPPORT UNIT

It's coming up to March, and in the deserts of Afghanistan the temperature is rising – so, too, is the dust. The Chinooks are resupplying troops on assault Ops with everything they need – rations, water, ammunition, mail and of course those fuel bollocks. It's heavy work for the men and women of JHSU. Major Phil Ritchie, the unit's OC, has himself served in Afghanistan with 47AD, and he brings that experience to his HQ, located in dead ground on the southern side of RAF Odiham airfield:

JHSU was formed in early 1982 soon after the Chinook was introduced – it became apparent that the aircraft's significant carrying capacity warranted a specialist support group. The unit deployed immediately on the Falklands campaign, sailing in the *Atlantic Conveyor*. It's unique – the only specialist in preparing, deploying and rigging underslung loads. We also set up helicopter landing-sites. Our remit is to support UK defence missions and tasks, worldwide. For that, we number three officers and a hundred Other Ranks – three-quarters of them soldiers and the rest RAF Movers. And we've a mixture of trades, too – RLC drivers, communications specialists, Sappers, infanteers, Gunners, Adjutant General's men, REME and Armoured Corps. That diversity helps – there's always someone who can connect with the ground forces.

All our people are volunteers, happy to break away from their primary trade for a two-year tour of helo handling. New recruits – one in ten is female – get a two-day course as rigger/marshaller in their home unit. This is followed by one week of instruction here as Landing Point Commander, and for the corporals and SNCOs, a further week as Helicopter Handling Instructor at JADTEU up at Brize. Included in the training cycle for everyone, and before deployment on Ops, is a stint on the detachment that we still have in the Falklands. We have a rolling rota of four guys down there now, working with a contract civilian helicopter operator. We pulled out of Iraq only late last year, but we have nine people always on Herrick on a roster for three months at a time – a senior NCO with a team of four hookers at both Kandahar and Bastion. And don't forget, we're worldwide – and on continual standby to support the UK contingent tasks, including military aid to the Civil Authority, Spearhead Lead Element and the Joint Rapid Reaction Force. Lead Elements are on two hours' notice to move 365 days a year, with the balance at varying degrees of readiness, but all at less than thirty days. The unit's been mobilized as a whole just the once in recent times, on Telic. We're self-sufficient in the field, and since 1982 have served in all fifteen of the British Ops mounted in Northern Ireland and overseas. That's something for the lads to be proud of.

Outside the HQ offices is the base hangar, doubling as workshop and stores. Ten caged pens house the Helicopter Underslung Load Equipment (HUSLE) kit for the two troops of five teams each, and a further storage area for reserve equipment – checked half-annually and ready-to-go for any call-out. Nets, slings, hooks and hawsers are meticulously examined for the slightest fault – to last out their planned operational life of four years they take some looking after. Nets cost £2,000 each, and are not often recycled – there's experimentation with one-tonne aggregate bags at £20 each, for carrying loose equipment.

In the training rooms next door, a section from The Rifles, who are going out in August as part of 1 Mechanized Brigade, are under five days' training as Landing Point Commanders.

Up the hill, on the grass of the airfield perimeter next to Runway 27 threshold, the Tactical Training Park is laid out with a variety of loads: armoured personnel carriers, a 105 mm light gun, a twenty-foot ISO container and various netted loads containing ballast. This is where the Merlins and Pumas from Benson and the Chinooks of Odiham come daily to hone their skills at heavy-lift. The troops come out in teams, kitted out in helmets, goggles, combats and heavy gloves, to brave the downwash a dozen times a day. They also travel up to Longmoor Camp and other training areas to do the same, wherever the terrain gives a good approximation of Helmand conditions, even down to the hail of stones and gravel. And they've just finished a two-week winter training exercise in Bardufoss, Norway, operating with Chinooks fitted with skids. Out there they faced cripplingly low ambient temperatures (which plunged even further in the wind-chill from rotors) and potentially lacerating shards of ice.

In Afghanistan, the unit goes out with the helicopters to select and prepare HLSs. On a recent mission, a team worked with 24 Danish Brigade to rig and lift a disabled Lynx eighteen kilometres distant from an FOB. They were twenty-eight hours out in the open before getting it back, slung under a Chinook. They can also fly on Chinook internal-freight missions – at a particularly high-risk HLS they'll look after the releasing and cutting of restraints and shoving out of the pallets, allowing the crewmen to concentrate on manning the guns. They retrieve downed UAVs in nets, and once, a capsized armoured Land Rover from the flooded Helmand river, full of weapons and ammo. Major Ritchie cites that instance, when Guardsman Murray volunteered for the job, as typifying the spirit of the men and women under his command:

> Despite all the hazards and hardships, there's a backlog of volunteers waiting to join the unit. A quarter of our manpower comprises RAF Movers from Brize and Lyneham, and among the remainder there are fifteen cap badges represented. This richness of skill mix means there's always knowledge of the kit being lifted, together with experience of pax and freighting routines and procedures – all backed up by soldiering skills. It's a two-year posting, but quite a few put in for, and get, a further year. Many are promoted while they're here, or soon after posting, and there's a lot of positive feedback from receiving units – they've acquired enhanced skill-sets, and hit the ground running in their next post.
>
> In theatre, the Troop Commander reports to the JHF(A) and contributes first-hand to the daily Support Helicopter and Battlegroup JMBs. We get excitement, pride and motivation from the job out there, and not just from special jobs, like hauling on the end of a handling line in the brown-out or landing in a Cab in front of the brick wall at Nowzad and heaving pallets off the ramp under fire. It could be simply enduring fourteen hours of exposure on the HLS at Bastion, outloading combat supplies to the FOBs. It's all in support of the men on the ground.

It's a tough three-month deployment for the hookers on Herrick, but as with 47AD, it makes for a strong connection with base.

ALL FOR ONE AND ONE FOR ALL

It's not only the Operational Headquarters at Odiham and Lyneham that rotate their personnel out to Afghanistan – the Air Movers do it, too. The SAMO at Brize Norton, Ruth Harris, has been deployed once in Iraq, and three times on Op Herrick:

> Being out nearer to the action has given me a good basis for understanding the needs of my current job. It stands me in good stead when I'm meeting the staff, most of whom work a twelve-hour shift system by day and night. And it gives me confidence when I have to fly into Afghanistan for a planning conference before each RiP – at the end of 'C' Flight's deployment it will be 3 Commando Group coming out of Helmand and 19 Light Brigade going in.
>
> And when we're working with the aircrews – getting the fuel weight from the captain and then calculating loading, passenger numbers and centre-of-balance for flight – I can understand their concerns because I've seen what they have to face on their missions. And I know from painful experience that we have to make sure that people flying in from Herrick are out and away from the terminal within the hour.
>
> It's key to the working of the home-base to front-line link that a large proportion of the people in the UK have been out there and done their stint on Ops.

One who has done that, more than once, is Warrant Officer Mark Taylor, Trade Standards Officer at Number 1 Air Mobility Wing (AMW) down at Lyneham:

> I was first in Afghanistan on Veritas, from September 2004 to January 2005. I went in a Hercules 'J'. I slept most of the way, but remember refuelling in Romania. I went into Camp Souter, the British military headquarters outside Kabul, to lead a small team of Movements guys. We worked with two armourers in support of the Resident Infantry Company, the RIC, which was manned by the Green Howards and then by the Worcester and Sherwood Foresters. We had to organize airlift resupply to British RIC detachments spread right across Afghanistan – and keep it going. We just had the one 'K' Model in Kabul to do that. We processed pax and freight at Souter, and often flew with them on to their destinations. We saw a lot of mountains and a lot of sand.
>
> We also organized convoys of armoured vehicles and trucks to move stuff from the camp up to the airfield – through the city, every day.

Kabul had had the stuffing knocked out of it by all the years of fighting between the warlords and the Russians – and the Talibs.

Then we had to get 3 Squadron's Harriers down to Kandahar and on to Bastion. The old 'K' managed everything in forty-seven loads – except the support kit. We had to use four chartered Antonovs for that. When we got down to Kandahar base, it wasn't much more than fields – full of shell holes.

It was an eye-opener, working with soldiers and aircrews, and having contact with Afghans and their way of life. There was a lot going on all right – we hardly noticed Christmas come and go. Anyway, by that time the lads just wanted to get the work done and go home. But I found that first deployment really rewarding, and enjoyable because of that.

Number 1 AMW has three squadrons. One of them is the HQ, with administration, Ops and planning functions. The others are 44 and 45 Mobile Air Movement Squadrons (MAMS), which have a deployable role, supporting the EAWs worldwide and providing the helicopters and freighters on Op Herrick with air-loading manpower.

They also man the cargo hangar at Lyneham, on a twelve-hour shift cycle every day of the year – day and night. Bulk goods arrive by truck and are then built into complete loads for air delivery within twenty-four hours. This is generally by Hercules, but for Herrick, chartered DC8s and Airbuses are used, plus a few ageing Boeing 707s. Parked outside the hangar are the DROPS (Detachable Rack or Pallet System) twenty-ton trucks with up-and-over hydraulic lift-on system – they can haul ten one-tonne containers out to the aircraft at a time.

Mobile Flights are deployed to Herrick for an eight-week tour of duty. In the words of the RAF Lyneham website, they are the 'unsung stalwarts of the logistical chain … providing essential support to the wider UK military'. As Trade Standards Officer, Mark Taylor is still very much a part of that:

I've been out three or four times since that first deployment – my job gives me a roving brief. Of course I still miss the family when I'm away – we all do. When the C-17 'Freedom Bird' brought me back in January '05, the whole lot of them met me at Brize. The children flew at me – made me sit in the back seat of the car, and held onto me all the way home. After that, I did nothing but sleep for twenty-four hours.

The Lyneham website recognizes the vital role of the Movers in the logistical chain, none more so than 'in support of Operation Pabbay – the repatriation of Service personnel who have laid down their lives while on operations'.

Mark's office is high up on the cargo-hangar wall, and down below, on the tarmac outside the terminal – in the pouring rain – a squad of pall-bearers are practising with an empty coffin for a repatriation scheduled for the next day:

Why do we all go out to Herrick? It's the job, we're professionals. And we do it for the whole team – our families, colleagues and mates.

MEDEVAC

There's probably nothing that shows better the working of the military machine than the co-ordinated efforts of the RAF on casevac and medevac operations, and on Op Pabbay.

The Lyneham Hercules are often involved in Helmand medevac missions. Dave Hogg explains:

The Chinooks and other helicopters bring the casualties in from the field. Sometimes they take them direct to Kandahar, but more often to Bastion with its top-class hospital – we've flown injured Afghan children the 600 kilometres down there from Kabul to make sure they get the best treatment. Once British casualties are stabilized at Bastion, the priority is to get them back to the UK, on the TriStar. But that can't operate from Bastion, so they're loaded onto a medevac Herc, with stretchers attached to the centre stanchions – it's usually not more than a couple, but we can take up to twenty comfortably. Walking-wounded come on board, too, usually travelling with a nurse escort.

Oxygen bottles and saline drip supports are integral, and the medics can access the stretchers from both sides. Normally it's a team of four – doctor or consultant anaesthetist, nurse and two paramedics. Each can handle a pair of patients. If it's more, we get what they call an enhanced MERT. Then it's a thirty-minute dash to Kandahar from Bastion.

On occasion we do a longer transit. Once, when the case was urgent, we flew the casualty the seven hours direct to Cyprus – to RAF Akrotiri. We got air traffic priority as soon as they heard our 'Hospital' callsign.

Vicky Lane has done her share of those escort duties. She's a Qualified Intensive Care Nurse and a serving RAF corporal. Based at the John Radcliffe Hospital in Oxford on the MDHU, she carries out regular operational tours with the CCAST unit at RAF Lyneham.

She declared an early vocation to become a nurse. At college she obtained a GNVQ in Health and Social Care. As soon as she passed the 17-year age limit for nursing, she entered three years of training at Bournemouth

University, graduating with an Advanced Diploma in Adult Nursing. After two years at a Bournemouth hospital as a qualified nurse (in her first year her Diploma was topped up to a BSc in Adult Nursing Practice), she called in on an Armed Forces Career Centre, and in April 2004 found herself at 22 years of age at RAF Halton, starting on a nine-week course of military training. She passed out as SAC. Then it was down to the MDHU in Portsmouth for one year of training as a military nurse. She moved through the wards before finally getting her wish to start Intensive Care nursing at the John Radcliffe in Oxford in July 2005:

> When I'm at the John Radcliffe I live in a house provided by the authorities, separate from the main nursing accommodation. When I'm at Lyneham it's a transit block, close to the CCAST unit. I'm on a rota with twelve consultant anaesthetists and thirty other nurses, ratio six female to four male, all ready for call-out. We spend one month at home, as first-on-call. That means we can be in the air from Brize in six hours, targeted to be back from Herrick within twenty-four hours.
>
> We always fly as a team of five. As well as the one doctor and two nurses, there's a flight-nurse assistant – usually an RAF medic – who gets involved in the logistics for the mission as a whole. Then there's a medical servicing technician – they're the guys who know all of our medical equipment inside-out and will fix any problems that we have in-flight. We fly as a team for a reason, and we won't fly without all its members.
>
> A call-out means a dash to Brize, lugging a ton of medical kit. It can happen up to three times in a week. Then we spend another month as second-on-call – in a supernumerary role at Radcliffe, ready on twelve-hour notice to be raised to first-on-call. It's a tough roster, and it wreaks havoc with the social life – but despite that, I love my job. It's up at the front-end, making a significant difference for the wounded.

After six months on standby in the MDHU, the nurses are liable to be called for three months' deployment at Bastion. Vicky was out there last year, tending the casualties the Chinooks were bringing in:

> Although we work closely with them, we're not a Bastion hospital asset – any NATO hospital within the area of operations can call on us to move any patient. Many – too many – of our charges are very seriously wounded, and have to be got back to specialist units in the UK as a matter of real urgency. The C-17s and TriStars with a CCAST team give them their best chance – the flights are routed direct to Birmingham

International, close to Selly Oak Hospital. They can be from the battlefield to intensive care in the Royal Centre for Defence Medicine within hours.

A FATALITY

Sadly, some of the victims of combat cannot be saved, even by the deployed medics, and succumb to their injuries out in theatre.

During the first week of March, the Helmand weather deteriorated rapidly. High winds stirred up the dust into storms and visibility dropped to less than a kilometre. But that didn't stop the MERT shouts. Frankie and crew were in the tent when the phone gave those two ominous rings.

'It was a soldier, critically injured in a fire-fight. We got there in good time and lifted him out OK. From the MERT in the back this time it was, "Hospital at Bastion – top speed!" followed by, "Pulse failing ..." and then – "He's dead." The engines had been on the stops, but now I throttled them back – no point in hurrying. We were all pretty quiet on the way home.'

At Bastion, the Op Pabbay link moved into action.

REPATRIATION

The procedures and ceremonials for Op Pabbay flights are almost continuous in Helmand. Immediately, private Internet and international telephone services are closed down, to spare families the distress of becoming aware of the incident before the official 'KIN-forming' process has taken place. At the same time, the body is prepared for repatriation by morticians from Kenyon International. For more than a hundred years, this private humanitarian assistance company has been offering a compassionate and dignified service for military deceased – from as soon as possible after death, up to the funeral in the home country.

An aircraft is then detailed for the repatriation. Deployed C-17s and Hercules have been used for the task, but most often pressed into service is a scheduled 99 Squadron C-17 shuttle from Bastion. Passengers and general freight are loaded first, and then the ceremony gets under way.

At the appointed time, the coffin – draped with the Union Flag and with regimental cap on top of that – is brought from the hospital mortuary and laid on a bier behind the aircraft. A squad of colleagues-in-arms then marches on, forming a guard of honour on three sides. Space is reserved for a score of participants from other units serving at Bastion – JHF(A) and 904 EAW among others, make sure to send a contingent, no matter what the nationality of the deceased.

With the Union Flag at half-mast, in a 'Sunset' ceremony led by the Task Force Commander, the soldiers bow their heads in formal respect to one of their number who has paid the ultimate price of duty. When the final notes of the Last Post have died away, the aircraft reverses up to the bier. With the guard at the salute, pallbearers from the regiment, escorted by two warrant officer volunteer escorts, lift the coffin to their shoulders, pause and slowly move up the ramp.

Inside the cargo bay, the bearers carry out a 'turning march', bringing the coffin slowly around, to be placed, foot forward, on a trestle. They again pause, before slow-marching off the ramp. Those on the dispersal watch as the doors close for the flight home.

Within the aircraft, the loadmaster and escorts make the coffin secure and install curtains to section-off the bier.

The parade stands at attention as the freighter taxis for take-off, and remains there until it has made a low-level pass over their heads. As the roar of the engines dies away, the normal business of the runway restarts. The soldiers slope arms and march off – back to their combat duties.

If a Hercules has carried out the lift from Bastion, it's just a short twenty-minute run to Kandahar. There, similarly respectful rights are performed to transfer the coffin, escorted by an officer or a warrant officer, to the base mortuary and then in due course to a 99 Squadron C-17, which stages direct to Al Udeid or Incirlik for onwards to RAF Lyneham.

There, the arrivals lounge in the Air Terminal will have been made ready by the Duty Air Movements Officer and team, assisted by the respective Front Line Command (RN, Army or RAF). Six groups of nine chairs will have be set out, each three-by-three around a low table. The glass windows along one side look out over the dispersal, and on the opposite partition wall there's a bravura display of enlarged photographs, with modern military themes. Further on, a door leads to a private space for waiting relatives.

At the appointed time, usually on the hour, the family group, together with assembled military dignitaries and an escort party from the deceased's home unit, files out to the apron – their eyes on the horizon for the distinctive lines of the incoming C-17 Globemaster. The pilots bring the aircraft over the airfield, cleared to fly past in full view of the waiting mourners, before banking, joining the circuit and dropping down the glide-path to land.

Out of sight on the disused runway, passengers and freight are off-loaded. After the Wiltshire coroner has gone aboard for the official procedures, the C-17 taxis to the apron. When the aircraft has come to a halt and its engines wound down, the ramp lowers, bringing into view the bier, still flag-draped

Wootton Bassett High Street. (Photograph by LA (Phot) Alex Knott, RN © crown copyright 2010/MoD, image from www.photos.mod.uk)

and with its escorts rigidly at attention. Borne on military shoulders down the ramp at the slow-march, the coffin is brought back onto UK territory.

The cortege winds its way through Lyneham base, the Union Flag bright through the hearse windows. Servicemen and women come to attention as it passes. And through the main gate and along the streets of Lyneham village, it's the same – out of respect for a young life lost in service far away.

Over the bridge and up the hill into Wootton Bassett High Street, traffic clears away and lines of silent citizens and schoolchildren crowd the pavements. Everyone knows when there's to be repatriation at RAF Lyneham – the dates and times are posted in shop windows and on noticeboards and passed by word-of-mouth. Shopkeepers and their customers come out to stand in tribute, and by the war memorial, alongside the half-timbered seventeenth-century town hall, military veterans stand in silent ranks. In the church, the bell tolls.

Kenyon personnel conduct the passage of the coffin through the coroner's office and on to their premises in Bracknell, before the final transfer to the family's funeral director. There, they may at last claim their own.

CHAPTER 11

Where is All This Getting Us?

ISAF ACHIEVEMENTS

On the top floor of the new Station HQ building at RAF Odiham, standing apart on the edge of the airfield, there's a room made available for receiving members of the public – official visiting delegations, special-interest groups and families of servicemen and women. In pride of place, standing on a central table, is a handsome, eighteen-inch-high gold and silver abstract statuette – a Millies Award. Introduced last year by the *Sun* newspaper, with support from the Prince of Wales and the MoD, the Millies are designed to recognize excellence in the military. In December 2008, the award for Best Unit was presented out in Helmand by the British Prime Minister – to the RAF Chinook detachment from Odiham for 'notable achievements on operational deployment'.

Today, with Group Captain Turner away commanding JAG at Kandahar Base, Group Captain Richard Mason, Acting Station Commander in his place, is making an audio-visual presentation – one of many given here to explain the role of the Chinook Force in Afghanistan. He is well qualified to talk about the Chinooks on OP Herrick, as for the past two and a half years he's been OC 18(B) Squadron, and in 2007 he spent five months as commander of the JHF(A), with responsibility for all British helicopters in Afghanistan.

February gales batter the Chinooks out on the dispersal, but in here it's snug. The chairs are comfortable and the coffee's good – all in stark contrast to the images coming up on the wall-screen, showing the whole spectrum of Helmand weather, from white-out to brown-out, as well as the Chinooks in operation, with all the discomforts and risks.

An armoured convoy of Mastiffs, Vikings and truck delivers the turbine to Kajaki Dam. (Photograph by Sgt Anthony Boocock, RLC © crown copyright 2010/MoD, image from www.photos.mod.uk

One set of pictures shows damage to a rotor-blade, a circular hole made by an RPG round that went through the blade in flight – and luckily didn't detonate:

> With the blade rotating at 400 mph and the Chinook doing over 100 knots, it was a hit at the extremes of probability. There is a statistic which states that we should expect to lose an aircraft once every 10,000 flying hours. We've completed that number and I would like to think that this rotor strike was the one we might have lost.

Other images show the achievements of the Chinooks in Afghanistan:

> In the twelve months from August 2007 to July last year, they moved 82,300 troops and 62,000 tonnes of mission-critical freight. Imagine the number of convoys that saved. In the same period they carried very nearly 2,000 casualties – which sadly included sixty-one dead. That said, that's an enormous number of lives saved when you consider that we are only called in to evacuate the most seriously injured.

A further frame stresses that the first priority of the Battle Groups on Op Herrick is to build security:

> Lasting security must be achieved by local forces – but for that, establishing the rule of law is a pre-requisite.

Elders from Musa Qal'eh look on as NATO troops emplane.
(Photograph by POA (Phot) Sean Clee, RN © crown copyright 2010/MoD, image from www.photos.mod.uk)

A video clip shows a night-vision action during Operation Spin Ghar in the Baluchi valley in October 2007:

This was a Deliberate Operation – an insertion of Battle Group 1 Royal Gurkha Rifles. They were carried by a fleet of five Chinooks. At that period we were involved in one of those Ops every seven to ten days.

Here's a picture of a 19-year-old infantryman, battle-scarred at the end of a six-month tour. I have spent the last thirteen years supporting the British Army, and I never fail to be humbled by the professionalism and courage of young men like this – humbled but inspired. It makes the RAF Chinook crews want to go the extra mile, and they do. We ask a lot of our crews and the engineers who support them, and they never fail to deliver.

Another clip shows a MERT in action:

This time, the soldier sadly died from his wounds. The soldier's mother in 'Tribute to the Fallen', shown on Remembrance Day last year, said how grateful she was to the crew for risking their lives in trying to save her son.

Moving to the positive achievements of Coalition efforts, a series of stills shows the successful progress of the giant turbine up to Kajaki Dam, and a group of laughing Afghan kids leaving school:

That's something that would simply not have happened under Taliban rule. And here's Sangin, on the Helmand river. In 2006 it was virtually destroyed by bombs and fire-fights – today, it's a bustling market town. Results in Helmand are tangible – please remember that. The RAF Chinook force is making a real difference.

Another senior RAF officer at pains to stress the positive side of Coalition achievements in Afghanistan is Group Captain Mark Heffron. He has had a varied career in the Personnel Branch, including service at Lyneham and Brize Norton, and at RAF Cottesmore, the front line of the Harrier Force. He served in the Overseas Secretariat in the MoD, where he was responsible for bilateral defence relationships between UK and India, Pakistan, Bangladesh, Sri Lanka, Nepal and Afghanistan. This, along with a tour running an element of the Chief of Staff SHAPE's outer office, qualified him to spend six months of last year with ISAF as Chief of Information Co-ordination and Strategic Communications:

I was employed by the Commander ISAF at HQ in Kabul to co-ordinate all the strategic messaging. I worked the information picture with the

Afghan Government, the United Nations, a number of embassies and Non-Governmental Organizations (NGOs), and within NATO and ISAF themselves.

Since his return, he has given presentations to among others, members of the Houses of Lords and Commons, on the situation in Afghanistan at the turn of 2009:

My responsibility at ISAF HQ was to promote a coherent and co-ordinated message to the nations of NATO and their people and media, and to international NGOs and the Government of the Islamic Republic of Afghanistan (GIRoA). A key objective was to seek to gain the support of the general public – British deployed forces depend a lot on the support of their families and the people back home.

Since ISAF assumed command in August 2003, the force has grown to be around 52,000 strong. Contributions come from forty nations – twenty-six of them from NATO. The United States provides by far the largest contingent, with Britain second. The Prime Minister has currently set a limit to UK combat troops on Herrick at 8,300.

There are three major tasks for ISAF: securing key areas from Taliban and insurgent control and holding them, keeping the routes of communication open so that cross-country movement is possible – already extremely difficult due to terrain and weather – and thirdly, building Afghan-led governance. They are key requirements for establishing the rule of law so that reconstruction of the country can make progress.

It's not only hostile forces that throw up obstacles to that progress. In Afghanistan, the population of over 31 million is diverse in ethnic origin and religion. Pashtuns represent forty-two per cent – they are mainly in the east and south – and the Tajiks, who are in the north, make up twenty-seven per cent. Hazara in the central mountains and Uzbeks in the north each account for nine. And of course, apart from the Hazara, those tribal groups overflow the country's boundaries into Pakistan in the south, Iran in the west and the Stans to the north. Religions also straddle the borders – with them, the great divide is between Sunni Muslims, at seventy-four per cent of the population, and Shi'a, at eighteen. In the struggle for hearts and minds, this diversity must be recognized and the needs of each group considered.

In the fight to make the country secure, a major problem is the border with Pakistan. It's 2,340 kilometres in length, and mountainous – hence it's porous. The majority of Taliban and other insurgent activity takes place in the south and east, below the so-called 'Pashtun belt'. On the plains to the north of that line, which runs roughly from Kabul westwards, it's local and regional power-brokers and criminals who hold sway.

Narcotics are a major factor in the country. Helmand Province is currently the second-largest poppy-producing area in the world. This factor is at the top of the ISAF priority list. To avoid their country becoming a 'narcostate', an Afghanistan National Drugs Control Strategy has been agreed with GIRoA. It has eight pillars, including the promotion of alternative crops (believe it or not, pomegranates and wheat can out-earn poppies), reduction of demand and treatment of addicts. International and regional co-operation are essential, as is public awareness of the dangers of reliance on the drug trade. Eradication is in the frame, but ISAF does not get involved in the direct destruction of poppy fields – the will for change has to come from the Afghan people themselves. So far, the strategy is working – since ISAF's arrival and support of the national strategy, poppy production has already halved. But it will take some time to stem the flow of opium – there's anything up to ten years' supply already in the system.

ISAF works at all levels in the country, with President Karzai and his ministers, Regional Governors, and the Mullahs – even with some of the more tractable Taliban leaders. But there's little significant contact with

Wheat and poppies compete for space. (Bob Ruffles)

religious leaders. Our main focus is on the Regional Governors. In making and keeping those contacts, our difficulty is that we, too, have a regional structure. There are five Regional Commands – Capital, that's Kabul and its immediate surrounds, North, West, South and East. In each of them, all of the forty or so ISAF contributing governments need to be involved in all decisions. Another difficulty is that some parts of the ANSF are more committed and better trained than others. On top of that, ISAF itself lacks certain capabilities and is perhaps short of numbers. Six hundred and fifty thousand square kilometres of mainly desert and mountain is, to say the least, a challenging area to secure for reconstruction and governance. We've only had responsibility for the entirety of the country for three years, but results so far are encouraging.

In three out of five regions the country is stable, and three-quarters of the significant actions, SIGACTs, are taking place in just ten per cent of districts. And the vast majority of those are being initiated by ISAF forces going after insurgents – our security forces are being concentrated in the hotspots.

That relative control is giving room for the main objective – reconstruction and development. The Kajaki Dam project, which is a US–British initiative, will provide electricity for 1.6 million Afghan households and ongoing jobs for 2,500 Afghanis. We work with other international funding agencies, the UN and the World Bank, but through our network of Provincial Reconstruction Teams we also deliver our own projects to plug gaps in the broader development framework and help win hearts and minds. There are twenty-six of these across thirty-five provinces, providing schools (since the start the number open has more than doubled, for girls as well as boys), rebuilding universities, repairing bridges and ensuring water supply. The GIRoA is looking to bring in oil and gas production expertise for developing, in due course, the country's huge reserves – the Chinese are showing interest here. HQ ISAF is developing a computer database for the 'Afghan Country Stability Picture' – 70,000 records so far – and there have been great strides on the medical front. Medical engagements, MEDCAPS, are designed to help Afghanis. It's a project of joint medical activity aimed at bringing immediate relief to those mainly in remote areas with poor access to the health system. There were close to a thousand MEDCAPS last year, in which some 60,000 patients were treated. This direct action is backed by sustainable activities, such as systemic training, coaching and mentoring of local medical staff.

In all this, working in conjunction with GIRoA ministries, and alongside those agencies undertaking reconstruction, ISAF is aiming to assist the building of a bilateral Afghan-Pakistan relationship. This stuttered with the fall of Musharraf, but the Pakistanis have now come back to the table.

ISAF seems to be steadily building confidence among the population, whose top priorities according to recent survey are security, drinking water and education. If the situation today is compared with the Taliban era, then many improvements can be seen. Then, there were 1,000 schools for a million boys, no girls, and 20,000 teachers – now there are 9,000 schools, with 160,000 teachers, for six million pupils, including 2.2 million girls. Then, eight per cent of people had access to health care, now that's seventy-eight per cent. Infant mortality rate was the highest in the world – now it's gone down by a quarter, with 89,000 lives saved.

On the economic side, there's now a banking system and a globally recognized currency, and non-illicit exports have gone up by 588 per cent. In the field of communications, mobile phone companies have tripled from the single provider under the Taliban, and there are now 3.5 million subscribers. Sixty-four per cent of Districts have Centres of Government that are linked to the Central Government network, and there are six TV and 104 radio stations where there were none before. In infrastructure, then the road network was 21,000 kilometres – much of it damaged – but today it's lengthened by fifty per cent, much of it repaired and upgraded. Four hundred and forty kilometres of canals have been rebuilt, and electricity production has gone up from 430 megawatts to 754.

The message is – all is not as dire as people may think.

AFGHAN HEARTS AND MINDS

Another group captain, Andy Turner, picked up a revealing slant on Afghan hearts and minds on his tour at JAG:

> There was a party at the District Centre in Kandahar to celebrate the eightieth anniversary of the extraction of British civilians by the RAF from Kabul. In conversation with an Afghan I asked, 'What was the golden age of Afghanistan?' He replied that it was 1981 – when the Russians were in occupation and there was stability.

SAC Ben Hayman, serving with the RAF Regiment in Kabul for the first time in the American–British 'liberation' of 2001, was given another perspective:

Even then, the Afghanis were wary of foreign troops and foreign objectives. I was in a troop securing a school. The adults let me know pretty firmly that it was irrigation schemes they needed, not schools.

Frankie can add more:

From the perspective of the Chinook cockpit, nothing seems to be changing much for the people. Yes, there are buildings going up at Bastion and Kandahar for us – but outside the bases, what's improving? It's still some of the children waving to us and some throwing stones, and women running inside out of the way of the flying-machines and the dust. And farmers not even looking up as we clatter over their heads.

What sort of future do they expect? Given the scale of the country, how can we hope to dominate the factions and make it all better? Meantime, most of them still can't read or write, or even have running water, let alone electricity. And against the hostiles we, their supposed liberators, have to sprint simply to stand still. We're helping to train the Afghan army and police so that they can take responsibility for the security of the new Afghanistan. That's the only exit strategy, as far as we can see – otherwise we'll leave a void that will put us back to square one.

Meantime, all we can do in our Cabs to secure the place for its people and make that possible is to be there day by day for the Coalition troops – take them in, deliver the resupplies, and then bring them out again. In my eyes, as long as the troops are risking life and limb in some really

Flaring out... (Bob Ruffles)

...to extract the Afghan troops. (Bob Ruffles)

arduous conditions, everything about my job is to support them. I'm there for the 18-year-old private living in a ditch.

One of the Hercules pilots working to the same ends, Dave Hogg, has the same difficulty in assessing the state-of-play from the Afghans' viewpoint:

> Although, as aircrew, I try to get an idea of how the ground war is progressing, what we get from our Intelligence briefs is a series of snapshots, which are generally specific to our particular tasking. And as that rarely varies day to day, I unwillingly find myself detached from the bigger picture.
>
> Our exposure to the local people is generally limited to our Afghan National Army passengers, and a few words exchanged with market traders on the base. We have to rely for what they think about it all, and what their fate is likely to be, on reports from *Sky News*.
>
> As to why we're here, I can't help thinking that if we weren't intervening in the country's affairs, it could become an uncontrolled breeding-ground for insurgent groups, with the population at their mercy – as they've been so many times in the past. Unfortunately, this isn't like a conventional war in terms of defined battle lines and ground won or lost – a tangible victory is much harder to see. It doesn't get any easier to work out what's needed to bring this conflict to anything like a satisfactory conclusion – either for us or for the Afghans.

Shepherds or insurgents? (Bob Ruffles)

On his first deployment, Morts can already see the point of view of the Afghans:

> They must be pulled in all directions. They are pressurized by the Taliban to fight – they've always been used to doing that and even to making money from it. Today's rate is twenty-five dollars a day, I'm told. It beats the pittance they make farming – unless it's poppies they grow, and they're being told in no uncertain terms that that's illegal.
>
> The story is that the Afghans outside the major towns have no idea what's going on and are likely to get most of their information from Taliban propaganda. But it's a plain fact that there were over 2,000 civilian casualties in the country last year, nearly a thousand of those reckoned to be down to Afghan and international forces. One lot of armed foreigners must be much the same as any other to them – they probably think we're Russians.
>
> Of course, we have very little contact with the locals – we meet them in the market, but they just want to sell you stuff, you don't chat to them. And out at the FOBs and compounds we see people who come to watch the Cabs come and go. Some of them are squirters – they're the Taliban or their collaborators – and they beat a hasty retreat. Some of the children throw stones. Why's that? Annoyed with us being in their country? Come to think of it – nothing new there. Helicopters get plenty of complaints in the UK – low flying, noise and that kind of thing. Can't

be much fun for the Afghans in all the dust we throw up. Still, I hope we're doing something to make their lives better.

Chomper also notices the children, and reckons that there have been improvements:

Last time I was out here, the first kids I saw were in a village near Gereshk – as we landed, they all ran away in panic. This time, those same kids are running out to welcome us. Are we making a difference?

We need to understand the point of view of these locals. Their country's been war-torn for hundreds of years – of course there's suspicion of another lot of foreigners coming in to meddle in their affairs. What do we have to offer that's different? It's got to be pretty powerful to win their hearts and minds – to beat the idea that armed resistance of the invader is the manly thing to do. Especially in protecting the tribe and its survival, which for so many of them depends on a good crop of poppies. And if they die in the attempt – then they become martyrs and reach salvation. All that makes a hell of a thing to fight.

Of course we're not set up to be the world's police force, and the Brits have got a pretty poor history in Afghanistan – but we might be having some positive effect.

Our motivation, in our Chinooks? Well, we're not the ones with our boots out there on the ground for six months at a time – in the dust and the crap, being shot at or worse, having our best mates killed right next to us while trying to make a difference. Be there for them, day and night in all weathers and under whatever fire – that's what we have to do.

John Edbrooke agrees:

When you sign up for the RAF you sign up to go into conflicts. In all my career, I've met no greater challenge and satisfaction than here in the Chinook force on Op Herrick. Of course, however hot, dusty and greasy it gets on the flight-line, it's nothing like as bad as it is for the troops out on the ground – in the dark, being dicked, waiting for the water and ammo to arrive. But working to make the flying-hours available to meet the task, getting the supplies out, being the lifeline to the troops – that's what it's all about. It's our job. And whatever the rights and wrongs of Herrick – or any other campaign – we took an oath that we'd do it.

CHAPTER 12

Getting On With the Job

WHEEL-CHANGE IN FLIGHT

One of the engineers working on 1310 Flight's early 2009 detachment is Ski McComisky. Eighteen months earlier, on the first day of September 2007, he had been called out to the flight-line at Bastion, where a Chinook was in trouble:

> Steve Hardie came with me. We saw this Cab in the hover over one of the pans. The crewman was leaning out over the ramp, pointing up to the forward left-hand wheel. We dodged round the side, crouching under the down-wash, to find that out in the desert it had picked up this ruddy great boulder – lodged between the tyres. The Cab couldn't land with that stuck there – it wouldn't have been stable and the rotors could have swung the whole lot over as they wound down. So the pilot had to keep it sat there in the hover.
>
> We had a bit of a chat with the crew, and the firemen off the fire-truck – they wanted to have a go with the heavy hammer. But it was about the size of a ten-pin bowling ball, and bashing it out might have caused serious damage. So Steve and I offered to get the wheel off with the regular drill. With the Cab resting on its rear wheels and the front hovering up above our heads, that's what we did. We removed the tie-down ring, and then the split pin, and got the wheel loose. We had to watch out for our toes as we pulled it off and the rock dropped to the ground. Then we put it all back together again and the cab was OK to land – which it did. It was a bit strange, doing the wheel-change routine with all that Chinook clattering away over us, but we'd done it hundreds of times before on the jacks, and the pilot kept it steady enough.

John Edbrooke reckons that Ski understates their achievement:

> The lads' quick thinking and practised skills, not to mention their strong nerves, ensured the safety of the aircraft. Not only that, they'd kept it serviceable, and it was straight away off on another mission. Ski received a Chief of Joint Ops Commendation for his leadership and initiative, and when returned from detachment, he went up to the House of Commons for a dinner hosted by the Aldershot MP Gerald Howarth, who's a Junior Minister for Defence. They did something really special that day at Bastion. But that's what we expect from our engineers – getting on with the job.

FORCE PROTECTION AT KAF

By mid-March in Helmand, 'C' Flight's deployment is half-way through. It was certainly cold when they arrived, but since then there's been no snow, and no icing – and now the temperature has already risen to 30 degrees in the day and scarcely drops below twenty at night. Dust, though, has become even more of a problem. In Fishhook resupply, the pilot of Number Two Chinook in Frankie's formation aborted ten attempts to land in the brown-out before finally succeeding with the eleventh. Now, the Met men are giving warnings of high winds, which will stir the powder into haze, and thunderstorms, which will toss the aircraft around the sky. They will also make life even more uncomfortable for troops on the ground, including the RAF Regiment on patrol in Kandahar's GDA protection zone.

Two who have been guarding the base over these past weeks are Senior Aircraftmen John French and Ben Hayman. For John it is his first six-month tour – Ben has been out here a number of times:

> We've got an escalating system of threat assessment, designed to warn of a specific threat from terrorist rocket attacks or anti-aircraft weapons, or both. In KAF the threat is further sub-divided into East and West areas. We get right up to speed on the threat level when we go out on patrol.
>
> There are about 40,000 people living in the GDA – in scores of villages within a fifteen-kilometre radius from the KAF wire. About twenty are classified as 'major' – they're given a codename after English towns. We patrol these villages continuously, alongside KAF's Canadian Task Force, as well as Afghan soldiers and police.
>
> We've got three types of patrol vehicle. The WMIK is a three-seat Land Rover with some armour and a lot of weapons. WMIK stands for

Weapons Mounted Installation Kit – a grenade launcher and a couple of machine-guns, one heavy and one a Jimpy, bolted on to the vehicle. It's highly manoeuvrable, and we like that, but it's not designed to be a tank. They've stuck some Kevlar plates on as well, but that's not much protection against roadside bombs. The Vixen-Snatch has a bit more armour but it's still a Light Protected Patrol Vehicle – the Vector is heavier. But to date, we've lost three men to IEDs, and a good few more have suffered life-changing injuries.

We go out for four to five days, led by a Flight Commander. We're tasked by the HQ Chief of Staff for either non-kinetic jobs, such as hearts and minds, veterinary and medical work, all aimed at getting the locals on our side – or kinetic, which means either 'hard-knocks' or 'soft-knocks'. Soft is where we work with Afghan interpreters to gather Intelligence. Hard means kicking in doors to grab suspects, and then holding the ground. With both types of action, the ANA and the ANP go in first.

We work closely with UAVs – Desert Hawk, Predators and Raptors. Of course, those are at their most effective when used in close support of ground troops, but it helps that Afghans in the GDA can hear and see them overhead, and know that if they go outside carrying a rifle they're liable to be zapped.

The Americans seem to have a different approach to us. They roar along the roads in their Humvees and half-tracks. We go more carefully, searching for mines and IEDs – more subtle all round. We've managed to pick up a smattering of Pashto – that helps us with the locals. But even so, a lot of them don't see much difference between us Brits and the Russians – many think we are Russians. It's best to be wary of the locals, though – the atmosphere can suddenly change for the worse.

We don't use the word 'Taliban' much. It means 'students', apparently – so we call them 'insurgents', or just 'terrorists'.

Bob Davies says that on an average of once a month, the HQ staff will go out with a patrol:

That's at the Squadron Commander's discretion. The six-month detachment is busy enough. For seven days a week the routine is pretty constant – get to the office, do some work, come home. The work ranges from the strategic to the tactical, and frequently we hear, 'It's all been changed!' There are continuous Deliberate Ops – mostly with just a day's notice, and that makes planning a challenge. It takes some keeping up with.

John French soon got used to life on base:

> There are plenty of facilities, but you have to think about where you do your shopping. Prices at the British NAAFI are steep as compared with the subsidized goods at other countries' PXs, especially the Americans'. We can pick up US dollars through Accounts, or by cheque, at a beneficial Forces' rate. But you couldn't use $100 bills even if you had them. They won't take them – too easily forged. Then there's 'pogs' – they're the plastic tokens used for small change, just on base. The Internet system's good – you can keep in touch with the wife when you get a bit of time to do it. But that's a mixed blessing – breaks my heart to see the kids on Skype.

'To date,' says Bob Davies, 'we reckon we've done a good job with scarce resources. Now, with the wind-down in Iraq, our footprint here will increase. But the relief won't last – in 2010 we'll be defending Bastion, too. We'll cope.'

The regimental motto of the RAF Regiment is *Per Ardua* – 'Through Adversity'.

More IRT shouts

In March, there's a general reshuffle of pilots and crewmen on 1310 Flight for the second half of the deployment. Chomper moves to fly as NHP on the Boss's crew, while Morts joins up with German. By the second week of the month, all the changes have bedded in, but the heavy work-load of the detachment so far has put several of the aircrew close to maximum monthly flying hours, and the Boss has to rotate tasking and call-out duties on the fly. He takes his crew on the shuttle to Bastion to relieve the rostered IRT, Frankie and team. She reports that it's been a busy couple of days for casevacs:

> We've been going full out – finding ways to shave minutes or even seconds off to make sure we keep in the golden hour. But it's been a close-run thing a couple of times. Yesterday the escort Apache held us off out in the desert for forty minutes. The patrol was coming under three lines of fire – they couldn't get the casualty out of the contact zone, and this time they weren't happy for us to fly into the middle of it. In the end, the troops dragged a stretcher all of 300 metres over ploughed fields to a spot where they could carry on the fire-fight while the

casualty was being loaded. Didn't help the bloke's chances, but we've checked with the hospital and he's going to be OK.

Then last night we got a call to Nawa, for four ANA wounded – they'd caught it when a rocket took out their main gate. It was red illume and the NVGs couldn't pick up much. I knew from the briefing about the hundred feet of phone mast behind the compound – but couldn't see a thing. The CINS is telling us we're there when these headlights flash up in the goggles – two sets of beams, in a sort of a cross. We reckon the lads had put them out there to mark the spot, and start to go in. But I don't like it at all – I've not seen anything I recognize. So, before I throw up the dust, I lift – and spot a marker a hundred or so metres to the left. The ANA had helpfully set it up in the compound, but behind a wall. We couldn't see it from down low. The headlights were there just by chance.

I knew where I was now, and despite the dustiest and darkest night of the det so far we landed OK. Then they brought out the casualties – two walking and two on stretchers. We can see their IR in the goggles – they're coming straight towards the forward rotors, thinking it's the back ramp as it's so dark. So I flick on the landing lights – strictly non-standard but without them that stretcher party would've been mincemeat. We got them on board, and swung round one-eighty to go out in the way we came – well away from that mast.

In such tight situations, it helps that everyone on board the Chinook knows who's in charge. The Boss explains:

The captain is at all times responsible for the safety of the aircraft and its crew – that's the rule. But we always discuss any other potential hierarchy questions on any particular mission at briefing. It can be critical. For example, ultimately it's the captain's call as to when the Cab lifts from an HLS on a trooping mission, but on occasion that has to be overridden from the troop leader down the back – people have been known to fall off the ramp, and a timely shout from the back could save a life. On one occasion I got that shout when a big soldier burst down the cabin to jump off, not wanting to leave his mates behind – a quick touch on the collective broke his fall and he was unhurt.

On casevac, the decision to take injured civilians or Talibs, that's down to the captain, who can refuse to take anybody. But outside of that, we'll always try to provide the service the doctor requires. Once, I was instructed from base to take an injured local to Lashkar Gah, but when the doctor told me that that would mean almost certain death for the poor man I took him to Bastion after all. That decision was straightforward, but often it's difficult, especially if it's a junior captain and the doc has a high rank. We have them all on the MERTs – on one shout we had a Harley Street consultant on board who was a Reserve brigadier.

Then there's the question of waiting for the Apache escort. We lift straight off the pans at Bastion, but they need to spin up their weapons and taxi for a take-off run on the helicopter strip – all that can cause delay and eat into the golden hour. Or the Cab captain may need to put the nose down for speed and leave the escort behind. It's the captain of the IRT Cab who has the authority for decisions like that.

On 11 March on IRT, the Boss has of necessity to put those principles into action. Chomper tells the story:

It was an IED, outside an FOB. We get the grid reference – it pinpoints a spot a few miles north-east of Gereshk, right in the Green Zone. An ISAF soldier has lost a leg and half of the other, as well as an arm. So we're off like a shot. As we start to descend over the river, we spot two plumes of grey smoke, just visible against the brown murk of the dust-haze. The Apache's been slow getting off and it hasn't got to the scene yet to clear us in – but we're already close enough to see the fire-fight down at the FOB and the Boss decides to start our run-in, low and fast. The Apache's not happy, but the guys on the ground say the man's in a bad way and we need to get in soonest. The Apache finally clears us in, but we're already there, calling to get the guns to stop firing. Number One sees green smoke at six o'clock so the Boss hauls her round one-eighty and sets down in a green field full of trees. The MERT's off and back in again fast, and we do a concealed departure, low over the Green Zone. It's top speed, cutting the grass out to the desert and then flat-out down to Bastion. The bloke made it to the hospital in time. The crewmen tell us he gave them a thumbs-up with his good arm. Later news is that he'll probably recover.

ROUTINE AIR-DROP

Since Op Herrick began in 2006, close to 200 military and civilian truck-drivers have been killed in ambush while making resupply runs by convoy. That's one of the very good reasons why the Hercules in Helmand fly air-drop sorties up to four or five times a week.

These are always at night, for greater safely from ground fire, and usually tasked to despatch one-tonne containers over the ramp using CDS. But there are exceptions, such as the leaflets dropped in January around Kajaki Dam. Captain Ross Edwards of 47AD Squadron explains:

Leaflets are custom designed, each targeted at 'shaping' a particular battle area. We used to call these 'Psy-Ops', but that's dropped out of use – they're 'Info-Ops' now. They're launched in boxes attached in a 'daisy-chain' to static lines. Some of the boxes are NATO standard and robust enough. Others are American and pretty flimsy – you have to handle those with care' otherwise it's a paper-chase all over the cabin. The lines rip out the sides of each box and the leaflets scatter in the slipstream. We despatch the boxes from the side doors – both doors for

Leaflet air-dropped at Kajaki. (Chris Stuart and friends)

an area drop, and just one if they are meant to fall along a road. We're doing a lot of leaflet drops in Helmand these days.

The main air-drop task of 47AD, the Movers of AMW and the Hercules of 904 EAW is to deliver Kandahar stock-piles of water, food, fuel and ammunition needed to satisfy the constant needs of troops on the ground. There are normally three days' notice of the scheduled resupply drops, but in an emergency the CDS can be rigged and loaded on a 'J' Model Hercules in one and a half to two hours. In any event, the Hercules pans are a hive of activity on the night of a drop. Up to sixteen one-tonnes, netted and with SC15 parachutes fitted, are shifted by fork-lift truck onto the Dash4 roller system – two tracks fitted in a space eighty-eight inches wide, from end to end of the cabin floor. The 47AD despatch team rolls the containers forward one by one, fits the restraining bungees and hooks each static line to an anchor cable running the length of the cabin roof, one for each 'stick' of containers. Finally, they insert a red-tagged locking-pin, attached by a cord to a stanchion above their heads, on the inner face of each of the two rearmost containers. The load is now safe and secure until the time comes to drop it into the void, somewhere out there in the wilds of Helmand.

Meanwhile, the aircrews will be in 904 EAW Ops Room receiving the mission brief. The pilots will peer at the Intelligence Officer's live-feed screen, fed with UAV pictures of tonight's destination, and up-to-date with details of perceived risk out in the field. Everyone is well aware that in January 2005 a Hercules over Iraq was shot down by enemy fire, at the cost of ten lives. In Afghanistan, drops are normally made from medium altitude, above the range of small-arms, RPG and smaller missiles, but circumstances of weather can always, as in the Fishhook mission to 42 Commando, force the pilots to fly lower to make the delivery. Intelligence will also tell the aircrews whether more than one pass can be made over the DZ – it's usual for the drop to be made in a single run, but hang-ups do occur, and then it's, 'Round again'.

The captain of the aircraft then carries out his external pre-flight inspection, making sure that the aircraft is fit to fly, before climbing up the rear ramp to inspect the load. At the same time, the second pilot will be programming the aircraft's computer and navigation interface – inputting the Point of Impact, the spot on the DZ where the first container should land.

Before long, the rear doors close, the turboprops wind up, and the Hercules taxis out to the Kandahar runway, busy as ever, even at ten o'clock at night. As the Hercules heaves its load into the pitch-black Afghanistan sky, the despatch crew settles down to wait for the call to action.

That comes soon enough. Fifty miles up the Helmand river, the pilots warn that it's twenty minutes to run to the target DZ, and the despatchers make a final check of the load. Squeezing down the narrow gaps between the containers and the cabin wall, they make sure that nothing has shifted in flight, that riggings are good and release locks tight. Then they wait for, 'Action Stations!' when it will be the duty of the Crew Commander, in full body-armour, to edge down the walkway between the sticks – not more than a foot wide – to remove the pins and show the red tag to the loadmaster, before edging all the way back again. They know from their training lectures that once, with a jammed load, a brave volunteer had to scramble across the top of the whole lot to ram the pins back in.

The pilots know the importance of drop accuracy. If containers land outside the DZ, itself the size of two football pitches, then the troops on the ground have to weigh the benefit of retrieving them from the desert against the real risk of a mine or IED strike, or even of running into a Taliban ambush. The Hercules aircrews are introducing an aid to accuracy called the Precision Airdrop System, PADS. This is a device about the size and shape of a one-litre water bottle, with an aerial on the pointed end and a radio transmitter in the main body. This is sent down by parachute, to measure the winds at height. These values are then fed into the navigation interface, and the lay-off from the Point of Impact is calculated. This kit is reducing the percentage of supplies lost in a drop, but it's not yet robust enough always to be of use. And as with all computers, accuracy of data-entry is vital – more than one case of pilot error has resulted in the drop ending up short. But no matter how accurate the despatch, there's inevitably the risk of scatter – obviously the containers don't all go over the ramp at exactly the same time, and then wind gusts are a law unto themselves.

Tonight, the captain knows that this particular DZ is, as with many, well removed from the FOB and surrounded by deep wadis – should any container drift into one of those, the only way to retrieve the goods would be to break the packs down and manhandle the stuff out. It's with much relief that he hears that the PADS has worked a treat and shown no unexpectedly strong winds down below. There's no need to plunge down into the darkness and run in at low level to get the load in. The Hercules can sit at altitude, safe from hostile fire. But there's still excitement to come. Releasing sixteen tonnes from the aircraft cabin at low level at night is a job not for the faint hearted.

Through their night-vision equipment, down there in the distance, the pilots can see the markers the troops have laid out on the DZ, and it's, 'Action Stations! Two minutes to drop.'

Radio contact has been made on UHF with the ground troops' Joint Forward Air Controller (JFAC), who confirms that it's, 'All clear to drop'. In the cabin, the Troop Commander does his 'rabbit run' down the narrow gap, removes the locking pins and holds them aloft. He's safely back to the forward bulkhead when the call comes: 'Fifteen seconds – stand by to drop!' With the rear doors confirmed open, the PNF presses the red-light button to arm the computer and the despatchers brace as the aircraft pulls up into a 7-degree climb. Then, in the cabin comes, 'Green on!' as the winch removes the release-locks, and 'Load moving!' as both sticks rumble on their inexorable gravity-powered way to the edge of the ramp. Static lines slap, drogue 'chutes snap out, and the delivery floats away on billowing silk to the waiting soldiers below.

Up above, there's a relieved, 'Load gone!' No hang-ups tonight. No struggling with a thousand kilos of wayward container. The loadmaster checks above and below before calling out, 'Red on – clear at the back – doors closing', and a reassuring, 'Load straddling'. The delivery's safely on the DZ.

The pilots reset the computer for Kandahar and the despatch team tidies up below. The loadmaster fires up the microwave – it's time for coffee and pizza on the way home.

OP AABI TOORAH PHASE 2

By the third week of March, the Royal Marines of 42 Commando have carried out fourteen Deliberate Operations, within which there have been eighteen full aviation assaults as an entire Commando of 550 men, and ten other operations at company level with 150. The three-week Fishhook phase of Aabi Toorah has scarcely been completed when, after a couple of days 'clearing up' at Bastion, they are launching the next. In the final assault before their scheduled relief at the beginning of April, the men are tasked with striking into a suspected insurgent heartland in the complex Green Zone of the Helmand river some way to the south-west of Lashkar Gah. The declared aim is one of '..disrupting the enemy's will and physical capacity to fight, degrading his stocks of weapons and equipment, and engaging with the local civilian population in areas not previously visited by ISAF forces, to establish their needs and improve regional security'. It's due to launch on 20 March, and will be a large-scale insert, utilizing among other helos the Chinooks of 1310 Flight.

By this time, even the 'Mighty Wokkas' are feeling the strain. Constant hauling of USLs, and scouring from dust, are taking their toll, and the ExCES men are having their work cut out to get the required hours available for tasking. Three of the aircraft have fuselage cracks, but John Edbrooke is determined that with help from his Dutch maintenance and repair colleagues there will be Chinooks ready for their part in the scheduled start of the Op – before dawn on Friday the twentieth.

Their efforts are not helped when a hostile round hits them again, this time on the night of Wednesday the eighteenth. It smashes through the blast-wall, skids into the 1310 Engineers' block, taking out a toilet, and ends up on the floor of the AAC building. Again it fails to explode, and through good fortune no-one's hurt, but it's a shock for all the men.

It was on the Wednesday that the Boss and his crew began to see signs of the imminent Coalition assault. With uncertain aircraft availability, crewing was subject to instant flex, and they found themselves tasked to Silab FOB – positioning a 105 mm gun in preparation for the Op. En route, a dust-trail could be seen billowing up behind a convoy of pick-up trucks with heavy machine-guns mounted on the back – the dickers were at work and insurgents were on the move. And back at Bastion, the rumour mill had it that to free up sufficient 1310 Chinooks for the action, 'they' (those in charge) might be reducing 1310's IRT and MERT commitment.

As if in contradiction, the Boss and crew were immediately called out on a casevac run, followed soon after by another. The second victim was a local national caught up in enhanced security operations prior to the Op who'd sustained a bad chest wound.

Back from those two shouts, the Boss and his guys attend the first two-and-a-half-hour planning session for what the pilots have dubbed the 'Marjah Op'. Marjah, a dozen miles south-west of Lashkar Gah, has up to now been the centre of an area controlled by the Taliban, and Coalition troops have operated only on its flanks, probing to determine likely enemy reaction. There's surveillance in progress and new maps need to be prepared. The work continues on the next day, Thursday, the eve of the insertion.

The JMB is set for 1300. The large number of interested parties means that the MT section's recreation tent has to be commandeered to accommodate sufficient 'bird-tables' – so named either because the maps are laid out to give a bird's eye view of the target, or because they get circled by planners all wanting their peck. No one quite remembers how it was. By this time of day it's a sweltering 30 degrees at Bastion, and the tent has no aircon.

As well as the 1310 Flight Chinooks, US Marine Corps CH-53 Sea Stallion and Royal Navy Sea King support helicopters have been tasked to take part in the Op, and their crews join the party. Also in attendance are pilots and observers of American HH-60 Pavehawk and AH-1 Cobra attack helicopters, who will be augmenting the British AH-64 Apaches. The 3 Commando Brigade Chief of Operations for Task Force Helmand outlines the plan:

> The target area is the Trikh Nawa district, a strip of land a few miles deep between Marjah and Nad Ali. An excursion into the area has been in the back of commanders' minds for a while. It has long been a region claimed as an insurgents' heartland – secure for training camps, weapons storage and narcotics trading. Successfully confronting enemy forces, securing the area and holding it in strength will be a major ISAF gain. In addition, when the RiP of 42 Commando then starts, the relieving Battle Group will be able to move in and, together with the ANA, continue the occupation of this key location. To ensure the element of surprise, the Operation will be launched by an aviation assault. It's considered that the benefits of stopping Taliban aggression so close to Lashkar Gah, and allowing the spread of legitimate Afghan governance, outweigh the considerable risks involved.
>
> The insertion will comprise co-ordinated drops from below and above enemy positions. The Marines, five hundred of them, partnered by approximately 400 troops from the ANA's 205 Hero Corps, will land on the initial objectives. They will then be reinforced by another Royal Marines company together with 120 soldiers of the Danish Battle Group

who will land in the desert, on the edge of the Green Zone. These forces will punch across the canal, clear an existing crossing and erect an infantry footbridge. Having thus secured a bridgehead, they will link up with the shock troops already on the objectives. The assault will then continue through agile ground manoeuvre, supported on the flanks by Royal Marine Viking armoured cars and Danish Leopard tanks. The operation will be prefixed by a leaked message to the Taliban, saying, 'We are coming and will come again with even more troops. This is just a foretaste.' Their commanders will then be shown that we can go where we want to and at a time of our choosing.

The plan for the helicopters is to insert as many troops as possible as quickly as possible into the heart of the enemy. A ground convoy will deploy this evening and sit out in the desert to the north of the target area, beyond audible range and the dicking screen. Under cover of darkness, the 42 Commando Echelon will advance into the desert to the north-west and establish the support leaguer. Then, the first helo wave will make simultaneous insertions of troops to two crossing-points over the canal. The second wave will fly directly into the Green Zone – a single three-ship not to be repeated unless in emergency circumstances. Once these first two waves are complete then further troops will be inserted to the desert north of the target area, ready to move up in support as required.

The Met man steps forward to talk about the weather. The gist of his message is that 'tomorrow it's likely to be another hot and shitty day across the province'. But he declares that tonight's going to be fine, and the Op is given the all-clear.

The Apache Operations Officer stands up to start the aviation brief. She shows satellite imagery and maps of each landing site, overshoot and abort plans, and details of compounds and planned disposition of ground troops. She then outlines the anti-aircraft weapons reckoned to be available to the Taliban – the usual suspects of small-arms, heavy machine-guns and RPGs.

Now it's the Boss's turn to present the SH mission brief:

Tonight we'll be inserting the 42 Commando Reconnaissance Force, together with their Kilo and Lima Companies, at half a dozen landing sites in enemy country. We've talked before about landing 300 metres from the compounds, to minimize the threat from small arms and allow the Marines space and time to get into battle order before closing with enemy forces. But partly due to the congested nature of the terrain in the Green Zone, but primarily so that the troops get into cover as quickly as possible, we're not going to do it that way.

My deputy and I have spent some time with the Royal Artillery in the UAV det. They very kindly gave some time to show us the live feed from the various sites. We've taken a look at possible ways in and ways out, the buildings we'd see at the 300-metre point, even the state of the crops in the fields we could land in. Absolutely superb – and now we know how we're going to do it.

He starts from the beginning, indicating which aircraft is parked where at Bastion, how the troops will find their aircraft, the comms check-in and so on. Then it's on to the vital part – how they plan to get six aircraft into each individual field:

To decide on this, we've talked to each company commander and asked him to draw on the satellite imagery exactly where he would like the Chinook to land if he could choose, and facing which way. We've also been shown the route the troops need to take as they disembark – we'll land with the ramp pointing in the most convenient direction, and the crewmen can show them the way. Disorientation could be disastrous, especially if they were to be attacked on the HLS. As a result of all that, this is the insertion plan we propose.

Now, in a brief time-window in an airless, stifling tent the Boss has to get the plan across to each crew – the exact field they're aiming for and how they will route in, the order in which they are to land, and on which side of which tree or hedge. They have to know what to do if they cannot make their landing, if they come under fire or, in the worst case, if an aircraft is shot down. He outlines the plans for an alternative landing site – an Apache will have a good look at the primary site, 'Pimlico', and if not content will advise a diversion to 'Wimbledon', the alternative not more than two kilometres to the south-east.

The Boss is well aware of the importance of such detailed preparation:

As I am potentially taking crews to face their death, there is a need for a direct no-faff delivery that leaves everyone in no doubt as to what is required of them. I have ordered them to land on a particular worm in a particular piece of land facing in a specific direction. If there are a lot of questions then the aim has been missed. The brief sets the tone for the Op – that's why planning can take far longer than the Op itself.

Finally the ninety-minute briefing ends, and it's time for the Rehearsal of Concept drill to see how well the crews have taken it all in. Junior Apache crews have been tasked with building a ten-by-ten-metre model out of blue paper-roll for rivers and the canal, and black tape for buildings and tracks. Hats have been made out of paper bowls to denote each aircraft – the Apache pilots dutifully wear theirs and the Chinook captains send forward their NHPs to do the honours. Each takes position and the Operations Officer fires random questions as they walk through the mission. Every detail is examined and the 'what ifs' considered. This continues until as many eventualities as can reasonably be expected have been covered. Then, at the request of CO JHF(A), they do it all again in silence, except for the Operations Officer who calls out the times into the mission. Such is the complexity of the plan, the CO needs to be sure that everyone, particularly the American crews, have fully understood the brief. It goes well. In the Boss's words, 'It's a silent aerial ballet on the ground, and almost miraculously, danced to perfection.'

There is now the question of 1310 Flight aircraft serviceability. The Boss wants five in order to have a spare for the Op, but needs to be careful. If the Chinooks can't cover the IRT role, that increases the long-term risk of losing it to the Sea Kings or Pavehawks. The engineers have been working like demons, and the whole requirement can be met by the tasking crew flying a machine up from KAF – it is due to arrive no later than 2200. Before he goes off for the compulsory crew-rest at 1900, the Boss and Frankie take another look at the six HLSs through the live feed. They're all quiet except that a pit's been dug next to 'Clapham', where three FAMs are lying in a shallow scrape lined with plastic, a motorbike alongside. Three cars pull up and their occupants get out for a chat with the men, one of whom is carrying a rifle. It's decided to watch the pit through the evening, with the possibility of a kinetic Apache strike if the men are still there in the morning.

Aircrews and troops stand down, and try for some rest before the off. Meanwhile, Mister Mallinson and the 42 Commando Echelon, supported again by MAOTS, are moving forward on the ground into the north of the Green Zone, to reconnoitre and lay out the desert landing-site, ready for the third wave. They're either 'two-spot' or 'four-spot', depending on the number of helicopters expected. The spots are set up at an angle so that the pilots can see them from the approach. There are no DZs to be prepared on this Op – the terrain in the Green Zone is generally reckoned too 'tight' for air-drops. In any event, once established in the area, the Marines can be resupplied by road convoy on loops over the eight-hour run from Bastion.

The 1310 Flight crews scheduled for the first wave insertion – time on target 0510 – endure an uneasy few hours of enforced rest. In the early evening, on cot-beds in the crowded surge tent, their minds are full of briefing details and the action to come. The odds are stacked against highly charged aircrews dropping off, but eventually most drift into a doze. The Boss and his crew are in the HRF tent, and his final conscious thought is that it's his elder son's fourth birthday tomorrow.

At 0300, the Boss wakes his crew for breakfast. As he, Chomper and the others pass the surge tent they turn on the lights to wake their now slumbering colleagues, before getting stuck into bacon rolls and muffins – and for one beefy pilot, even at this ungodly hour, pie and chips. The Boss and Frankie have a final chat with CO JHF(A) and CO 42 Commando, and get an update on what has been seen through the night by the UAV. The FAMs have gone and Clapham is in play.

At the Chinook pans, everyone is up and running for the start-up. The engineers have done their job – they have three Chinooks ready for the task, and the two in reserve. The second of these was on its way over last evening, pressing on in a thunderstorm, when it was struck by lightning. It had to limp back to KAF for repairs, and the engineers and crew finally got it to BSN with half an hour to spare – half-hoping that one of the front-line helos would break and they'd get to see some of the action. The Boss acknowledges their stunning effort, and wishes everyone good luck. 'There's a place for Dame Fortune on every Op.'

By 0430 the three Chinooks have lifted and moved to their embarkation spots. Forty Marines, in full battle-order and loaded down with upwards of 100 kg of weapons and kit apiece, file onto each Cab, psyched up for the final thrust of their deployment.

At one minute to lift, a late call comes from ATC – a C-17 has reported being shot at just to the south of the airfield. It's probably spurious, but just in case, the route out gets changed – outbound to the north, and then looping around through west before arriving to the south of the combat zone. At thirty seconds, the Apaches line up on the helicopter landing-strip, and spot on time the formations roll. Apart from the brief route-change message, everything's done in radio silence.

The Chinooks hold below 400 feet, to deconflict with the Apaches, which are at 500. The US Marines' Sea Stallions lumber behind – they're even bigger than the Chinooks but carry about the same number of troops. The Apaches start to climb and the Boss holds the speed back so as not to overtake. Two miles out from BSN, all IR strobes are turned off – the helo force is now blacked out. Fifteen miles to run to target – the darkness is still intense, but before long it will start getting light. Ahead, the enemy forces will be soon be stirring – and moving fast when they hear the beat of the approaching choppers.

As the formation of three Chinooks and two Sea Stallions turns onto the final heading for Clapham HLS and counts down the miles to run, the Boss edges to the right of the track line to give the formation room to turn onto a northerly heading – the troops want to come off the ramp facing south. He's now expecting to see the bridge detailed in the brief – but it's still too dark. He turns when the CINS gives him the mark, and the two other Chinooks peel away as planned and make for their spots for a simultaneous drop a kilometre to the west.

Chomper is tracking the route on the print-out of the briefing imagery and sees a rutted field he recognizes. The computer shows just a third of a mile to target, and the Boss brings the formation down to 50 feet, slowing to 50 knots. He's looking for a rough area of mud, a different texture among the green cropped fields. There it is! But there's a tree to the right – he's too far across. Approaching the ground, he slides left to make room for Sea Stallions on the right. Up comes the dust. He checks the slide as he lands on and drops the ramp. One of the Sea Stallions gets in beside him – but the other's missed its approach in the brown-out and has to go round again.

Down the back the Marines are already on the move – they hit the ground and make for a ditch to find cover. There's no tracer to be seen yet. The ramp closes and Number One gives the all-clear, but the Boss waits on the ground – the second Sea Stallion is coming in to land and he doesn't want to kick up more dust than he has already. The Chinooks to the west are already lifting off as the Sea Stallion gets in second time around. The Boss and formation lifts, joins up with the two Playmates and clears to the north, away from enemy fire. On the ground, the Marines close up and move off to secure the area. The Apaches maintain station, unseen high above Marjah, as the five-ship speeds back to Bastion to pick up more Marines. So far – so good.

For the next wave, the Sea Stallions are to route back to Clapham and drop off the Marines' CO and his TAC grouping. The Boss is to take a three-ship formation of Chinooks to Pimlico, south of Clapham and deep in the Green Zone. But while the troops are boarding, a call comes through on the secure radio. The Apache reports that Pimlico is swarming with enemy forces, and the formation is to divert to Wimbledon. Number Three switches off its IR strobes to show the aircraft is loaded and ready. Frankie at Number Two does the same, followed by the Boss, who lifts. With no Apache to slow them down this time, the formation speeds south at low level and 140 knots.

As they near the Green Zone, tracer is seen coming from right to left across the track – the troops have gone into action. The routeing must be changed, and Chomper does some fast work on the CINS. This time the troops want to come off facing north, so it's a southerly heading as the three Chinooks run in at 130 knots, one and a half nautical miles to run. Adrenalin's in full flow, the formation's tight and all eyes are scanning compounds as they flash by. They've rehearsed this so many times that all the Boss needs to do now is nail the approach and give them the best chance of staying in close – then all the troops will be off and away in thirty seconds. At just under a mile, he starts a gentle flare, a couple of degrees nose up, just enough to show the Playmates he's slowing – they mirror to perfection. At half a mile, he's back to 100 knots – there are the four compounds, two on each side of track, guiding them in. One field gone and one more to go to the target – there's the ditch from the satellite imagery. The field is cropped wheat, selected to minimize the dust – but it's rutted for irrigation. Speed back, and down to one foot – speed zero, and onto the deck. Even before the nose drops the ramps are down and the troops on their way. One man stumbles – the field's wet and the mud cloying – but he's right away up and off again, scarcely breaking step.

Frankie is off, heading south and then crossing the Boss's nose out to the west on the prearranged track. His ramp is travelling, and he and Number Three lift too. Suddenly, there's tracer to the right, where Frankie is, Wellsing as she goes. A call on the radio: 'Tracer nine o'clock!' Now there's tracer everywhere, and shells fly over the Boss's Cab. He's at seven spans' distance when a long burst comes up between the aircraft. Frankie is clear and out in the desert – a few more seconds and they're all across into safe airspace.

As they route back to Bastion, elated from the action, but becoming quieter as adrenalin levels drop, the Apache sends a sitrep. 'Heavy callsigns under contact by small-arms and RPG.' The chatter continues as the attack helicopters relay enemy sightings to the Marines, at the same time engaging the Taliban ordnance with lethal effect. It's not going to be an idle day for them, with targets aplenty. The action at Trikh Nawa is left behind, and the Boss and formation descend into Bastion. The sun comes up and the goggles come off. In defiance of the Met man, the morning is beautiful.

The three Chinooks make 'quickstops' onto their spots. Number Three has a bullet-hole in the aft pylon, but it could have been much worse – it's reported from the ground that the RPG passed within a metre of the tail. The next load of troops is to go to the desert leaguer laid out by the Commandos' Echelon overnight to the north of the Green Zone – almost a routine move. One mile out, with a light early-morning mist shrouding the sand below, they can see Danish vehicles marking the landing site. It's dusty, but they pull off a copy-book formation landing. With troops disembarked, it's back to BSN, where all the helicopter crews meet up, to debrief and share with their commanders the satisfaction of a difficult job well done. The 1310 Flight people go off for a cup of tea, before, within the hour, the Boss and his crew are again on routine tasking – a long resupply run up the Helmand river to Sangin, Musah Qaleh, and Kajaki Dam.

Sergeant Eames says that life on the HLSs that night was exciting:

> We had the Apaches and the other attack helicopters clattering overhead, and the Cabs, the Sea Kings and Sea Stallions kept going all night, getting the guys in. It was dirty, and dangerous – being sand-blasted by hundred-mile-an-hour pebbles under all those helos, and choked by the brown-outs. The muck takes at least five minutes to clear, and often ten if there's no wind. It took one American Chinook three goes to get in. It was quieter when they came back to get the lads out three days later.

The extraction is scheduled to start on the morning of Monday 23 March. The day before, the weather takes the expected turn for the worse, with massive dust-storms bringing the visibility down to practically zero. But by that time the ISAF assault force has gone a long way towards achieving its objectives. The strategy has worked. The canal crossing-point is established, providing a ground-based supply-route to control the area. The Taliban are taken by surprise and divided, and in their confusion they reveal their locations for the attackers to strike. They fall back towards Marjah, their stronghold, and mount a determined defence. It takes the Marines all of twenty-four hours to advance just 100 metres, but after a full three days of hand-to-hand fighting – supported by mortars and 105 mm light guns, ISTAR resources and numerous attack helicopter missions – the robustness and tenacity of the Regional Command forces enable the ISAF commanders to declare the enemy 'comprehensively beaten'.

Lieutenant-Colonel Stickland starts systematically to withdraw his men, keeping 'one foot on the ground' with a covering group. Sub-units tramp to desert pick-up points where Viking vehicles, and Sea Kings and Chinooks collect them for return to Bastion.

Mission accomplished – extraction begins. (Bob Ruffles)

Reporting to the 0445 mission brief for the extraction, the Boss is pleased to see an improvement in the weather. Yesterday, on a tasking run from Bastion up to Musah Qaleh, the dust over Lashkar Gah forced him down to zero feet. On the way back, as lightning started to crackle in the dust, the Marine Lynx escort called up to report he was low on fuel. They opted to go for Gereshk to top his tanks up. The Chinook sat on the ground waiting with rotors running before they lifted as a pair, the Boss and Chomper using the CINS to grope their way home. At three miles out they got a visual sighting of base and flew onto the HALS. One hour later, all Ops were called off due to the weather.

This morning, the target is a desert grid-reference six nautical miles north-west of Marjah – 'Piccadilly'. The first Commandos are to be lifted out in four waves, by three 1310 Chinooks. The formation lifts in the dark at 0555, escorted by two Apaches – on the HLS approach, instead of sand it's mist that's the problem. But the Commandos have circled the Vikings to mark the spot, and they land without incident. As the battle-stained and weary troops haul themselves and their kit out to the aircraft, they are accompanied by a curious goat. The Crewmen shoo it off, and the first wave is on its way to

base, the men savouring the moment of return from their last assault Op –
on this deployment at least. On the second run, the goat tries again, and this
time actually gets a hoof on the ramp – but a crewman's boot is an effective
deterrent and the forlorn animal abandons its attempt. On the third and
fourth runs the wind is getting up again, helping to blow the brown-out
away, and today's final group of Marines have a more comfortable tramp to
the ramp.

Two days later there's a debriefing, and with all his men withdrawn,
Charlie Stickland sums up the whole assault:

> The insert before dawn shocked and dislocated the insurgents. Through
> aggression, agility and guile we removed significant numbers from the
> battlefield and psychologically paralysed them across the central
> Helmand belt. Then importantly, we left at a time and place of our
> choosing, with the enemy wondering where and when we would strike
> again.

Following Operation Aabi Toorah 2, the District Governor Habibullah is able
to hold a Regional 'shura', a formal assembly, with the Nad Ali District
Community Council and the elders of Marjah. Security and development are
top of the agenda.

Troops extraction from Kajaki HLS. (The Boss and friends)

CHAPTER 13

Reliefs in Place

42 COMMANDO ROYAL MARINES

By the end of the first week in May, the tramp of 42 Commando's boots is no longer to be heard over Chinook ramps in Afghanistan, but echoing through the streets of the Brigade's home city of Plymouth. On Thursday the seventh, still in desert camouflage and with Colours unfurled as is their privilege, the Marines quick-march along the Royal Parade in front of the Lord Mayor in his regalia and through crowds of cheering people. It's to

RiP begins – the Black Watch emplane at KAF... (Photograph by SAC Neil Chapman, RAF © crown copyright 2010/MoD, image from www.photos.mod.uk)

mark the Commandos' return from their seven months in the deserts and Green Zone of Helmand, Kandahar and Uruzgan.

A few days after Aabi Toorah 2, a RiP began, bringing in the soldiers of the Black Watch to take over as Regional Battle Group (South). The departure of 42 Commando from Kandahar, starting on 16 April, was according to the CO an occasion for mixed emotions:

> On our way out, there was a bubble of anticipation. We travelled by Slovakia Air to the Gulf and then by C-17 into KAF – the boys were keen

... and deplane at BSN.
(Bob Ruffles)

RiP for 42 Commando Royal Marines... **(Photograph by POA (Phot) Sean Clee, RN © crown copyri̇̇ 2010/MoD, image from www.photos.mod.uk)**

...and into action for the Black Watch and ANA. (Photograph by Cpl Rupert Frere, RLC © crown copyright 2010/MoD, image from www.photos.mod.uk)

to get on with it and make their mark. Coming back, it was the more everyday RAF TriStar to Cyprus for two days' decompression. When we finally made it home, we were enormously excited at the prospect of being reunited with our families and friends – but we'd lost three comrades in Afghanistan, and that was sobering for us all.

Back in the Bickleigh Barracks, there's time to reflect on the Herrick Ops. Having now completed three tours in three and a half years, Lieutenant Colonel Stickland readily confirms the importance of the air in support of ground manoeuvre:

> It would be more convenient for us if more air-drops could be done by daylight, and accuracy is better when they come in at a lower altitude – this would have been ideal on the Fishhook operation. But the service is generally top class. When we were out in the bundu with the Australians in the Mirabad Valley, beyond Tarin Kowt, the Hercules parachuted a drop of twenty-two full loads on the fourth night. That meant we could remain on the ground unchallenged and uninterrupted, allowing the insurgents no freedom of manoeuvre. The Chinooks were an absolutely fundamental component of our actions – we conducted a total of nineteen full-scale Commando aviation assaults during our tour. Then, together with the Sea Kings, they were also crucial to our sustainment in the field, zipping in with two-fifty-kilo pallets of essentials whenever we needed them. Without the air and aviation assets to support and enable us, our success would not have been possible.

When he was in Helmand this time, Danny, the CO's driver, completed his seventh year in the Royal Marines:

> When we're not on assaults, I feel safe for most of the time out there. The bases are well secured, and outside the perimeter the Engineers clear whole areas of mines – we're trained to deal with any that are left ourselves. Going out on Ops, you're psyched up and they're bloody great, those helos. The main thing out on the ground is the physicality of the job. The body-armour and the kit make every movement a sweat. The good thing is, though, you keep fit – you don't need any formal PT. Different back here though – you have to schedule it in.

Danny can look forward to twenty-two years' service – the officers can expect to serve longer than that, depending on achievement and seniority. Lieutenant Colonel Stickland, who joined in 1987, is coming up to the end of his allotted two years as CO. By the autumn he'll be posted, most likely to Whitehall:

I came into the Marines direct from school in Kent, looking for a leadership challenge and adventure in an élite organization. I have certainly found both – indeed, life as a servicemen is in many senses more a vocation than a profession. After six months in Iraq, my first deployment on Herrick started in September '06, as Chief of Staff for seven months to the UK Task Force. The operational theatre was extremely immature, and a key early focus was understanding the dynamics and actors fuelling the insurgency. There were fewer IEDs then than now, direct and indirect fire were the principal threats. Air-drops were not really on – the country was too restrictive around the FOBs, with no room for DZs – so we relied heavily on the Chinooks for resupply. It was a frenetic period – consolidating in Gereshk and Lashkar Gah, holding Garmsir and pushing the enemy line further

Ilyushin 76s join the transport team at Kandahar. (Bob Ruffles)

south and then seizing Sangin on 7 April 2007 in a final bold action of the tour. In relation to that deployment the use of air assault was limited.

This time, the Commando Group found it hugely rewarding to serve as Regional Battle Group – reporting direct to the two-star NATO Regional Commander, General de Kruiff, and having the luxury of a draw on wider NATO assets, particularly the Dutch, US and Canadians. We conducted a number of operations with 3 Battalion, the Royal Canadian Regiment, with whom we're maintaining close ties. In addition, J Company gained experience from being detached to Kabul and Lashkar Gah.

RAF and 1310 Flight flags fly at Bastion. (Madonna Walsh)

But the major difference between this and previous deployments was not being tied to FOBs. The dynamic nature of the actions, and their rapidity and shock effect, gave the Marines a distinct psychological and physical advantage. They were able to dance from fire-fight to village shura and make a real difference. May they continue to do so.

After leave and recuperation, the Marines of 42 Commando, under their new Commanding Officer, will get down to 'conducting low-level training in preparation for a period of high readiness' – but a future date with the Airbridge can never be far from their minds.

THE AIRBRIDGE

The Royal Marines have not been the only unit on the move. From the beginning of April, the 9,000 men of 19 Light Brigade have been in transit from Northern Ireland to Op Herrick, to take over from 3 Commando Brigade as the lead formation of UK forces in Afghanistan.

The RiP means a surge in the work of the Airbridge. Dave Hogg had an insight when he took a month away from the Helmand treadmill for a spell at Al Udeid, serving as Chief of Staff to the Hercules Detachment Commander:

> These posts are filled on a continuous rota by 24 and 30 Squadron officers. We live and work in the same accommodation as the aircrews. My job was to manage the detached Hercules crews and co-ordinate the flying programme, based on the requirements of the Forward Movements Control Centre. It gave me an insight into the workings of the Airbridge, and particularly the C-17 crews that slip there. All kinds of factors affect the scheduling. Crew duty, crew rest and crew rotation come into it, and when I was there the snow in England threw another spanner in the works. The blokes told me that when there's an RiP going on the system creaks a bit, but they manage.

1310 FLIGHT COUNT-DOWN

The RiP also pushes up the workload of the 1310 Flight Chinooks at Kandahar with a series of shuttles to and from TFH HQ at Lashkar Gah, as well as to all the FOBs. While these are going on, the IRT and HRF call-outs don't ease up, and Deliberate Ops continue. The ExCES men have managed to keep the Chinooks in the air to meet that workload, despite those fuselage cracks, and the damage from small-arms fire. Three have taken bullets – rotor blades have been hit twice and one round punctured the aft pylon. Charlie's

Freedom Bird – troops from 16 Air Assault Brigade take the C17 Globemaster… (Photograph by Sgt Anthony Boocock, RLC © crown copyright 2010/MoD, image from www.photos.mod.uk)

machine even took a slingshot rock in the rotor – she and her crew thank their lucky stars it wasn't an RPG.

On the day after the Aabi Toorah extraction, the Boss and his crew are on IRT – with no shouts. But the next day they're into Gereshk at the double to pick up an Afghan girl, the victim of a suicide bomb. As the deployment moves to its final fortnight, the American Pavehawks start to take on more of the casevac missions, easing the pressure on the 1310 crews – timely, as more of them are coming up to the limit of their hours.

Fatigue is making itself felt, too. But on occasion, aircrews find themselves happily spending a couple of days at Kandahar as duty crew, when, if they're lucky, there's perhaps no more than a twenty-minute air-test to fly. This leaves time to catch up on sleep, laundry and regular meals – although the baguettes at the new French patisserie remain very popular. Paperwork is not, but it has to be done. Forms 541, the daily Operational Reports, are a task for junior officers – for those who enjoy creative writing they're a breeze, but for most they're a chore. The Joint Personnel Administration system (JPA), newly implemented on Oracle to track records, expenses and allowances, follows them out to Kandahar, where it continues to tax both brain and patience.

There's a development in the inter-Service flagpole-raising contest. Up at Bastion one morning, a determined bunch of Navy Sea King crews, hauling manfully on ropes as good sailors can, succeeds in lifting into the vertical a swaying mast with banner flying. It teeters dangerously – but is finally made fast. It's taken nearly two months, but they've beaten the RAF's 36 feet.

On Ops, the surface-to-air missiles continue to fly, and the mountain scenery offers its mixture of hazard and exhilaration. There is no let-up in early-morning lifts and also in technical niggles. One 0555 departure is pushed back to 0625 owing to the Apache going unserviceable. Another time, a shuttle to Bastion has a fuel pump problem on arrival – the engineers can't

...for the journey home. (The Boss and friends)

Relief for the Gurkhas. *(The Boss and friends)*

find the right replacement part up there, and gravity refuelling delays the departure up to Kajaki. Watching *The Tudors* on the TV in the surge tent goes some way to ease the pain of that delay.

Sorties continue to the now safer area of Nad Ali and Marjah, but the odd RPG is still seen, and pilots fly circuitous routes to avoid pattern setting. Crews continue to spot suspicious eight-vehicle convoys carrying FAMs with guns, and on occasion, a government Poppy Eradication Force convoy of trucks. The last day of March sees a three-ship formation of Chinooks, following a day-long sortie to all the FOBs up to Musah Qaleh and back, flying through the rain over the Red Desert, and letting off steam by test-firing all their guns.

The first day of April finds the Boss and his crews planning for another Deliberate Op, this time with Canadian and American troops in the mountains out of Tarin Kowt. It's decided there's probably no need for a paper-hat walk-through, and sure enough, after an hour the commanders are satisfied that the crews know their stuff. By this time in the deployment, they most certainly do.

But there's a difference in that the crews are expecting a 'black illume' insert. This is a new development, and the idea is that a parachute-flare lights up the darkness so that the terrain can then be seen as clear as day in the NVGs for the critical period of landing on. In the event, the inserts are made in the early dawn and all goes well. Then, the planned last two days of the Op are cancelled, and following this, the most notable events are the Padre's ride in Frankie's aircraft to see a bit of the action, and the appearance on the menu at the Tarin Kowt bistro of the *filet mignon*.

The days are fast counting down for the Boss and his people to return to the UK, and there are signs that the repetitive workload is beginning to drain even 'C' Flight's reserves of adrenalin. Then, the Airbridge brings in their colleagues from 27 Squadron's 'A' Flight to relieve them, and the handover starts.

HOMECOMINGS

The men of 4 Force Protection Wing have already been relieved and have returned home. SAC Ben Hayman says that he has no problems adjusting to deployed life on arrival on Op Herrick, when spirits are high and the prospect of action excites. It's on the way back when the emotions kick in – when the memory of mates blown up comes to haunt, and home-base routine is in prospect:

> To start with, travel from Helmand can be a pain. Airbridge flights are a bit hit or miss. Seats are block-booked in advance – you're OK so long as your name's on the list, but if it's not, you fight to get a place. Then, some TriStar flights are delayed or turned back. By the time you've been decompressed in Cyprus, and then got home, the bubble's burst. The feeling comes over me that says, 'When I finish my service in three years, what am I going to do?' Take six months off, and never wear a uniform again – that's what.

The man with overall responsibility for Personnel, Manning and Welfare matters for all British servicemen and women on Operations, worldwide, is Group Captain Mark Heffron. Following his tour in Kabul, he was posted to Northwood, reporting to Brigadier Mike Hickson as Deputy Assistant Chief of Staff of J1 Division.

Apart from Herrick, the division currently has around twenty Operations to support. Manned by army, naval, and air force staff, it has the job of augmenting the deployed forces – receiving the request from operational units, obtaining the necessary governmental and military clearance from

Whitehall, and then identifying the augmentees in personnel lists. A maximum period of 104 days is then given to the RN, Army and RAF, in order that cover-in-post, personal affairs and deployment procedures can be put in order in good time. This manning process is continuous and constant, and in overdrive this spring, as the Prime Minister has authorized an increase in British troops on Op Herrick to 9,500 in order to increase security for the Afghan presidential elections due in August.

Once in theatre, personnel are entitled to the Deployed Welfare Package, which extends from telephones and the Internet to gymnasium and NAAFI facilities for the 9,000 people employed across Afghanistan. For the FOBs and dispersed units, the aspiration is to provide the same facilities, including computer terminals, phones, shelves of books, and gymnasium equipment. For all, there's the all-important British Forces Post Office. In the week before Christmas, two Boeing 747 loads of family mail were processed through RAF Northolt and delivered to Kandahar – on average seventeen parcels of gifts, newspapers, magazines, books and DVDs for each serving man and woman in the British force.

For the troops' further diversion, the MoD sub-contracts to the Buckinghamshire-based charity Services Sound and Vision Corporation, whose mission is to entertain and inform Britain's Armed Forces, wherever they are around the globe. SSVC transmits satellite TV through its British Forces Broadcasting Services (BFBS) arm, a unit whose live radio programme is scheduled to start at Camp Bastion in October. In addition, its Combined Services Entertainment (CSE) organization, 'dedicated to boosting morale', brings comedians, bands and dancers (and the occasional 'Page 3' girl) to enliven the routine of those on Herrick bases.

Joint Forces Support Staff are deployed in theatre, tasked with addressing all personnel issues hands-on, but Group Captain Heffron says that there is also full realization of the increasing need to extend welfare support for those returning from deployment. For all the larger deployed units, but not yet for the smaller, or for individual augmentees, J1 is also responsible for Post-Op Decompression.

In-depth care is essential for all the wounded, but top of the list for continuous attention is repatriation of the dead. It's J1 that employs Kenyon International, and oversees Operation Pabbay. The Division, in more ways than one, strives to take end-to-end care of its charges.

Charlie Thompson, back again from Herrick and now OC Deployable Aeromedical Response Teams (DARTS), is another who finds coming home in some ways more upsetting than going out:

After all the harrowing experiences and hard work on a deployment, you have to fight for a seat on a flight alongside everyone else. But at least you're coming home, and back to your family. Then, after a couple of days of euphoria, you realize how tired you are, and you're on a short fuse with family and friends both. You're on leave, and don't know what to do. I've found myself standing in the queue at Tesco's listening to people complaining about the most trivial things, and asking myself, 'What's it all about?' It takes me a good couple of months to recover.

The medics and nurses work in the front line all the time out there. We see them all – 3 Para, 16 Air Assault Armoured Brigade, 42 Commando – going out to the combat zone in the Cabs. And see them back in as well – many badly injured, or worse. Then there are the IED victims, often caught close to Kandahar and Bastion.

I'm due back in Helmand in March next year. The pre-deployment training lasts six to eight weeks, sometimes longer than the deployment itself. It's broad-based – weapons, fieldcraft, 'dunker' immersion drills, survival and interrogation, as well as advanced trauma techniques. It all adds to the load.

On base and on deployment, I do a lot of running – that makes me feel better, as does a game of squash when I'm at Lyneham. I live in the Mess with two dogs. Not an ideal arrangement, I suppose – but they're great company.

Captain Chris Trinick is back at the Household Cavalry barracks in Windsor, and has words of praise for the casevac operations in theatre:

The only way for the ISAF forces to make a difference for the Afghans is to keep boots on the ground and make the locals feel secure. Then they can get on with rebuilding their country themselves. That means our soldiers will be continuing to put themselves in the line of fire – and relying on the helos and the MERTs to pull them out if they get hit.

The RAF crews do the job well, and in challenging conditions. Once at Garmsir, we were told by JHF(A) to change the HLS three times on the one IRT shout. It was a mystery – we'd already cleared a desert box for the Cab to come in. But there we are. Our flyers do an outstanding job.

Corporal Vicky Lane has had to cope with another of her regular returns from a spell of nursing in Helmand:

You might think that at the end of a CCAST call-out from UK, once we've brought our charges safely back to Selly Oak, the job's done and it's time to relax. Sadly this isn't the case. First is an emotional meeting with the patient's family – we'll usually be the first contact they have with someone who has looked after him. After about an hour the Welfare Team take them off to visit the victim, and we set off for Lyneham.

By now we'll have been up for thirty or more hours, and on the journey we'll probably take the chance to grab forty winks, before getting back to base. There, we'll have to replenish the whole kit, clean the monitoring equipment and put it back on charge – get it all ready for the next mission. After that there's a report to write and then we'll have a quick chat and debrief about the mission. The whole team will be asked how they felt the trip went and if there are any issues for follow-up. This gives you a chance to offload any worries before you see your family. Only after all that do we get stood down – just for a day or two. For me, the first thing is the shower and bed!

After a formal deployment, it's different. The medevac flights in Helmand are a lot shorter, but more frequent – certainly more than one a day. We move a lot of Afghan nationals, Afghan army and police – those patients often have poorer general health and condition in the first place and are consequently sicker. Back home, as soon as possible there's a formal debrief with section commanders – I told mine that despite everything, I had a pretty good tour. Then you're free to go on leave.

I had four weeks off – looking back that was probably too long. I was so used to minimum sleep and busy days that just doing nothing was really hard. The first week or so, I visited family and friends. Then I went on holiday – then I just got bored!

Sergeant Mark Evans of the JHSU also recognizes the sense of deflation following a detachment:

There's a strong camaraderie on Herrick, and that, and the excitement, fade a bit when a deployment ends, especially when men and women return to life in their respective barrack blocks at Odiham. It helps that ORs and NCOs live in the same block, and that helos hover most days over the Tac Park – although more contact with the Chinook squadrons who train with us there would be appreciated. Of course, like us, they come and go so much that it's hard to build much of a relationship.

Still, there are plenty of exciting missions flown in the UK – not to mention the Falklands detachment. And we're a proud outfit. The Americans don't have a specialist unit – they get just four weeks' helicopter support training as part of their normal job. But the Canadians have seen what we can do, and now they want a JHSU. We've shown the way and have every reason to be proud. Aside from the special lifts, there's the continuous RiP trooping flights and freight resupply to handle. In one week on this last go, 100,000 tonnes of USLs were carried in a week, and we moved 1,000 pax.

Within a year my troop will be off again to Helmand – could be sooner. They keep our detachments at only three-months to keep us fresh, so we're available for a second stint each year. It'll be more 0400 starts, with loading and Intelligence briefings. There'll also be more long days being bruised and buffeted by a swinging hook or a flying rock, legs turning to jelly from the effort and arms semi-paralysed from static – all in the filth of the brown-out. And after all that there'll be tasking conferences, and working up to midnight preparing USL kit for the next morning. But we'll be back in the front line, where it counts.

Dave Hogg is reasonably relaxed at the prospect of returning for his sixth deployment, at Easter:

In the Hercs, we're generally a long way from the blood and guts of the battlefield and the kind of front-line action that the Chinooks and other helicopter crews see. Of course we do a lot of aeromedical evacuation, compassionate transfers to get servicemen and women home a.s.a.p. – and the most emotional of all, sunset repatriation flypasts for battle group survivors that have lost friends and colleagues. But after six detachments in Helmand, the greatest psychological pressure I've had is from the endless repetition. It's now very rare for the Hercs to fly to outlying airstrips – this time I've been to just the one, Tarin Kowt.

And it's usually much of a muchness when we get back to Lyneham and straight away into the post and pre-deployment loop again. There'll be the annual medical examination and keeping our jabs up to date, and usually a trip to the stores to pick up the latest kit – they're improving that all the time. And of course we'll be subjected to the biannual weapons-handling check and another annual bout of Force Protection training.

We'll be incarcerated in the simulator and bombarded with emergency drills, and we might even get a couple of flights. There are the continuous Aircrew Categorization rides – even after eleven years of flying I still find those nerve racking. And perhaps something exciting will come up. The 'J' crews have a rolling roster for a stint on six-hour standby – comes up on average once a month for each of us. It was on one of these that a French Exchange captain and his crew flew up to Stornoway to collect a mother expecting twins – she had to be got to hospital in a hurry. It made the headlines at the time. We were particularly proud of that one – seems the weather was too bad for the helicopters to get in. Good old 'Fat Albert' managed it.

However, on returning from this detachment I'll be changing squadrons, which will mean more training and exercises before being deployed again. I've got something different to look forward to this time.

Apart from deployed service stress, another pressure on Lyneham people is the now certain knowledge that the base will be closing in 2011, and the units moved to Brize Norton. There has been, and still is, full consultation with servicemen and women and their families, and with the 3,000 civilians who work on the base, and there'll be support as the clock ticks down to the move. But it's a worry for the people out in Helmand, and for their families back home. Warrant Officer Mark Taylor of AMW is one for whom the problem has been solved:

I'm being posted in a couple of months to JADTEU up at Brize. I'll be a Project Officer in the air-portability section. That'll suit me and the family very well – but I'll miss Lyneham. It's the friendliest camp I've known in the RAF – fitted me like an old pair of slippers. It's probably because the whole place has a common objective – operating the Hercules. We've felt at home in the Wootton Bassett area too – the old two-up-two-down house we're doing up in our village will still be there for us when I retire. That's due in 2017, after thirty-seven years' service.

I hope by then Afghanistan will be sorted. In hindsight, the positive mood we had at the end of my first deployment in 2005 was remarkable. It soon wore off. But it was exciting out there. I remember that after disembarkation leave I warned back into the Mess, picked up a newspaper and some coffee – and sat down to read. I was soon saying to myself, 'What am I doing here?' The job back home suddenly seemed so humdrum.

For Chinook ExCES engineers, up to now the return date for each man has varied. Last December, SAC Phillip West had a long wait:

I was due to come home for Christmas but there was a mix-up and I finished up still at KAF. It was relatively quiet in the FOBs. Welfare parcels arrived – WI cakes and woolly hats – and there was a Christmas dinner menu in the cookhouse. Religion was there if you wanted it, but not forced. When I finally made it back to Brize, it was freezing cold and the TriStar cargo doors broke – had to wait two hours for the baggage.

Ski McComisky, who has spent two Christmases in Helmand in three years, says he doesn't count the days on detachment:

I just take each one as it comes – that is, until the days remaining get down to single figures. That's when I start looking out for my replacement – we can't leave until he arrives. When he does, we try for a quick handover, within the day if everything's in order. Then it's the lottery of getting a seat on a flight home. They give the highest priority to troops leaving for R and R – tour-expired travellers get the lowest. But I was lucky with the flight this time – the same TriStar that brought in my replacement took me home.

Westy says that for days after his arrival back at Odiham he felt he ought to be doing something to keep busy, and was happy to ease back into work:

I live in the Junior Ranks' Mess, where there's still a military chef, not one of your contracted civvy firms – the food's much better for that, I reckon. Mind you, it'll be the scran at Kandahar again before long. I don't mind that – it's out there that I can really get into doing my job. It'll get me in good nick for Cosford, and my next stint of trade training.

Ski says he has a good feeling when he gets back:

There's none of that dust in the air here, and the Guinness is good. I'm moving out next month to live with my long-term girlfriend. I've been able to save for the house – out of the money I've earned from the one year of my life that I've spent on detachment. There's the tax refunds, stretching back to 2006, plus £12 a day tour bonus, plus Operational Allowance of £10 per day. And all that time I've not been spending anything – our food and accommodation on Herrick is free. On top of that, they give us one extra day's leave for every nine days worked in Afghanistan – I've got more than thirty days of that to come. That's not bad, is it? I'm comfortable taking the money – after all it's payment for six tours and a job well done. I'll be back for my seventh with 27 'B' Flight first of August. Who knows, by then I might make corporal.

Warrant Officer Edbrooke is due to take the TriStar on Saturday 11 April – his replacement arrives on time, but his flight home, as sometimes happens, is cancelled. This delays his return until the Sunday, when two passenger loads now need to be moved. An extra, reliable C-17 is brought into the schedule, and John gets a seat on that:

It's been a hard-working detachment. I've managed the odd visit to the Boardwalk, but not had much time to take advantage of its attractions – anyway, it gets so you can't stand the smell of pizza and burgers. We've beaten the serviceability target right to the end. We've had cracks and bullet holes, but mercifully none of the Cabs has taken an RPG this time. For once, I haven't flown any sorties on this detachment, but with all the Deliberate Ops, we've seen a lot of the troops and the RAF Regiment in and out of the Chinook pans. We've also seen them, and blokes from other engineering shops, when they come on the scrounge for tools.

There's been a lot of IRT work as well. That's always been something special – where you come face-to-face with the front line, through the injured and the fatalities. Our work with them is not for the faint hearted – though the medics and crewmen do their best, after a MERT shout there's always something of a mess for the engineers to clear up.

When I get back to the UK, there'll be a two-day debrief, followed by a couple of weeks' leave, followed by some kind of adventure training – the lads will possibly be surfing at St Mawgan this time. Decompression for us is being enhanced – the powers that be have realized that to ease the transition back to work and to sustain our level of effort there's just as much need for us as for aircrews for a planned exercise of recovery, and improved quality of life back at base.

But I know that my family will have got on with their lives while I've been away. As usual they'll have had good support from neighbours, and from the Station – my wife works in the Logistics Supply branch. So my decompression leave is going to be table tennis. I'm on the Odiham team of three for the inter-station RAF 'A' Cup – it starts in a couple of weeks.

Then, when I'm back at work, I'll be monitoring the Commendations that JHF(A) put forward after the special efforts of two of our men on this det. And we'll see how the reorganization of ExCES onto a flight-by-flight basis is going. It's to be called 18/27 (Engineering) Squadron. Mirroring the aircrew flights should rebuild the sense of identity that was lost when we were removed from the flying-squadrons a few years ago. But I probably won't be part of that for long – I'll be posted by the

'I dossed down on top of the cargo.' *(Bob Ruffles)*

autumn. This could have been my last Herrick deployment. My motivation's still strong – it's the love of the lifestyle that pulls me into work. When I have to stop, my wife and I plan to retire to Devon.

RIP FOR 1310 FLIGHT

The target date to board the homebound Airbridge for 'C' Flight is 10 April, Good Friday. However, as the relieving aircrews one by one refresh their theatre qualification, many of the tour-expired men can be released a little earlier.

On the Easter Saturday C-17, John Edbrooke meets up with many of the 'C' Flight aircrews. But Mister B beats them all back:

I was crewed up for the second half of the detachment with German, and on Friday we got up for Ops briefing at 0300, and lifted at 0730 for a three-hour mission. Then it was into the Cambridge Lines to pack bags and to the Terminal at 1400 – with most of the flight. Once there, they told us the TriStar was still sitting U/S at Brize and we'd have to wait until 2230 the next day. I'd been here before, so rather than sit around, I sought out alternative means. The blokes at AMW told me that a Sea King was to be airlifted back to Brize in a C-17 – so I got myself on the waiting list. Long story short, my initiative was rewarded with a place on the flight, taking off at 0300 that night.

We flew via Turkey, and not having the thermal mattress and arctic sleeping bag you really need for a good night's sleep on the floor of a C-17, I dossed down on top of a cargo container – a bit warmer up there.

Having handed over an operational JAG, Group Captain Turner has come back on the same flight, and on arrival at Brize at 0930 on Sunday morning, he offers Mister B a lift down to Odiham, which is gratefully accepted. He gets home while the rest of 'C' Flight is still waiting at Kandahar:

It's a joy to land safely back at Brize, but the real moment of elation was the lift-off from KAF. When I get back to the house, seeing Mrs B and the family is a relief, but I don't want to talk about the det for a while. I'll probably get the photos out at the weekend.

No one tour ever seems the same as another. This time, there were quite a number of Deliberate Ops, with the Cabs being used by a variety of organizations, including the Americans and the Canadians. We did about four months' work in two. I did have a few days off in February, but even then, it wasn't sitting around drinking coffee – accumulated admin filled that time. But I prefer it like that. With all the work, February and March flew by – no need to count the days.

But there still doesn't seem to have been enough investment in 1310 Flight's operating infrastructure – the engineers work in particularly rough conditions. At KAF it's mostly in begged, borrowed or stolen accommodation, and at Bastion, it's out of a Portakabin. And they're always desperate for spares. They've done better than ever for us over the last three months – it's about time their efforts were rewarded with the respect they deserve. There's a lot of civvy engineers now doing the Primary Chinook Servicing at KAF – this may save money overall, but the high tax-free salaries they offer tempt our RAF guys to leave and come back as contractors.

The weather at the start of the det wasn't as cold as it might have been, although there was snow on the hills. Then, by the end of March, it got up to 30 C in the daytime, and along came the storms and floods. So that damped the dust down a bit – just right for the incoming detachment.

Rocketwise, it was quiet for the first two weeks at KAF, and then we had ten to twelve in all, usually a couple in each salvo, three to five at the most. There were none at Bastion. In the hours I flew, the Cab sometimes came under heavy machine-gun fire – other crews reported RPG attacks, but there were no strikes.

In line with all my previous detachments, the crews I was on brought in no British casualties, just American and Afghan – I'm getting a reputation as the one to fly with. A colleague, who shall be nameless, is known on the other hand as the 'Grim Reaper' because he seems to carry so many British injured, and worse. Maybe it'll be a little easier for 'B' Flight on IRT, with the American 101 Airborne and their Pavehawks moving into KAF.

Now I'll take a couple of weeks' leave before getting back into the old routine, thinking already about the next det due in December. I reckon there'll still be a challenge with manning – there are so few new crewmen coming in. On this one, four had to be borrowed – one of those was new and was keen for experience, one came forward because his wife is expecting a baby later in the year and he wanted to get on an earlier det, and two just volunteered to help out. There'll be more of that sort of patching through unless more trainees come through the pipeline. Despite all that, the spirit on the squadron is good, especially among the crewmen.

Ginger agrees with that:

My best friends are among the crewmen I joined up with, and a lot of those are here at Odiham. I've got good pals among the civvies we know around home, too – it's one of the advantages of living off base. It means at weekends I can be a normal person, and that helps with readjusting to home life on return from detachment. Not that I need much help. Even with all the horrors and stresses out there, I don't have bad dreams or any other trauma symptoms. It's a case of saying, 'That's squared away – that's that done.' Getting home from Kandahar is actually the worst nightmare – it can be a case of hitching a lift in a C-17, like this time.

I have to say that I enjoyed the det. Right from the start it was very busy, with long operating days, very little time off and constant retasking at short notice. Our 1310 Cabs were first off in the morning and the last to land – we'd fly for ten hours a day and live on caffeine. I'd seek out the more dangerous missions – if you're in this sort of job I reckon you should be looking for the more exciting stuff. I didn't get to fire the guns in anger, but came close.

On one insertion, we knew that Taliban were in the area. Then I saw one of them, running – and I had him in my sights. We did come under fire – but I lost him. At 180 mph and fifty feet there's not much hope of drawing a bead on anything.

With all the Deliberate Ops and IRT shouts, I clocked up a lot of hours on this deployment. Now I'm back, and it's all admin. I've got reports to write on everyone on detachment – mostly generic, but specific for those new guys who are struggling a bit. It gives people a chance of mixing the coming home to loved ones with some work – helps with any domestic strain. But as I say, I slot right back in. It's a pride in the job thing, and my civvy chums seem to respect me for it.

I enjoy life on the squadron – good people, in a good working environment. They're saying that for sustainability, every member of aircrew graduating from OCF has to do at least a six-year Chinook tour. Well, I've done nearly nine years already. I'll go on – if I weren't happy I'd go somewhere else. I'm turned on by the sense of achievement – making a difference.

Morts found his first detachment rewarding:

Time went quickly, and it was a great experience all round. I even did a score of take-offs and landings. Arriving back at Odiham Officers' Mess is a bit of an anti-climax. I'm off to London tonight, and then from Friday I'm away on leave for three weeks in Indonesia, pursuing my passion – surfing.

Then, it'll be squadron life until PDT starts again in the autumn. It's back again to Helmand in December – this time, if all goes well, as a captain. I learned a lot in double-quick time on this detachment. There's still much more to learn – but it was good to find out I could cope.

Chomper has similar captaincy ambitions to Morts, but his own special memory of his second detachment:

We were in the middle of all the shit at some HLS or other, off-loading the poor sods going into battle. Then, a completely unexpected waft of poppy scent blew in on the rotor draught, and came through the cockpit window – very refreshing. It was completely surreal – we could have been in the middle of a Suffolk meadow. Then we lifted off again, back into the murk of the dust-haze. By the time we get back in December, the poppies will all be gone – harvested to make bloody opium.

The Boss handed over authority for 1310 Flight on time, but then the RiP pressure demanded more aircrew, and he and Frankie were tasked to fly on the day of scheduled departure, inserting a Black Watch dawn assault to the north of Kandahar. But they were clear of duties in time to catch up with their delayed colleagues on the Easter Sunday TriStar. Back at Odiham, Frankie finds there's been a change – her 'other half' has been posted to Air Command, and is moving in:

That's nice, isn't it? Really helps to put Helmand out of my mind. But I usually manage that – although once, on holiday in Antigua, I was brought up short. I had come back off a 'B' Flight det two weeks early, as I was transferred to 'C' and due to go back with them to Herrick in eight weeks' time. One evening by the pool, there was this news report on TV saying that a Chinook had crashed in Afghanistan. I had no way of knowing whether or not it was the guys I'd just left out there – my mates. But they'd got it wrong – it turned out to be a Nimrod. A relief in one way, but still very bad news indeed.

It was a busy det this time – not as much flying for me as previously, but I throttled back to concentrate more on my training role, bringing some of the younger guys on. I even flew as co-pilot on a high-end Op for one of the newer captains – better for them to learn from our past mistakes rather than let new people make the same mistakes again. We did a lot of casevac missions — eight to ten in the first week and then at least one a day. My crews and I did fifteen, but we didn't come under fire, except for that kid with his slingshot. We did have a bird strike, though. That was on the Fishhook Op – took out the centre window.

We flew home on the TriStar with the Boss and his crew – there was no goody-bag on arrival at Brize like there is at KAF, but it was comfortable. Not like the time I hitched a lift on a Globemaster via Qatar, when we had to sleep on the floor – but the loadmaster served up an excellent curry, for all that.

It will be my last full deployment for a while – I've got a new job, as Squadron Standards Officer. But before that, it's decompression. We're not going to make it to Ascension Island – it's to be the 'Padres' College' near Andover for an overnight of chat and good eating. But after that, I'm off to South Africa for three weeks with my man.

The Boss is home from his busiest detachment yet, having gone past 1,600 hours on Chinooks:

> Everyone's back now. It was a long trip home for the last of us. We were some time in Departures at KAF, watching the 'Going Home' video. It's on a loop, endlessly pointing out that returning 'warriors' are not invulnerable – although they may feel so after conquering all in Helmand – and warning them to be careful after a few drinks.
>
> Then it was a two-hour flight and a stopover of another two, before four to Akrotiri. There we had two more while the crew slipped and soldiers disembarked for their two days' decompression. Another four hours to Brize made it fourteen in all – with the three-and-a-half time difference we didn't land until ten o'clock in the morning. All the family except the dog were there waiting – a joyful reunion. I'd brought home a variety of gifts, including a Unicef shoulder-bag and a mug from the new French patisserie at KAF. They'll join the ISAF bears from a previous visit.
>
> 'I'm allowed to slot back into the household routine in my own time. For quite a few days, 'Daddy's going to work' means for the children that I'm off again for another unimaginable length of time – and there are tears. I recognize the strain that these deployments put on families. For me, I'm just 36, and already a veteran of the Afghanistan action. From 2010, and my sixteen-year point, we'll have to see.

The day after 'C' Flight's homecoming, the washing-lines in the back gardens of Odiham's married quarters are weighed down with desert-camouflage kit. It's the same sight every ten weeks.

CHAPTER 14

On and On ... and On

'C' FLIGHT BACK HOME

After their arrival back from Op Herrick at Easter, the men and women of 'C' Flight, together with the returned ExCES engineers and the Troop of Hookers from JHSU, had their weekend at the 'Padres' College' – the Tri-Service Armed Forces Chaplaincy Centre at Amport House. As an alternative to the beaches and adventure training in Cyprus offered to soldiers straight from Kandahar, the Chinook Force has negotiated these two quieter days in the peace of the Hampshire hills.

After arrival for lunch on the first day, the programme included a debriefing from the Boss and a lengthy chat with the Padre from Odiham. After dinner, the whole crowd strolled down for an evening in the local pub. The next day, half the group spent the morning go-karting, while for the others it was croquet on the manicured lawns.

Frankie says that there was a chapel available, and books on the spiritual side of things, but, apart from the saying of Grace at mealtimes, no one pushed religion at them:

> The Padres do a lot for the families when their nearest and dearest are away on duty, and they train, deploy and live with us in Helmand. They're there to offer a response to someone in pain or worse, worried about home, or just needing someone to be angry with. They're the first ones to say they don't have all the answers.

POSTINGS

For the Boss, this gathering was to be his last chance to wind down with the troops, for his number had come up for Staff College. By the beginning of

May he'd handed over 'C' Flight to his successor and was a student at a desk once more. After ten years, he finally had his break from Operations, but his family still suffered his absence, on a weekly commute. There were ructions each time he left wife, children and dog to drive up to Shrivenham. And it's odds on that the roster for Herrick will catch up with him again, sooner or later.

After her three weeks in South Africa, Frankie took up her new job, and was soon organizing visits from the STANEVAL 'trappers'. But she then got word in the autumn of a New Year posting to Benson – as the Chinook pilot on the Operational Evaluation Unit. It's a two-year job, and she got it, she says, because she's tactically minded. She won't be far from the action. She might deploy for a month next year to keep current on the Chinook and the latest tactics – and, as 'C' Flight starts to gear up for its next detachment in December, she's offering her services to the new boss:

> It's sad to watch guys with kids having to go out there over Christmas. It's not certain I'll be needed, but I've been on every 'C' Flight det so far, so it would be the first without me. But in any event they'll be fine – and you have to move on!

John Edbrooke is another with a new job. He is to be posted in October, for his last two years in the Service, to RNAS Yeovilton on the Chinook Project Team. His task will be to put in train any modifications coming along for the current fleet – integrating logistics support (including spares) and engineering training:

> I knew that the deployment in the spring was to be my last, so I took steps to help 'engineer' this posting – why not? It fits – handy for my house in Devon, and I'm well qualified for the job. But I was on tenterhooks before I finally got the drafting notice, right at the end of August. I'm going to have to give my body-armour back, but I'll hang on to the rest of the desert kit – always likely I'll make at least one Herrick visit before I've finished.

LOSSES

Since Mister Edbrooke came back from his last detachment, there have been two RAF Chinooks lost on Op Herrick, both within one week in August. One went down five miles south-west of Kajaki, caught finally by an RPG. The crew was unhurt, and to deny the aircraft to enemy forces it was blown up where it lay by an air-launched missile. The other suffered a heavy landing during an air assault at night. Ski McComisky, back on his seventh detachment, was on duty in the hangar at Kandahar when the call came:

It was four weeks into the tour – thirtieth of August. I'd only that day been moved to the night shift. One of the corporals had broken a leg and they'd shipped me across to cover – with acting stripes. At about five in the morning, this message comes in that a Cab has gone down in the desert, somewhere up north, east of Sangin. The sergeant gets me and three of the lads to rustle up the emergency tool-kit, grab weapons and desert survival stuff, and we're off on the Sea King to Bastion.

We fly on to the crash site and get there about ten o'clock – already bloody hot. There's the Cab, looking like a stranded whale. The story we're given is that it was one of a three-ship insert of the Rifles on an air assault. What had looked to the pilot like a nice flat area in the half-light had turned out to be a wadi. As it landed on, the fuselage finished up straddling the gully, and the force of the impact shunted the whole nose section upwards by several inches. No one was injured, but it must have been a nasty moment for the crew – and for the twenty blokes in the cabin.

It's a bit of a worry for us, too, out there in the desert. We're used to being in the rear, in a nice secure base, surrounded by blast-walls – not in the field of fire, miles outside the wire. But we've got the soldiers from the Rifles to protect us. The other two Cabs have pushed off back to Bastion earlier, taking the third crew with them, and the troops have formed up in a defensive ring – up on the sand dunes above the wadi. The Sergeant Major's marching up and down – calm as you like, keeping everything in order. He tells us the assault's been put on hold – but there are suspected hostiles not far away.

We take a look at the Cab and soon see that the force of the impact has severed all the flying controls. There's no chance of getting it flying again – the machine's a write-off. So we get on with making it ready to be lifted out. We hump out the heavy stuff, including the guns, to reduce the weight – even cut the blades off with this heavy power-saw. That's something we'd not done before. While we're doing that – wallop! An RPG lands not more than a hundred yards away. The Rifles Sergeant Major tells us that's the fourth this morning – makes us sweat even more.

We carry on pulling out the sensitive stuff – and the valuable and reusable bits. But then the message comes through that there's no Cab available to do the lift and it's been decided to deny the machine to the enemy. So in the afternoon, more helos arrive – bringing in the Sappers to blow our Cab up. They take us out, with the stuff from the wreck and most of the soldiers – back to Bastion. By the time we get to Kandahar, the whole thing's taken close to twenty-four hours. It's been a long, hot and nervous day – and we've been shot at.

The next day, they show us a video of the broken Cab out in the wadi – taken from a UAV, right overhead. You can see Sappers scuttling up the sand-banks, looking for safety behind the dunes, where the Rifles are. Then there's these bright flashes all along the fuselage as the charges go off – the whole thing goes up like Guy Fawkes' night. It's a sad moment for us. We've looked after that machine for years, and there it is, lying in the desert in flames. It was the one that got an RPG in the rear pylon last year – perhaps it was jinxed.

But we had to get up and crack on – and we've learned something from it. If it happens again, we'll know what to do – cut the machine in half and lift it out bit by bit.

It made us all think, those five hours out on the ground. We get times on detachment when we hit a wall – when it's a struggle to get everything sorted, spares delivered and the Cabs in the air. But we'd got a better idea of what it's like to be out in the heat of the desert and under fire. There's no danger now we'll ever take the ground troops for granted – the risks they run and the jobs they take on. After all, it's them that it's all about – that's why we're there, keeping the Cabs going.

When he came back on the Airbridge in the second week of October, Ski was able to carry his kit through his own front door. He and his girlfriend have moved into that house they'd been planning to buy. He's still wearing his acting corporal's stripes, and should be confirmed in the rank by the time he goes out to the heat and sand again. He already knows that his next stint is to be in May next year.

Mister Edbrooke says that Ski is now in the group of engineers affiliated to 27 Squadron's 'B' Flight – Jericho manning is in full swing. He also says that the two lost helicopters have been pretty quickly replaced:

A couple of Cabs were taken out to Kandahar in two C-17 loads. Despite those two losses, and serviceability problems, the flying-hour task is still pretty much being met out there.

And more Chinooks are on the way. Our Mk 2/2As are in for mods – like getting the new 714 engines – and will become available soon. And the issue with the Mark 3s in storage at Boscombe Down has been resolved – the first of them will be here in November. It's a different machine and the aircrews will need retraining, but they should be on the flight-line by Christmas. Fifty-three engineers are in training for the new machine – they're to have a month in school and then they'll be here in post when the first aircraft arrives. Someone has done some effective prioritizing at MoD. There'll be more to come – some tough choices are being made at last.

The reorganization into 18/27 Engineering Squadron has worked – the Commander JHC came down to kick it off and we're having a few beers in 27 Squadron crew-room this evening to get to know each other better. My replacement's a warrant officer who's been at Odiham before. I'm leaving confident that the outfit's in good shape and that down at Yeovilton the RAF lifestyle will still be pulling me into work. By the way – we won that table-tennis Station cup, hands down.

Squadron Leader Bob Davies is another who's been posted – he's now at PJHQ Northwood:

Since the spring, for the RAF Regiment men out in Afghanistan the situation has changed dramatically. The expansion of their base protection duties, expected in 2010, has already happened. The wind-down in Iraq has released the forces necessary to increase our footprint, and now we're defending Bastion, too. Tragically, almost as soon as we got there, one of our men died in IED contact while out on patrol. He was with 34 Squadron and was the two hundred and nineteenth British fatality since the conflict began. We have to keep going, of course, but the only long-term solution is going to be security and economic growth provided by Afghans for Afghans. In that respect the new Commander ISAF, General McChrystal, seems to have it absolutely spot on.

THE CONTINUING STRUGGLE

On the first day of August, as planned, Major Chris Stuart moves from High Wycombe to take over as Officer Commanding 47 Air Despatch Squadron at Lyneham. Later in the year he'll be making a short visit to Helmand, to familiarize himself with the current situation:

I know already that the use of air-drop has reduced considerably. 19 Light Brigade worries that deliveries fall too far away from its safe area – so it has to be our aim to increase accuracy. The snag is that at the same time we have to reduce costs. We hope to bring in the GPS-controlled system used by the American military, which can deliver supplies within 200 metres of a secured area – but that needs a £30,000 box of electronics attached between the parachute and the payload suspended underneath. The pay-off would be that with loads landing that close to an FOB, and well within the range of a Mark 19 grenade-launcher or 50-calibre machine-gun, no Taliban is going to risk trying to plant IEDs on the DZ. The system would also allow the drop to be made stealthily, from a remote distance, out of the range of the Taliban's current surface-to-air missiles. That's what the Americans are doing.

Meanwhile, 19 Brigade is relying mostly on convoys, and chartered Russian helicopters – but they're expensive at eleven and a half million dollars US for three hundred hours. And two have recently been lost – one crashed at KAF and the other was shot down. Now, they'll only go where the threat level is low.

Another potential area for development is the UAV. The Predator can already carry a payload of nearly 600 kilos, so it doesn't need much of a leap of imagination to conceive of air-supply robots. And the Americans are reintroducing lower-cost 'chutes, made out of mail-bag type material. Didn't Bill Slim do something like that in Burma?

But there's still a heavy workload for us on Herrick, working with the Battle Groups on their Ops. I'll be going out on deployment myself before long to get a taste of that. Soon, we'll be starting the planning for another major task – moving the squadron to Brize Norton in 2011. Already one of our main concerns is – will we be able to take our Dakota with us?

The two RAF Regiment men from 4FP, SACs Hayman and French, are already in training for their next spell in Helmand, in April next year. Then, after another twelve-month turn-round, they'll expect to be off again. It's much the same for Vicky Lane, the CCAST nurse. She's fully back in the routine at the John Radcliffe Hospital:

When I came off leave, I was given a shift or two to work with another colleague – just to get me back into a normal working pattern and to bring me up to speed on any changes. The civilian staff have been great – welcoming, and keen to hear how things went in Helmand. And for me, it's a relief to be working in a steady, safe environment again.

The CCAST system is currently up for change. They are looking to reduce the fatigue issues by pre-positioning two nurses in Kandahar. However, as things stand currently, we're still flying the route. I don't mind that. I've been a nurse for seven years now, and on CCAST for three. Obviously I don't wish injury on anyone, but this is the job I've been trained to do, and it's challenging and educational. It's an honour and a privilege to bring these sick and injured troops home.

When I go out next, it'll be as a sergeant – I'm delighted to say that I've just got my promotion.

Change is also in train for Major Phil Ritchie and the men and women of the JHSU:

They'd been talking for more than twenty years about merging us with MAOTS – well, now it's been done. After many attempts, all the interested parties got together last November and the OC MAOTS and I were tasked with sorting out the details. We found cultural differences, which were inevitable, and operational benefits, which were compelling. The new unit's to be called the Joint Helicopter Support Squadron and will be based here at Odiham.

The fourteen guys in MAOTs – five of them are flight lieutenants, the remainder non-commissioned aircrew – are deep specialists in the employment of support helicopters. They're currently based at Benson but they handle all types, including the Chinooks in Helmand. They've been going forward with combat troops, establishing the HLSs, and calling the Cabs in for casevac and other emergencies.

JHSU Troops have traditionally been centred on the USLs in the base area, but are increasingly being deployed forward to recover damaged equipment, including downed aircraft on occasion. Putting the two together will offer a single source of service over the whole spectrum of SH asset use – from the operational to the tactical – under a single chain of command. MAOTS moved down here on the first of September, when we declared Initial Operating Capability. I'm OC the new squadron, and we'll be working up to Full Operating Capability by 1 April next year.

Now that the Merlins have been upgraded and are going out to Helmand, and with the Pumas working-up in Kenya just now and expected to be there in December, we're guaranteed Herrick deployments for as long as the Op lasts.

COMMANDERS' VIEWS

By the autumn, Squadron Leader Paul Curnow is posted, but earlier in 2009 he was the Officer Commanding 'A' Flight of 18(B) Squadron. A navigator by trade, he was one of just four remaining on support helicopters, a role that he describes as 'professional co-pilot'. He saw Chinook service in Kosovo, Sierra Leone, Bosnia and Iraq, and from 2001 had completed a total of six detachments in Afghanistan – from October to December 2007 he commanded 1310 Flight on Herrick. Recently, he was the driver of the 1310 Flight badge application, and was delighted when it was given Royal Consent on 1 April. He holds firm views on the flight's central position in Chinook aircrew life:

> Individual squadron ethos at Odiham has been difficult to generate, with aircraft ownership and engineering support centralized. The five flights are the actual operating units and they take the identity generated by the personality of the Flight Commander and his senior people. That's reinforced by the fact that we seldom meet other flights, even those of the same squadron. We train, take leave and go on detachment as a unit. We have our own shoulder-badges – ours says we're the 'A-team'. About the only time we overlap is on 1310 Flight changeover.
>
> Out there on 1310, that strong identity continues – it'll be even more so now the engineers get rostered in parallel with us. Their commitment is already seen in the feats of support they achieve, and the workload they shoulder in theatre. Yes, it's 1310 Flight that's the focus.

Also by the autumn, the OC 27 Squadron, Dom Toriati, has been promoted to group captain and posted to a desk. He puts a slightly different slant on the roles of flight and squadron:

> Although our people take on the identity of 1310 in Helmand, they're not islands – they need the support of the Odiham command structure. There's a balance to be struck between the intense relationships and spirit built up in the war-zone and membership of a squadron back here. The formal badge for 1310 Flight is a strength – it brings engineers and aircrews together, working to a common aim. But for forty-two weeks of the year the guys live and work in a squadron that's had a strong identity for many years – as a unit, it is still important for morale. It exists to ensure that its flights are properly prepared and supported for deployment – fully manned, carefully balanced and ready for operations.
>
> I know this from experience. I've been on the front line for much of my twenty years' service in the RAF, and since I took over 27 Squadron, I've been out to fly with our crews on Afghanistan Ops. Then I had a four-month tour last year at KAF, as CO of JHF(A), giving me a chance

to find out about the wider picture, but at the sharp end. In his Odiham role, a Squadron Commander's flying duties are important – he keeps current for deployment and standby duties and carries out formal checks of aircrew readiness for Combat Ready status. Other duties are critical, too. Apart from a lot of admin, form filling and report writing, the OC has a whole raft of personnel duties – maintaining discipline of course, advising on people's careers with a helping hand where necessary, and most important, welfare. It's vital to support the guys before and after deployment, and I was always available on the telephone for worried wives and families.

It seems to me that personnel issues are the key to sustaining the Chinook effort in Afghanistan – and elsewhere. Remember, apart from Herrick, the Chinook Force has a commitment to support operations worldwide at very short notice – like the mobilization for the Lebanon evacuation in autumn '07. Training is continuous – for the desert of course, currently in Morocco, but there's also been amphibious training this year off the Turkish coast, and preparation for arctic conditions, in Norway.

Now we're out of Iraq, obviously the overwhelming priority is Afghanistan. The more troops we send there, the more work there is for helicopters. The main challenge for the Chinook SH Force is sustainability. The critical path is the availability of personnel, both ground and air – combat-ready aircrews and engineers are at a premium and regularly deployed. Our expectation is that each man and woman will deploy on operations once per year, but people occasionally get sent back for unscheduled extra visits to fill the gaps created by the unforeseen, such as illness or domestic issues. To keep them going, we're striving to improve their quality of life when they get back home. Supporting the morale of our people is essential for motivation, and for their focus on the task in hand.

Andy Turner says that the job of CO JHF(A) in Kandahar in many ways parallels that of a Squadron Commander at Odiham. The aims are identical – get the Chinooks into action, and keep them there. The same goes for his roles as CO JAG out in the field and Station Commander back home:

There are twelve hundred people living on this base – at any one time a third of them will be serving overseas. The PR presentations we give next-door, here in the HQ, talk about the continuous operational delivery that's required of them – the relentless expectations that the bosses, and the public, have of our men and women.

Of course, those expectations are met. Look at individual efforts like SAC McComisky and his wheel-change at night, keeping the Cab in the air – and group achievements such as 1310 Flight delivering a high number of flying-hours each month. It's all linked, of course, to pride in the Service, which is something that can't just be taken for granted. This Afghanistan campaign has been going on now since November 2001 – that's two years longer than World War Two. The presentation also talks about the stresses and strains on our people, not only the physiological – we get a lot of neck and back injuries – but also the psychological. They see death and they dish it out, year by year.

The best way for them to confront their demons is to talk about it – that's really what the decompression programme's all about, but we also make sure to look for those who need further counselling, and then provide it. They and their families also need constant and visible support for their efforts, and to help in that, we have regular Family

'C' Flight march in Odiham Village Parade. **(The Boss and friends)**

Days on the station, showing the mums and dads – any relatives in fact – a bit about what their sons and daughters do day by day.

They also need the support of the British public, so we're constantly badgering the media – they're certainly becoming more supportive these days. But to help build positive relations with our local area, we have annual Open Days here on the base. This year, 4,000 out of the 5,000 people of Odiham village came – a magnificent response.

Especially with the uncertainty about plans to relocate all helicopters at Lyneham – now shelved because the Defence Budget can't afford it – this local engagement is priceless. It brings us tactical freedom, for example to fly at night. It brings tangible support – such as discounts in shops and cinemas – and most importantly, it gives moral support. The servicemen and women and their families deserve it, and certainly need it.

Every year, our personnel march in the Odiham village parade – in June the squad was drawn from 27 Squadron's 'C' Flight, fresh from their three-month Helmand deployment. Now, they're already getting ready to go back again in December, just nine months since the last time. That's the treadmill they're on. They'll find changes – the Afghan presidential elections have stuttered, the conflict has expanded to Pakistan's Swat Valley and now Waziristan. No one would dare to predict when and how it will end.

As we say in our presentation, the Chinook has become one of the key combat platforms of choice, which has built an insatiable demand for more. It's relentless. But we're there and we'll do our job. It's swimming upstream – but the view is, we must keep swimming or we've had it.

'C' FLIGHT OFF AGAIN

For Morts, the eleven months since he last started PDT has flown by:

I suppose it's because the year's split into five blocks. The month's downtime after deployment seemed to be over before it had started, and before you knew it we'd done two more on National Standby and another couple on R1 – that's when you're on twelve hours' notice for operational tasks, including supporting the Army on exercises. Then, it was a bit more leave before September arrived and PDT started all over again.

271

Resupply continues – underslung Land Rover. (Bob Ruffles)

Our date for the Airbridge is December 14, and we'll be taking over 1310 Flight by the twentieth, just in time for Christmas. I had hoped to be going out as a captain, but it now seems unlikely. There just haven't been the flying hours available to complete the syllabus. There are these twenty-odd key skills – like general handling and USL, plus flying with NVGs and on instruments – and we must show we're competent in them all before we can be passed Combat Ready. Some can be practised in the simulator, but not everything. Then there's the air check with the OC. That's not a big worry – four out of five of us pass, and the others mostly just get referred for further training, or to gain more experience – but aircraft availability's the snag. There's no fat in the system. And now, PDT's started ... Still, we're off for desert flying in Morocco on Saturday – I'll get some hours in on that. I'll be qualified to fly in Helmand, but fully Combat Ready? I doubt it.

Of course, I'm looking forward to the det – back into action again, and a chance of bumping into more old friends from training. For a start,

RAF ground-attack Tornadoes from Lossie have arrived to give the Harriers a break after five years – I know a fair few Tornado pilots.

But I hope I'll see some changes for the better out there. Look, when I signed up for a sixteen-year permanent commission I knew all about the Afghanistan business, and the prospect of six years or more of deployments – but it'd be nice to know there's been progress, that we're making a difference.

After all, along with my mates from training, I'm in one of the first intakes of aircrew not to see anything much other than Afghanistan. The old Boss had seen the lot – Belize, Sierra Leone, Iraq and the Falklands. We've just seen Afghan sand and mountains. But that's where we are, and we must get on with it. From what we get in the briefings and the press, ISAF's efforts are not exactly going on fast-forward. But it's a positive that we're now starting to review our strategy. Perhaps they should make a real effort to understand the viewpoint of the people – it's taken them eight years to realize it might be a good idea to start talking to at least some of the Taliban.

Christmas Day at KAF – 47 AD men rig ration packs, diesel fuel, and crates of festive fare. **(Chris Stuart and friends)**

Still, one thing's absolutely for certain – I'll know not to take quite so much kit out with me this time!

Chomper's captaincy hopes seem to be coming to fruition. He has qualified as fully Combat Ready, and is slated to deploy in December, crewed with the new OC 'C' Flight:

The new boss is long on helicopter experience, but short on Cab hours. In effect, I'll be sharing the handling pilot duties as he beds in – I'll have moved, if you like, from being the senior co-pilot to the junior captain. On the last detachment, the repetition was in danger of bringing frustration and even boredom – now, I'm looking forward to the challenge of extra responsibility. It should relieve any monotony and focus the mind.

Of course, the excitement of going out to life on the front line is always there. To tell the truth, there's always a bit of the boys' holiday about it – the banter and the comradeship. Mind you, there were signs last time that bureaucracy was on the march, and we hear that it's still the case – police pulling guys over for speeding on the way to an IRT shout, off-duty people having to change into uniform for all meals in the cookhouse, that kind of thing. It wouldn't surprise me to find that an edict gets put in place banning our flag-pole efforts at Bastion.

What won't have changed are the IEDs. The Taliban and their collaborators have learned that they can't beat us in face-to-face battle, so they're using these roadside bombs more and more. They cause terrible injuries, but on the plus side for us is that we've got lots of good guys who know how to find most of them and put them out of action – and they're getting better at that all the time. And then there are the suicide bombers. But it seems that it's not the Afghans themselves that are keen to blow themselves up – they leave that to the insurgents.

German will be on 1310 Flight duty for Christmas too – something he hadn't expected:

I was supposed to be posted to Shawbury, for the instructor's course. But I've just been told there's a log-jam up there, and I've been put off until the middle of next year. It's a bind, but there's nothing to do but accept it – and move on. So I've been volunteered to fill in for a chap who has special reasons not to be away for the first half of the det. He'll come out and I'll come back at the end of January – unless it all gets changed again. Such stuff happens.

It'll be my sixth stint in Afghanistan. I keep myself motivated because that's the professional thing to do – part of our task is to keep smiling for our colleagues, and the blokes out on the ground and in the back of the Cab. I have to admit it gets harder every det, but in December there'll be a few new young pilots going. It'll be good to be able to show them the ropes – should help spark the interest up again.

I suppose it will be more of the same work this time. The winter ought to be quieter, but there's been all the hoo-hah over the election, these bloody IEDs all the time and then this terrible thing about the five soldiers getting shot by an Afghan policeman. The ISAF assaults into Taliban strongholds have been stirring up the hornets' nests for sure, but at least we're showing the Talibs they've got fewer safe havens – fewer nice cosy spots where they can set up their evil training camps. And it shows we've got the stomach for the long term. Not just us – the Americans sent in an extra 20,000 soldiers and Marines in the spring and summer – so there are close to 60,000 of them there now. And they're talking about making a further surge to 100,000 before long.

I'm not sure where it's all going, especially for the Afghans. They must be fed up with it all, to say the least – nothing but war and destruction since the Russians came in nearly thirty years ago. Until we can show there's a government they can have confidence in, they'll not trust either side. And then, the people in Helmand don't necessarily see themselves as Afghans – it's all tribal stuff for them.

I try my best not to make it worse for the locals when we're coming in low and fast in the Cabs. Of course, my first responsibility is the safety of passengers and crew, but if I can avoid filling their homes with dust, and make sure I don't bombard them with flare discharges, or destroy their crops – then I will. We don't want to be fuelling the next generation of Taliban.

Ginger is getting ready for his fifth spell in Afghanistan:

I feel much the same as I did the other times – as if I've only just got back from Helmand and already it's time to go again. It's a strange feeling when it gets to just a month to go – your stomach starts to feel like you've swallowed a brick, as you realize all the stuff you've got to get done before the off. We've just spent practically the whole of October on Exercise Jebel Sahara in Morocco, working with the guys in the Royal Gibraltar Regiment – good experience in desert Ops for the new crewmen, but eating away at domestic life. Then, last week it was Force

Protection, and at the weekend we're up to Yorkshire for five days of bad-weather flying. It makes every minute at home all the more precious.

Of course, yesterday's news about the Afghan policeman is on everyone's mind. It makes us wonder why we're bothering. We carry these guys in the back of the Cabs every day. The ANA soldiers are recruited outside their area of operations, but these policemen are all locals and have family and tribal pressures. On top of that, they're paid less than they could get from the Taliban. All that makes us wary of them – anyone who isn't shouldn't be in this job. At the very least, we'll be expecting to see some new weapons control procedures put in place.

The flight's looking a bit different this time – a new boss, and Frankie off and away. And three or four others will be tour expired before Christmas. At the same time, there's a lot of young crewmen to train. About time too. We've only had the one new guy since the beginning of last year – in the same time, four or five have left us. It's put a heavy demand on those who are medically fit, Combat Ready and willing to crack on – but that's life.

I'm not looking forward to December, and the final week before we go. At that point, all you can think about is the det – you get to the stage where all you want to do is get out there and start the count-down to coming home. But I know that my mind will get in focus when I get back into the job. I'll crack on all right.

Mister B will also be returning to 1310 Flight in December, for his seventh tour:

I'm OK with that. The UK Chinook Force gives me an annual plan – I know where I am at any time of the year and it defines my way of life. I can schedule my out-of-squadron activities in the gaps – like triathlon events and biking. We've just done a London–Southampton run for the Not Forgotten Association – raised a stack of cash for ex-Service disabled.

It's going to be mighty cold this time – more than the last det. There'll be a lot less dust, but a lot more mud, and snow in the mountains – you'll sweat with humping stuff on the ground and then freeze in the Cab at altitude. It needs a lot of skilled work with layers of clothing – you make sure there's the biggest of big parkas and cold-weather trousers to go over your body-armour. And you check your Cab's got the heater working – they sit idle for most of the year and can be a bit creaky when first brought back into action. But most of the hot air from that gets blown over the ramp – what doesn't comes out in the cockpit and cabin under the seats, so at least the pilots and the pax get a warm bum. For us, we've got the heater exhaust to hang on to. In a Red Desert transit from Bastion to Kandahar at altitude, and with those side doors open, the cold's disabling. Hands gripping the exhaust pipe act as a sort of heat pump for the body – it can save the day.

There's going to be a number of new crewmen on this det who'll need to learn the Herrick ropes – three of them are going out almost immediately after their six months' instruction. There'll be quite a few young pilots as well. It'll mean a big training load for me and Ginger – but I reckon we find that kind of challenge helps with making it through the ten weeks.

The workload's increasing for 'UK plc' out there. IEDs are getting more and more numerous, and the Talibs better and better at aiming them. Of course, to hold territory, soldiers have to manoeuvre on the ground, but army commanders – British, US and Canadian, too – are not so willing to take to the road to get in and out. They prefer to hop on a Cab, a British one for preference. Those bus runs can get a bit tedious for us, but we'll do them – it keeps the guys out of the convoys.

The casevac work isn't tedious at all – it's grim, but for us, satisfying. It's in serving our soldiers where we're making a difference – not sure what we're doing for the Afghans, yet. You can see that poppies are thinner on the ground, being replaced with maize – but then, those corn stalks give cover for the Talibs. It's difficult to win, out there.

Of course, we'll keep trying – for our mates, and the men up to their ears in it out in the field, if for nothing else. It's getting harder and harder, but we'll go out and get on with it as best we can. No dramas.

Index

1310 Flight RAF
  'A' Flight 18(B) Sqn 267, 268
  'B' Flight 18(B) Sqn 50
    at Kandahar 77, 81, 91
  'A' Flight 27 Sqn 48, 124, 247
  'B' Flight 27 Sqn 52, 72, 253, 257, 259, 264
  'C' Flight 27 Sqn
    'Cambridge Lines' 77, 78, 121, 137, 162,
      170, 189, 255
    Airbridge to Kandahar 52-7, 69-70,
      74-6
    Camp Bastion 92, 95-108
      Helmand Reaction Force (HRF)
        125-30, 145, 162, 164, 185, 243
      Immediate Response Team (IRT) 80,
        92, 125, 130-6, 142, 144, 149, 220-30,
        245, 249, 254, 258
    combat fatigue 245
    Combat Readiness 52, 124-5, 272-6
    countdown to departure 51-2
    decompression leave 259-60
    groundfire 121
      machine-guns 130, 164, 257
      Rocket-Propelled Grenade (RPG)
        130, 133, 146, 233, 246, 257
      slingshot 245
    Insert at Bahram Chah 181-7
    Joint Mission Brief (JMB) 144, 175, 227
    Kandahar arrival 77-83
    Op 'Aabi Toorah' 173-80
    Op 'Aabi Toorah' 2 226-36

Op 'Diesel' 80, 137-49
Op 'Oqab Sterga' 146
Op 'Pakula' 165-70
Rehearsal of Concept (RoC) 144, 230
returning home 255-60
Theatre Qualification
  sorties 91-108, 123
formal crest & motto 45-6, 268
history 45, 124
identity 268
manning 45, 50
42 Commando Royal Marines 38, 226
  under the air-drop 38-40, 240
  Bickleigh Barracks, Plymouth 38, 240
  Cole, L/Cpl Danny, driver & rifleman 40,
    240
  Eames, Sgt Philip, Unit Armourer 39-40,
    174, 179, 234
  Logistic Hub 39, 160, 175
  Mallinson, W/O David, Echelon Sgt
    Major 39-40, 174, 230
  Morton, Maj Justin, Quartermaster 38,
    40, 160, 175
  Op 'Aabi Toorah' 173-80
  Op 'Aabi Toorah' Phase 2 226-36
  returning home 237-43
  Stickland, Lt Col Charlie, CO 158-60, 175-
    6, 180, 234, 236, 240-3
904 Expeditionary Air Wing (EAW)
  RAF 80, 115, 173, 179, 194, 201, 223
    at Kandahar 223

'Albert Square' 78
Cochrane, Sqn Ldr Pete, Hercules
   Detachment Cdr 109, 112, 115, 117, 127,
   158-61, 179
history 45
night air-drop mission, Helmand 222-5
medevac mission, Helmand 199

A

Afghan National Security Force
   (ANSF) 74, 128, 211
   Afghan National Army (ANA) 31, 130,
     136, 142, 181-8, 213, 219, 221, 227, 276,
     279
   Afghan National Police (ANP) 31, 90,
     130, 142, 181, 213, 218, 219, 250, 275-6
Afghanistan
   Balkh 58, 60, 63
   demographics 209
     Hazara 61, 68, 209
     Pashtun 60, 209, 210
     Turkmen 61, 64
     Tajik 61, 209
     Uzbek 61, 64, 209
   geography
     'Fishhook' 157, 173
     Ghorak Pass 144
     'Green Zone' 80, 168, 238
     Hazarajat mountains 70
     Helmand mountains 17, 44
     Helmand River 72, 80, 95, 138, 196
     Highway One 95, 96, 103, 132
     Hindu Kush 60, 71, 96, 168
     Mirabad Valley 240
     Red Desert 89, 95
     'Triangle' 44
   Govt of the Islamic Republic of
     Afghanistan (GIRoA) 209-212
Helmand Province
   Bahram Chah 181
   Garmsir 159
   Gereshk 44, 103, 222
   Herat 58, 60, 61, 63, 73
   Lashkar Gah 44, 142, 164, 235
   Marjah 80, 227, 236
   Musa Qal'eh 44

   Nad Ali 80, 236
   Now Zad 44
   Sangin 44, 80, 172, 208
   Tarin Kowt 165, 167
history
   'Great Game' 61-64
   1st & 2nd Anglo-Afghan Wars 63-64
   Abdur Rehman 64
   Ahmed Shah 61, 95, 168
   Ahmed Shah Masood 68
   Alexander the Great 58
   Babrak Karmal 67
   British East India Company 61
   Daud Khan 67
   Dost Mohammad Khan 61, 63
   Genghis Khan 60
   Hamid Karzai 69, 71, 73, 74, 210
   Mohammad Najibullah 67, 68
   Mughal Empire 60-1
   Northern Alliance 68-9
   RAF and the evacuation of Kabul 65
   RAF in 3rd Anglo-Afghan War 65
   religious beliefs 60, 209
   rise of the Taliban 66, 68
   Russian retreat & aftermath 67-8
   Sher Ali Khan 63
   Silk Road 60
   Soviet Decade 67-8
   Tamerlane 60
   Ulag Beg 60
   UN-backed peacekeepers 69
   Waziristan 66-7, 271
   WWI 64-5
   WWII 65
   Zahir Shah 65, 67, 71, 73
   Kabul 42, 44, 48, 60-73, 88, 198, 210
   Kandahar Province 44
   Kandahar City 61, 63, 64, 73, 89, 95, 212
   Khowst 71
   Mazar-e-Sharif 58, 63, 68, 71
   Mullahs 74, 210
   Uruzgan Province 238
weather
   dust-haze 145, 218, 222, 259
   flood 72, 196, 256
   heat 33
   thunderstorms 172, 231, 235

Air resupply history
   Borneo Campaign 1962-66 153-4
   Burma Campaign 1942-5 45, 151, 266
   Kut-al-Amara 1916 150
   Malaya 1948-60 152-3
Airbridge Operations
   Al Udeid 190-1, 202, 243
   Bahrain 70
   departure for Kandahar 69
   descent into Kandahar Airfield 74-6
   Incirlik 190-1, 202
   Relief in Place (RiP) 237-260
Air-drop 154
   accuracy 88, 154, 157, 224-5, 240, 265-6
   Container Delivery System (CDS) 38-9,
      155, 157, 160, 223
   research & development 155, 265-6
   dropping zone (DZ) 38-9, 158- 60, 175,
      180, 224-5, 230, 241, 266
      Kajaki Dam 157
      Sangin 158
   inventory 34, 154-6
   leaflet 'Info-Ops' 193, 223
   parachute recycling 155-6
   statistics 154-5, 192, 265-6
Al Qaeda 66, 69
   attack on New York 14, 68
   Osama bin Laden 41, 66, 69
Apache, attack helicopter 17, 25, 91, 99, 121,
   124, 130, 132-4, 138, 145-6 168-9, 175-6,
   186, 220, 222-35, 245
Armoured vehicles
   Leopard tanks (Danish) 228
   Vector 219
   Viking 174, 228, 234, 235
   Vixen-Snatch 219
   WMIK 174, 180, 218
Army
   16 Air Assault Brigade 69, 71, 159, 189,
      249
   19 Light Brigade 57, 197, 243, 265
   3 Para 44, 50, 71, 85, 125, 158, 172, 249
   47 Air Despatch Squadron 156-8, 192-4,
      223
      Edwards, Capt Ross, Ops Officer 192,
         223
      harness pack practice 33-7

   manning 192
   Stuart, Maj Chris, OC 193, 265-6
American forces 41, 44, 58, 69, 72, 73, 80,
   86, 165, 219, 245, 246, 275
Army Air Corps (AAC) 47, 91, 124, 132
Australian forces 165, 167, 170, 240
Black Watch 57, 238, 259
Canadian forces 89, 173, 218, 242, 246,
   277
Danish Battle Group 196, 227, 234
Gurkha troops 92, 93, 130, 153, 208
Household Cavalry
   Trinick, Capt Chris 161, 180, 249
Netherlands forces 167, 242
Prince Harry 73
Royal Artillery 99, 229
The Rifles 195, 263-4

B

British Forces Broadcasting Services (BFBS)
   131, 248
British Forces post Office (BFPO) 248
Black Hawk, US Army helicopter 85

C

C-17 Globemaster, freighter
   Airbridge operations 75, 141, 156, 190-1,
      243, 254, 256, 264
   MEDEVAC & Pabbay operations 200-2
   specifications 190-1
Chain of Command
   Air Command 46, 51, 154
      Stuart, Maj Chris, SO2 154
   Battle Group (South) 38, 159, 161, 180,
      238
   Battle Group (North) 39
   Joint Aviation Group (JAG) 80, 88, 91,
      141, 176, 212, 269
      Turner, Gp Capt Andy, CO 80, 88, 90,
         187, 188, 190, 212, 256, 269
   Joint Helicopter Command, JHC 45, 265
   Joint Helicopter Force Afghanistan,
      JHF(A) 45-6, 72, 80, 92, 125, 130-1, 138,
         141-2, 144, 176, 185, 196, 201 249, 254,
         269

Joint Tasking Group 161
Land Command 45
Permanent Joint Headquarters (PJHQ) 46, 154
Regional Command South, RC(S) 44-5
  HQ at Lashkar Gah 123
Regional Commands 211
Task Force Helmand (TFH) 161, 243
China 60, 67
Chinook, heavy support helicopter 15
  armament 28, 51, 94, 164
  cabin 19, 28, 32, 41, 93-4, 96
  defensive aids 72, 121, 133
  engines & rotors 19-20, 28, 94, 96, 142, 172
  flying controls 20, 93, 123
  losses 55, 80, 262-4
  modifications, 2010 264-5
  operating payloads 28, 92
  RAF service 41-2
Chinook airmanship
  bird strike 21, 172, 177, 259
  dust landing 91-3, 182, 184, 218, 221, 232
  formation flying 20-26, 146, 169, 177, 184 232-3
  hill flying 21-8
  icing 18, 27
  lift-off 20, 94
  low flying 21-8
  night flying 93-5, 106-8, 121, 133, 164, 221
  shutting down 96
  start-up 94
Chinook operating procedures
  casualty evacuation 27, 130-6, 220-1
  crewmen's duties 19-20, 94-6, 100, 184
  evasion techniques 21
    'Wells' manoeuvres 26, 29, 73, 233
  in the hover 20, 27-8, 95, 217
  palleted-freight delivery 28-9
  troop insertion 24
  underslung loads (USLs) 96-104, 177
  winching 27

D

Decompression 50, 57, 240, 247-8, 254, 260, 270
  'Padres' College', Amport House 261

E

Expeditionary Chinook Engineering
  Squadron (ExCES) 19, 833
  at Kandahar 85-8, 226, 243
  at Bastion 126, 131
  project 'Jericho' 83-4, 264
  Edbrooke, W/O John 84-8, 141-2, 216 218, 226, 254-5, 262264-5
  Hardie, SAC Tech Steve 217
  McComisky, SAC Tech Daniel 84, 253, 270
    crashed Chinook recovery 263-4
    wheel-change in flight 217-8
  Odiham Blade Bay 142
  West, SAC Phillip 252-3

G

Germany
  in Afghan history 64-6
  ISAF troop commitment 73
Great Britain 41, 60, 209
  Anglo-Afghan Wars 63-5
  British East India Company 61
  Browne, Des, UK Defence Secretary 73
  in the 'Great Game' 61-4
  ISAF troop commitment 41, 73, 209, 248
  Jones, Kevan, UK Under Secretary for Defence 30, 32
  media 30, 74, 149, 271

H

Harrier, close air-support 80, 92, 158, 198, 208, 273
Hercules, transport 32, 41-2, 46
  air-drop capabilities 37-40, 44, 154, 173-9 192, 222-5, 240
  at Kandahar 45, 58, 78, 92, 108, 114-20, 168, 199-202

cabin 34, 96
'J' & 'K' models at Lyneham 33-8, 252
RAF service 33, 42
Hercules airmanship
'K' Model start-up, taxi-ing and take-off
33-5
'J' Model start-up, taxi-ing and take-off
119-20
night flying 120, 225
tactical landing 37
Hercules operating procedures
air-drop 33-6, 40, 157, 222-5
medevac 32, 199
resupply shuttles 108, 114, 115-20, 117,
124, 160
HESCO Bastion blast-walls 96, 126, 154,
193

I

Improvised Explosive Device (IED) 154,
159, 165, 219, 222, 224, 241, 249 265, 266,
274, 275, 277
India 60-1, 63, 65-66, 73, 150-1, 208
Amritsar 58, 61
Indian Ocean 49
Punjab 61
Insurgents 44, 67, 70, 73, 80, 133, 138
168, 172, 180-1, 185, 209, 211, 214 219, 226,
274
attack on Indian Embassy, Kabul 73
'dickers' 123-4, 146, 164, 169, 169, 216,
226
suicide bombs 31, 73, 149, 245, 274
Taliban 31, 41-4, 58, 64, 66, 74, 78, 96,
103, 121, 124, 128-30, 132, 138, 144, 149,
164-5, 168, 172-3, 181-2, 189, 208-12 215,
219, 221, 224, 227-8, 233-4, 258, 266, 273-
7
in winter 57, 72
International Security Assistance Force
(ISAF) 41-2, 61, 67-9, 115, 117
achievements 205-12, 234, 273, 275
Bases
'Dwyer', American base 80, 174-187
Bagram, Kabul 70-1
Camp Bastion (BSN) 92, 96, 108

development 44, 55, 80, 84, 125-6,
256
flag flying competition 125, 245, 274
Hardened Aircraft Landing Strip
(HALS) 146, 222, 235
IRT & surge tents 125, 130, 182
hospital 30, 126-9, 199, 200
Kajaki Dam 104, 124, 154, 157, 164, 208
'Kamp Holland' 167-9
Kandahar Airfield (KAF) 44, 77-80, 126
'IronMan' challenge 162, 164
'Boardwalk' enclosure 79, 81, 83, 254
airfield defence 88-90, 126, 218-9
facilities 55, 71, 81-3, 162-3, 220
Cambridge Lines 77-8, 137, 162, 255
Fryer, Air Cdre Andy, Base
Commander 86, 172
rocket attacks 88, 92, 192, 218, 257
Musa Qaleh 44, 72, 104, 172
Nawa 105, 142, 221
Nolay 123, 164, 172
Sangin 44, 72, 104, 123, 142, 158 159,
172, 208, 242
hearts & minds 209, 211, 212, 216, 219,
249
McChrystal, General Stanley,
Commander 2010 265
reconstruction & development 41, 74, 211
Significant Actions (SIGACTS) 211
task 74, 209

J

Joint Air Delivery Test & Evaluation Unit
(JADTEU) 156-7, 194
Johnson, W/O Scott, Project Officer 156
Roberts, Cpl Ioan 157
Joint Helicopter Support Unit (JHSU)
'Hookers' at Camp Bastion 97-103
Evans, Sgt Mark, Troop Leader 97-102,
250-1
Murray, Guardsman William 196
RAF Odiham base 194-6
Ritchie, Maj Phillip, OC 99, 194, 196, 267
statistics 196, 251
Underslung Loads (USLs) 92
105mm light gun 99-103

Air Portable Fuel Container (APFC)
157
Helicopter Underslung Loads
Equipment (HUSLE) 195

L

Lynx, UK Marine helicopter 123, 164, 235

M

Merlin, Support Helicopter 157, 195, 267
Mi27, Russian heavy-lift helicopter 180
Mi-8 HiP, Russian support helicopter 85

N

Narcotics 74, 138, 181, 187, 210, 227
opium 73, 124, 149, 176, 210, 259
Poppy Eradication 164, 210, 246
Navaids and Radios
Chinook Integrated Navigation System
(CINS) 95, 121, 168-70, 182, 184, 221,
232-3, 235
Forward Looking Infra-Red (FLIR) 114
FM 17, 24
Global Positioning System (GPS) 21, 93,
95-6, 133, 138, 170, 182, 91, 265
Ground Collision Avoidance System
(GCAS) 114
'Kill Box' map 19, 21, 24-5
maps 19, 21, 24, 36, 81, 132, 167, 227-8
Tactical Air Navigation (TACAN) 169
Traffic Collision & Avoidance System
(TCAS) 35, 114
UHF 17, 22, 25, 95, 161, 182, 225
VHF 28, 161
North Atlantic Treaty Organisation (NATO)
15, 42-4, 71-2, 73, 115, 161, 209,
242
North-West Frontier 63-6, 71, 74
Durand Line 64-66
Faqir of Ipi 66
Islamic Emirate of Waziristan 67
Khyber Pass 63-5, 81
Leeson, Lt Frank, Khassadar Officer 66-7
Waziristan 66-67, 271

O

Operations
'Aabi Toorah' 173-80
'Aabi Toorah' phase 2 226-236
'Achilles' 72
'Diesel' 137-149
'Enduring Freedom' 68
'Herrick' 44, 56, 199, 207, 209, 216, 253
Insert at Bahram Chah 181-7
'Oqab Sterga' 146
'Pabbay' 198-204
Kenyon International 201, 204, 248
Wootton Bassett 204
'Pakula' 165-70
'Spin Ghar' 208
'Telic' 45
'Veritas' 68-9, 156-7, 197

P

Pakistan 67, 67, 68, 73, 208, 212
Afghan-Pakistan border 42, 44, 60, 66, 73,
80, 103, 209
Asif Ali Zardari, President 74
Baluchistan 181
Musharraf, General Pervez, President
117, 212
Swat Valley 271
Pavehawk, American attack helicopter
163, 227, 230, 245, 257
Permanent Joint Headquarters (PJHQ)
deployed forces augmentation 248
Deployed Welfare Package 248
Heffron, Gp Capt Mark 208-12, 247-8
Hickson, Brigadier Mike 154, 247
Persia (Iran) 58, 60, 63
Personal armaments & kit
body-armour 32, 56-7, 69, 74, 81, 92-3,
116, 131, 192, , 224, 240, 262, 276
desert camouflage kit 52, 69, 237, 260
Night Vision Devices (NVDs) & Goggles
(NVGs) 81, 106, 116, 131, 146, 160, 164
Model 112 personal radios 81
personal weapons 31, 51, 57, 85, 92, 93,
121
standard 'Herrick issue' 85
survival kit 16, 93

Pre-Deployment Training (PDT)
   Chinook crews
      PDT programme 50-1, 109
      winter flying, Cairngorms 15-29
   Hercules crews
      'hot & high', Sierra Nevada 109-12
      PDT programme 251-2
Puma, support helicopter 157, 195, 267

R

RAF Air Mobility Wing (AMW) 197-9
   at Kandahar 223
   Cargo Hangar at RAF Lyneham 198
   Taylor, W/O Mark, No.1 AMW 252,
      197-9
RAF Mobile Air Operations Teams
   (MAOTS) 175, 230
   merging with JHSU 267
RAF Regiment 50, 89, 220
   Camp Bastion 220, 265
   Kandahar Airfield 76, 78, 88, 89
      Kandahar Ground Defence Area
         (GDA) 89-90, 218
   MERT force protection 32
   No.4 Force Protection Wing
      Davies, Sqn Ldr Bob, Chief of Staff
         88-90, 219-20, 265
      French, SAC John 218, 220, 266
      Hayman, SAC Ben 212, 218-9, 247, 266
      Neame, Flt Lt Jason, Flt Cdr 88
RAF Squadron personnel
   18(B) 'B' Flight
      Curnow, Sqn Ldr Paul, Flt Cdr 267-8
   24 Hogg, Flt Lt Dave 113-4, 115-20, 199,
      214, 243, 251-2
   27 Toriati, Wg Cdr Dom, Sqn Cdr 46, 189,
      268
   Duncan, Flt Lt Alex 189
   27 'C' Flight
      'Boss' 16-29, 50-2, 55, 57, 69-70, 74
         joining up 46-7
         on Herrick 72-3, 78, 80-2, 91-115 122,
            125, 137-48, 160, 161, 162 168-72,
            175-80, 180-7, 188-9 220, 221-2, 226-
            36, 245, 247
         return 260-2

'Chomper' 52-3, 57, 69-70, 75-6
   joining up 54
   on Herrick 77-8, 81123, 125, 164,
      168-70, 185, 187, 216, 222, 231-5
   return 258-9, 274
'Frankie' 57, 70-2
   joining up 50, 53-4
   on Herrick 78, 80, 82, 91, 105, 108,
      125-6, 130-6, 144-9, 163-4, 177, 201,
      213-4, 220-1, 230-6, 247
   return 259, 261, 262
'German' 17-27
   joining up 47-8
   on Herrick 124-5, 144
   return 274-5
'Ginger' 20-9, 51, 53, 56, 70-1
   joining up 49-50
   on Herrick 80, 82, 108, 149
   return 257-8, 275-6
'Mister B' 20-9, 50, 52, 53, 56-7, 70
   joining up 48-9
   on Herrick 77-8, 80-1, 91-115, 130-6,
      145, 148, 162-3
   return 255-6, 256-7
'Morts' 21-29, 54-5, 56-7, 69-76
   joining up 48
   on Herrick 77-81, 91, 121, 144-9,
      169-70, 177, 182-4, 215
   return 258, 271-4
'Richie' 123, 131, 134
30 Cochrane, Sqn Ldr Pete 109, 112, 115,
   117, 127, 158-61, 179
61 Patton, Flt Lt Stu 113-4
99 Eyers, Flt Lt Marcus 190-1
216 Rushworth, Flt Lt Tim 191-2

R

RAF Stations
   Benson 48, 51, 125, 175, 195, 262, 267
   Brize Norton 70, 89, 156, 190, 194, 196,
      200, 252, 259, 266
      Airport of Embarkation 52, 55-7, 69
      Harris, Sqn Ldr Ruth, SAMO 190, 197
   Lossiemouth 15-20, 28-9, 55, 273
   Lyneham 30-2, 33-8, 42, 45, 46, 89, 109,
      113, 117, 126, 156, 192, 196, 199-200,

250-2, 265, 271
  Air Terminal 197-9, 202-4
  Daly, Flt Lt Louise, PRO 30
Odiham
  'Millies' Award 205
  18 'B' Sqn OCF 47, 48, 49, 50, 54, 85,
    258
  Mason, Gp Capt Richard, Stn Cdr
    (Acting) 205-8
Odiham Village Parade 271
Shaughnessy, Flt Lt Leigh, PRO 7
Turner, Gp Capt Andy, Stn Cdr 80, 88, 90,
  187-8, 190, 212, 256, 269-71
Shawbury 47-8, 54, 274
RAF Tactical Medical Wing (TMW)
  Critical Care Air Support Team (CCAST)
    126-9, 266
    Berry, Wg Cdr Robin, nurse 126-9
    Lane, Cpl Vicky, nurse
      199-201, 249-50, 266-7
    on call 200, 250
  Deployable Aeromedical Response teams
    (DARTS) 248
    Thompson, Sqn Ldr Charlie, OC 129,
    133, 248-969
  'golden hour' 30, 132, 182, 220, 222
  Medical Emergency Response Team
    (MERT) 30-33, 83, 127, 249, 254
    casevac training, Lyneham 30-3
    Haslam, Flt Lt Matt, nurse 30-3, 129
    Herrick missions 129, 132-6, 199, 201,
      208, 222, 226-7
Royal Navy 38, 45, 85, 138, 153, 227, 245
HMS *Illustrious* 70
Russia 60-68, 71, 168, 198, 212, 219, 275

S

Saudi Arabia 67, 68
Sea King, support helicopter 19, 22, 85, 123,
  125, 130, 138, 157, 227, 2 30, 234, 240, 263
Sea Stallion, US Marine Corps support
  helicopter 138, 227, 231-2, 234

T

Tajikistan 60

Telecommunications 189
  calling home 82, 145, 189
  Internet 55, 81, 123, 189, 201, 220, 248
  Skype 82, 83, 189, 220
Tornado, fighter-bomber 16, 19, 85, 273
TriStar, Airbridge transport
  at Brize Norton 56, 69
  en-route Kandahar 70, 74-6, 191-2, 247,
    253
  medevac 32, 144
Turkmenistan 60

U

United Nations 41-2, 73, 209, 211
  air embargo and sanctions 68
  Peacekeepers 69
United States of America (USA) 67, 68, 109
  Al Qaeda attack on New York 41, 68
  Bush, President George.W 73
  ISAF troop commitment 41, 73, 209, 275
  Op 'Enduring Freedom' 68

U

Unmanned Aerial Vehicles (UAV) 92, 219,
  224, 229, 231, 264
  }Predator 71, 138, 196, 219, 266
Uzbekistan 60, 64